Real
Powys

To Reg and George

Also in the Real Wales series
Editor: Peter Finch

Real Aberystwyth – Niall Griffiths
Real Bloomsbury – Nicholas Murray
Real Cardiff – Peter Finch
Real Cardiff Two – Peter Finch
Real Cardiff Three – Peter Finch
Real Liverpool – Niall Griffiths
Real Llanelli – Jon Gower
Real Merthyr – Mario Basini
Real Newport – Ann Drysdale
Real South Pembrokeshire – Tony Curtis
Real Swansea – Nigel Jenkins
Real Wales – Peter Finch
Real Wrexham – Grahame Davies

Real
Powys

mike parker

series editor: peter finch

Seren is the book imprint of
Poetry Wales Press Ltd
Nolton Street, Bridgend, Wales

Explore 30 years of good books at
www.serenbooks.com

© Mike Parker, 2011
Preface © Peter Finch, 2011

The right of Mike Parker to be identified
as the Author of this Work has been asserted
in accordance with the Copyright, Designs
and Patents Act, 1988.

ISBN 978-1-85411-553-9

A CIP record for this title is available from
the British Library

All rights reserved. No part of this publication
may be reproduced, stored in a retrieval system,
or transmitted at any time or by any means
electronic, mechanical, photocopying, recording
or otherwise without the prior permission
of the copyright holders.

The publisher works with the financial assistance
of the Welsh Books Council

Printed and bound by CPI Group (UK) Ltd, Croydon CR0 4YY

CONTENTS

Series Editor's Introduction | 7
Introduction | 10

CENTRAL – RADNORSHIRE

County Town | 16
Llandrindod Wells | 21
Penybont | 24
Rhayader | 29
Elan Valley | 34
River Wye, Safn-y-Coed | 38
Llanelwedd | 42
Rhulen | 46
Aberedw and Llanstephan | 48
Heart of Wales Railway | 54

EAST – ENGLISH BORDER

Offa's Dyke | 64
Sycarth | 67
Bride of the Border | 70
Churchstoke | 74
Hay-on-Wye | 77
Clyro | 81

SOUTH – BRECONSHIRE

County Town | 88
Beacons | 92
Crickhowell | 97
Penwyllt | 101
Epynt | 105
The Wells | 109
A470, Erwood: Save Our Toilets | 113
Cilmeri | 116
Llanafan Fawr | 120

WEST – FFIN CYMRU CYMRAEG

Ystradgynlais	130
The Devil's Staircase	133
Pumlumon	136
Dyfi Junction	141
Esgairgeiliog	145

NORTH – MONTGOMERYSHIRE

County Town	154
Welshpool: Relocation, Relocation, Aryan Nation	159
Gwlad y Plygain, Gwlad y Punk	164
A New Town for Mid Wales	171
Llanidloes	178
Staylittle and Dylife	183
Machynlleth	188
Llanbrynmair	194
Red and Green	198

Works Consulted	203
The Photographs	206
The Author	208
Index	209

SERIES EDITOR'S INTRODUCTION

Powys, land of the marches, the liminal hinterland, the sealess centre, the green uplands. The largest county in Wales. A place where the language thins and streaks. Where the English midlanders come walking. Where the ancient Welsh have their blood in the soil.

This place runs all the way from a border just beyond Merthyr Tydfil in the post-industrial south to an artificial line drawn across the hills just before you reach Y Bala and Llangollen. It's a county that contains more versions of the Welsh accent than Ben and Jerry have ice cream. Landlocked bar a corridor that hits Cardigan Bay, just, on the Dyfi Estuary. It's the place where most of Wales faces up to its English neighbour. There's a long land border with Herefordshire and Shropshire where places that were once hill-dominated Welsh – Oswestry, Shrewsbury, Hereford – now languish in the Anglicised and arable shires.

This was one of Wales's great kingdoms, fought over through the centuries in much the way Poland has been. Powys's borders squashed and shifted, manipulated, bent, removed and changed. For most of the twentieth century Powys did not exist. In its place were the proud counties of Brecknockshire, Radnorshire and Montgomery (plus a sliver of Denbighshire). Local government reorganisation reinstated Powys in 1974 and scrapped all that. In 1996 it again manipulated the county's edges, pasting in pieces from Clwyd and Denbighshire. The county moves like breathing lungs. Wales without the cities and the wreck of industry. Wales of the brochures. Where you cycle and walk and lose yourself in the rain and the hills.

I decide to cross it once again, just get the flavour. Harri Webb presciently called this place the green desert. You can go miles without encountering a soul. Turn off the main highways, such as those are, and you'll be lost in a maze of B roads and back lanes, tracks where grass still grows in the road's centre, hedges, thickets, fields in endless number. People? Hardly a one.

Is there a capital? Hard to say. There are places I've travelled to that are certainly centres – Brecon, Newtown, Llanidloes, Welshpool – but none of them really transcend the localness of their locations. If they have hinterlands then those are truncated. Do any of those places represent the idea of Powys? Could they hold the palace of the king, the office of the country poet (if there was one) or be the seat of government power? No.

In Newtown there's the remains of industry, a shopping centre, and evidence of the world's first mail order business. Its population of 13,000 plus makes it the county's largest conurbation. At Brecon there's a military presence, stone buildings, leisure canals, and literary history. A buzzing, tourist destination. Yet no sense of Powysness or feeling of regional authority. Brecon looks south. In Welshpool – Y Trallwng – the border is a mere four miles distant and the Georgian architecture gives a sense, unbacked by history, of Anglicisation.

That leaves Llandrindod. A smaller place than any of the other claimants. With a population of just over 5000 it's about as significant a county town as Cowbridge might be in Glamorgan. But that's what it is. The seat of government in Powys. A town right at the heart. One almost at the geographic centre of Wales, come to that. It's the place where national meetings are often held. The misery of travel is shared by everyone having to do it. As far down the A470 as it is up. If it were actually on that road, the only thing we have in Wales that connects the north with the south.

Llandod, as most end up calling it, is one of the run of Victorian spa towns that grew up in a line near the River Irfon. Along with Llangammarch Wells, Llanwrtyd Wells, and Builth it was the place you came to for the taking of the waters. Sulphur, barium, chalybeate – substances that lifted melancholy, improved sight, repaired the skin, strengthened digestion, and renovated the broken. Welsh snake oil. It flowed, still flows, in Powys's wells towns. But there are few takers.

In Llandrindod today the pump rooms have closed. You can drink the salty fluids at open air fountains at Rock Gardens. Two hippies and a retired couple with sandwiches were the only others present the last time I visited. At Llangammarch the wells have been subsumed by farmland. At Llanwrtyd they have been abandoned. At Builth they have been closed. At the chemists I buy a packet of multivit and a bottle of Ginseng extract. Packaged, portable, convenient. The wells' modern replacement.

With energy replenished I head on. This county is full of ancient wonder. At Builth, up beyond Wyeside, once the town's Assembly rooms and now an arts facility and cinema with an uncertain funded future, is Builth castle. Rarely heard of this massive series of medieval earthworks are some of the most impressive in Wales. Not a stone of this first Norman and then Edward I installation remains.

It was fought over by the Normans and the Welsh for several hundred years before being abandoned as a ruin after a great fire in the 1600s. The stone was filched. Filched comprehensively. I walk the ramparts accompanied by sheep. There's nothing here but grass.

Along the southern run and with its own well still extant is the village of Cilmeri. B&B, G&B (Bed and Breakfast; Gwely a Brecwast) announces a sign in this place so near to England and so far from the traditional Welsh heartland of the north West that you stop for a moment and wonder. Then it becomes obvious. Cilmeri. This is place where Llewelyn the last Prince of Wales was beheaded. 1282. The end of something. His head was taken to London, paraded in the streets and then hung on a poll outside the Tower. Welsh independence was over.

The site is marked by a great standing stone, erected in 1956, and has been the centrepiece of nationalistic revival and expression of Cymric certainty ever since. The sign, in two languages, has the words *legend of* totally obliterated from a board which reads *Information relating to the legend of Prince Llewelyn can be seen in the village layby*. Legend! This is no tall story. Llywelyn ein llyw olaf is real.

Far north from here, at Berriew in Montgomery, still Powys, the present Prince of Wales occasionally stays with friends at a great house. In 2003 he called together and assemblage of poets in an attempt to recreate the role of Royal Bard. The prince of Wales had a Royal Harpist so why not also a poet. Royal patronage of the arts has been a Charles constant. The poets present persuaded him that such an appointment would be politically difficult and culturally divisive. Which language would the bard compose in? Which royal line would he or she serve? After due consideration the Prince retreated. Wales saved from contention. In due course Gwyneth Lewis became the country's first National Poet, a Welsh appointment. The Prince moved on to Llwynywermod in Carmarthenshire. The kingdom of Powys connection dissolved.

North of Machynlleth, beyond the Berwyn mountains, is Llanrhaeadr-ym-Mochnant. The parish of William Morgan, the man who first translated the Bible into Welsh and possibly the Welshest place in the county. As different from Hay on Wye, Y Gelli, nestling on the southern border as can be. Powys might be desert but it's a desert of contrasts. A place where travel at speed is impossible. You walk this place, you amble. Slow. Time to think, to consider. Mike Parker, the man who gave us the *Rough Guide to Wales* and then travelled the country in a camper van for television suggested to me that Powys might make the perfect subject for a Real series psychogeography. Despite the fact that county is the opposite of conurbation, that its combined total population comes to something just over a third of that of Cardiff's, and its highest building is a four storey hotel in Llanwrtyd Wells, it is diverse enough to deserve the treatment. Doubting this to be possible I read Mike's outline. Then I changed my mind. You are holding Mike Parker's magnificent result. Powys, as real as anywhere with wall to wall tarmac and endless buildings. Read on.

Peter Finch

INTRODUCTION

As ever, it started with the map.

"It's definitely time to go off-map for a while". Writing those final words of *Map Addict*, my three hundred page love letter to the Ordnance Survey, I truly meant them. I'd had two years with my head buried in their didactic depths; it was time to breathe easy.

It didn't last; it never does. I spent the next week obsessively cutting maps up (perhaps in the way that a spurned lover turns the scissors onto their ex's suits or skirts in revenge). I wanted to wallpaper the stairs going down to my basement kitchen in a huge, continuous OS Landranger map, scale of 1:50000, starting with the Llyn peninsula in the hall, and then papering all the way down to the back door. It took days, and two dozen maps (the back door is just the other side of Swindon). Very costly wallpaper, all in all. Worth every penny, though: the one-and-a-quarter inches to the mile map of most of Wales and a large slice of England is quite beautiful. Visitors would hover spellbound on the stairs, while I took to sitting on different steps, coffee in hand, and letting my eyes and mind roam the land.

The thing that hit me first, was just how big, and how lean, was Powys. My adopted county filled the massive stairwell, mile upon mile of apparently not very much, its tiny settlements dwarfed by the frantic blotches of population that surround it. 123 miles from top to bottom; nearly thirteen feet at that scale. A green black hole in the middle of the map, I wanted to fall in and see where it took me. The idea for a *Real Powys* was born, half way down the stairs. Peter Finch, the series midwife who kicked it all off with *Real Cardiff*, wasn't so sure. The *Real* books had intentionally loitered on urban pavements, the traditional psychogeographer's playground. Could a landscape of such sweltering green possibly tell us much about where people and place collide? I felt sure that it could, it did. It does.

Some stats. The county of Powys is just over two thousand square miles, a full quarter of the Welsh landmass. Half the size of Jamaica, more than twice that of Luxembourg, bigger than thirty-one sovereign nations. A quarter of Wales, but home to just 4.4% of its population. 65 people per square mile, against a Welsh average of 365, and an English figure of over a thousand. Numbers like that get people very twitchy and avaricious; commentators concluded that it must be the main reason that, in 2008, Powys was named as Britain's happiest place, in one of those meaningless surveys that folk only take notice of if it confirms their boasts or fuels their paranoia or prejudices. We need only look down the rest of the list to feel the flickers of doubt: yes, Powys is tops in the happiness department, but Manchester is next and Cumbernauld fourth. The most miserable place to live in Britain, apparently, is Edinburgh.

Other stats that might, or might not, tell us something: 59% of Powys residents live in villages, hamlets or isolated dwellings, compared with a Welsh average of 17%, and 11% for England'n'Wales. 16.5% of the population are self-employed, double the Welsh average, and 11% work in agriculture, forestry or fishing, nearly four times the Welsh figure. They're working difficult land: 96% of the county has EU 'less favoured area' agricultural status, against 79% for Wales as a whole (the 4% that's half-decent is all in little indents hard against the border). Despite its green image and credentials, Powys has the highest rate of car ownership in Wales: only about 15% of households do not own a vehicle. On behalf of those drivers, the council have to look after just shy of four thousand miles of public roads, as well as 5745 miles of off-road rights of way (together, the flight distance from the county's own Llandegley International Airport[1] to Alice Springs in the middle of Australia. Thankfully, the flight path is not blocked by the same amount of barbed wire and bullocks as are Powys rights of way).

Talk to people from Gwynedd, Ceredigion or Carmarthenshire, Cardiff, Swansea or the Rhondda even, and they'll sometimes pooh-pooh the idea that Powys is proper Wales at all. Pale and The Pale. Limbo-land, mongrel, half-English, they say, yet the ratio of Welsh speakers in the county is marginally higher than it is across the nation as a whole. In some areas – *plygain* country in the northeast of Montgomeryshire, the old Cyfeiliog district towards Machynlleth in the west, the south-west of Breconshire around Ystradgynlais – the percentage figure climbs into the sixties. Or they point to the low ratio of residents actually born in Wales, the third lowest of all 22 authorities at 56%[2]. It's all soap-dodgers, dream-weavers and down-shifters[3], they say, folk drunk on the promises of weekend property supplements, but that forgets that very many diehard Powysians had no choice but to be born in Henffordd or Amwythig, Hereford or Shrewsbury, and so count in the statistics as English. In Bangor or Brynaman, such an indignity would spark petitions, campaigns, headlines, martyrs. In Powys,

INTRODUCTION

they shrug, sniff and carry on with the baling.

What it lacks in people, it more than makes up with in sheep. Like flecks of God's dandruff across His rounded green shoulders, there are said to be a million in Radnorshire alone, making the county's sheep-to-person ratio a meaty 50:1. Cue the jokes. This middle tranche of Powys, Harri Webb's 'green desert', is the medieval anti-kingdom kingdom of Rhwng Gwy a Hafren, Between Wye and Severn. Rhwng Cymru a Lloegr, then and now, heaven and earth as well. Rhwng Powys a Brycheiniog too, the powerhouses either side, now more or less coterminous with Montgomeryshire and Breconshire[4]. Any difficulties between them were nothing to the trouble that came from the east, from over Offa's Dyke, that eighth century trip wire that still demarcates two very lovely, but very different, nations. The gentle landscape is pocked with the pustules of strife, the castles, battlefields, trenches, forts, vantage points, lonely churches and dark whispers in a quiet sky.

Powys has taught me the true meaning of *hiraeth*, and an attack of it comes on now before I've even left home. With time between trains in Birmingham once, I was hurrying back to New Street station, and stopped to buy a *Big Issue* from a seller at the bottom of the McDonald's ramp. He was chatty, and I had to apologise that I was a bit pressed for time, as I had a train to catch, and they were only every two hours. "Where are you going then?" he asked. "Home," I said, "Machynlleth in mid Wales." He sighed. "Bet you can breathe there. Really breathe, you know."

Notes

1. See the Penybont, Radnorshire account.
2. Only Conwy (54%) and Flintshire (51%) are lower.
3. Or another major group of incomers, for whom the only statistic that much matters is that Powys is 99.3% white.
4. The three counties were amalgamated into Powys in 1974, surviving as district councils of the new county until 1996. Since then, Powys County Council has been a unitary authority.

CENTRAL

Radnorshire

COUNTY TOWN

The enduring Ruritanian quality of the smallest, poorest county in the land is only amplified by the eternal dilemma as to which of its pinprick settlements qualified as the county town. Although Radnorshire's population has remained steady at between eighteen and twenty five thousand for the past century or so, the competition for capital status meant that, at various times, Old and New Radnor, Rhayader, Presteigne and Llandrindod were all able to claim the modest prize.

Radnorshire was a product of the 1536 Act of Union, Henry VIII's attempt to hammer the lawless Marcher lands into the English system. The new county's jurisdiction largely covered the old Welsh tribal kingdom known as Rhwng Gwy a Hafren[1] and its birth was uncommonly bloody. The 'hanging bishop', Rowland Lee was appointed as President of the Court of the Council of Wales and the Marches, wasting no time in bringing his theories of muscular retribution to this part of his new domain in particular. To be fair, the area around the woods and hills of the Radnor Forest had an especially venal reputation as a hiding place for outlaws, but his response was swift, brutal and indiscriminate. Lee later boasted of having hung five thousand Welshmen during his brief reign[2].

Come the arrival of the new county, New Radnor was named as its shire town, while it shared the job as home of the Shire Court with Rhayader. The arrangement didn't last long. On only the second sitting of the court at Rhayader, one of the visiting judges was murdered, and the decision was immediately taken to re-locate court sittings from the wild west of the county to Presteigne, just inches from the border with England. Presteigne took the job on full-time from the late 1600s, and the Assizes (successor to the Shire Court) continued to sit there until 1971. Narcissus Luttrell, in his *Brief Historical Relation of State Affairs* of 1681, called Presteigne the 'capitall town' of Radnorshire, and this was the generally held belief until the county vanished from the administrative map in the local government reorganisation of 1974. Even so, when the Local Government Act of 1888 constituted elected county councils for the first time, the new authority in Radnorshire chose to meet in the growing town of Llandrindod Wells, initially at the Pump House Hotel, and then, from 1909, in a bespoke, brand new redbrick headquarters on the High Street, now the town's police station and magistrates' court. When that became too modest for their needs in the late 1940s, they took over the grand old Gwalia Hotel a few yards away, which remains the local offices of the county council today. As proof that what goes round comes round, when the new Powys County Council swept away Radnorshire and its cohorts in 1974, they took over the old Pump House Hotel as their headquarters[3].

Presteigne and New Radnor are the best places to find the ghosts of this most spectral of counties. The spirits are a great deal darker in New Radnor, for there is something scarred and yearning about this eerily quiet village, wedged into the windy gap between the lowering bulk of the Radnor Forest and the wide open Walton Plain[4]. This is not a natural place: it knows it and still sulks plaintively over the fact. New Radnor was established as a ready-made seat of power, a plantation castle and town designed to bring the ordered, supercilious ways of the English into the very skirts of the dark Welsh hills. It usurped the name of Radnor from an ancient hilltop village three miles away across the plain, known now as Old Radnor[5], and tried to boost its fledgling credentials with the sheer heft of its castle and its courtly ambition. There it is on John Speed's map of Radnorshire in his 1610 Atlas, the *Theatrum Imperii Magnæ Britanniæ*, that depicted and described each county in England and Wales, together with one hastily-drawn plan of the newly-acquired Scotland. Every county is given a double-paged map, decorated with text, illustrations of some principal sights, armorial bearings of its noblest families and a bird's eye illustrated street view of the county town and/or cathedral city. Next to the bustling streetscapes of Nottingham, Winchester or York, together with loving portraits of their attendant counties, the sparse Welsh divisions and their tiny capitals look raggedy indeed, but none more so than New Radnor and its still quite new shire. The small grid of town streets, which remains the layout today, is filled with just a dozen or so houses, a market cross and the church, encircled by 'the Ruines of the old wall'. Above them sulks the squat red fortress with five towers.

The plan was that New Radnor would become a major centre for the county and far beyond, but it never took off. Despite its status, for over three hundred years, as an incorporated Borough[6], its paltry size, controversial pedigree and crucial place on one of the most disputed borders of the age continued to thwart progress. Its only real contribution to the life of the county was as the home of a notoriously brutal jail in the most intact of the castle's corner

towers. New Radnor was never blessed; bloodshed and strife were the most regular visitors. Shire town status soon dribbled away to Presteigne, and the medieval grid of streets, even now, is full of gaps that were never filled in. The stonework of the castle, last recorded in situ in 1840, was stripped and used for building materials, and now there's just a pitted green mound looming large and gloomy over the place, like the mountain that people can't stop themselves drawing and building out of mashed potato in *Close Encounters of the Third* kind. In 1843, excavations for the new church turned up dozens of beheaded skeletons, believed possibly to have been victims of Owain Glyndŵr's inevitable attack on the castle. Something creepy hangs in the air, and it's not entirely the fault of the hideous church, one that the Pevsner guide calls "an extreme case of unsuitable rebuilding".

True to form in this place of eternally unfulfilled ambition, the railway only latterly limped into town in 1875, the last of Radnorshire's tiny branch lines. It didn't even properly reach the place, but spluttered to an apologetic halt in a field half-a-mile short[7]. Plans were to continue it through to Aberystwyth, but the money ran out and the tracks never went any further. Late to the

party, and one of the first to leave: the line was closed to passengers in 1950, years before Beeching. New Radnor's one and only concession to cosmopolitan gaiety comes in the shape of a soaring, Victorian Gothic memorial to the area's nineteenth century MP Sir George Cornewall Lewis, a prototype, it is said, of the Albert Memorial in London. Yet even that is fenced off now, crumbling and dangerous.

The imposition of an alien settlement on the emerald embonpoint of Radnorshire has never worked too well: New Radnor and its latterday cousin, Llandrindod Wells, seem to prove the point. A visit to Presteigne only underlines it. Where New Radnor is silent, sour and even spooky, Presteigne lies back in the gentle swells of its landscape like a society beauty posing for a close-up. Being slap on the border, which runs along the River Lugg at the back of the parish church, the town likes to play up to both its Welshness and its Englishness, and succeeds in mixing them into something even more rare and pretty. You fair dance around Presteigne, while New Radnor only ever encourages you to trudge under an unseen burden.

The county town touches are at their most winsomely Ruritanian. On Broad Street, the portico of the 1829 Shire Hall displays just enough municipal muscle, but in a scaled-down version that can only make you smile. As the Assize seat until 1971, this was one of the oddest little outposts of the Circuit, and must have come as welcome relief to the more ponderous responsibilities of Chester or Birmingham. A superb museum, recreating the building as a Judge's lodging and courtroom of the 1870s, lives there now, and long may it do so. It is a beautifully calibrated crescendo of evocative sights, sounds, smells and experiences that culminate in going downstairs into the flickering gas-lit kitchens and cells, before climbing out and straight up into the Georgian courtroom dock where the trial of William Morgan, accused of duck theft, is under way. In the entire history of an independent Radnorshire Constabulary (1857-1948), the force dealt with only four murders. Of far more regular urgency was 'the tramp nuisance', the incarnation at the time of Radnorshire's eternal band of outlaws. The Chief Constable of Britain's most tinpot police force drew himself up to his full height when, in January 1877, he gave the order that "members of the force are earnestly requested to search every tramp they meet in passing through the county. The roads actually swarm with them... Robberies are occurring every day, invariably committed by tramps".

In Presteigne today, you're far more likely to be harassed by a folk singer or a face painter than a beardy old gentleman of the road. This town, neither here nor there, has become a most politic cluster of creatives, 'not real' as writer and enthusiastic resident Ian Marchant[8] had it, but who needs reality all of the time? After ambling around the handsome streets, admiring the profusion of posters for upcoming events, ducking the rain in the impressive parish church, and gathering quite a helpful crowd in the post office (Llanandras Swyddfa'r Post a Siop – Swyddfa'r Post Gyntaf yng Nghymru, as it says on the hand-painted sign, under a fluttering Union Jack), I retire to the cosy Jacobean Radnorshire Arms, despite one lady's concern that it might be beyond my budget. £3.75 for a pot of tea and an absolutely perfect toasted tea cake is a treat I'm willing to lavish on myself when I'm already having so much fun. As I wait at the bar, a gaggle of young local mums is laughing at a nearby table. "Stacey coming down?" one of them asks in a furzey border accent. "She'll be down," says another. "I saw it on Facebook, 'er status update, says she's gagging for a drink." The modern age has even reached little old Ruritania, and all is well with the world.

LLANDRINDOD WELLS

The county town of modern Powys is pure hallucination. Coming off the spur A4081 from the A470, it suddenly looms across the fields like a mirage, a fake film set of redbrick suburbia and Victorian turrets in raggedy Radnorshire. A few minutes later, you arrive in the town and cannot be entirely sure that there is anything behind the stentorian façades. Will pushing open the door of a shop send the whole simulacrum tumbling, a domino effect of shammery?

Go up to the golf course, past the ornamental lake, past the original Holy Trinity church[9] and high up on the lane beyond. From there, look down on the town hovering lightly over its landscape, anchored by its surrounding bowl of Cambrian hills, as green and gnarled as time itself. Cut one of the invisible tethers, however, and the whole shebang could float off into the ether. This lack of rootedness is both the best and the worst thing about Llandod[10]. It is best because it allows the town to be above and beyond, to have a history that is fiercely autarkic, almost entirely independent of anywhere or anything else. It is worst because it is forever an awkward incomer, a patched-up frock-coat of a town that's gone slightly to seed but still thinks it's somebody special.

In the pine green Metropole, long the embodiment of a gracious heyday, there's Sade crooning over the tannoy to a line of suits queuing up for a buffet lunch. They hop from one shiny-shoed foot to the other and laugh too loud at each other's jokes. It's conference time; here, there's always someone to confer with. No-one takes the sulphurous springs these days, so the hotels have to plump themselves up with businessmen, bureaucrats and political anoraks. You can't imagine that Llandrindod, many of its inhabitants as rootless as the town itself, voted too enthusiastically for devolution, yet the Assembly has been its saving grace. Our new governance means lots of new all-Wales bodies, all of whom come to Llandrindod for days gathered around a PowerPoint presentation and a bit of blue-sky thinking. It's ideal: two-thirds of the way down the A470 and equally (in)convenient for all.

'The hygienic Capital of Wales', where you could once have a Hot Sulphur Douche for 2/6 or a Local Peat Pack for 4/-, came to an end when the spa shut in 1971, after over two hundred years of activity. Fortunately for a town that was peering into an abyss of

superfluity, Ted Heath was busy at the time mucking around with the county boundaries, and in 1974, Powys was born, with Llandrindod as its much relieved capital. The council took over the vast Pump House Hotel as their headquarters, bulldozing it in the late 1980s in order to build their Legoland palace HQ. The two pepper-pot towers at the front of the building are the hotel's old boiler house, the sole survivors of *la belle époque*.

A trend was set, and the tiny capital of a banana republic was born. Muncipality was to be the town's saviour. The lavish Gwalia Hotel, down by the entrance to Rock Park, has metamorphosed into the county council's Radnorshire offices. The similarly grandiose Ye Wells Hotel, on Spa Road, is now all Coleg Powys. Next door, St John's church has become Powys County Council's Economic and Community Regeneration Directorate, which further spills over the road and into a suite of offices in Tom Norton's swaggering 1911 automobile palace. Between these and the main council offices is a largish, dullish outpost of the Welsh Assembly Government, its car park announced by a screech of signs that holler and nag in two tongues. Whitehall, Rads: a far cry from the muscular, moustachioed entrepreneurship that the plaque at the town's railway station attempts to conjure up, celebrating its '1990 Re-Victorianisation'[11].

Tom Norton, he of the glorious, curving Art Deco garage, was the modernist king of Llandrindod's golden years between the wars[12]. Nothing was beyond his ambition, including setting up an aerodrome in the Rock Ddole Pßark. His mantra was the gleaming, streamlined future: now the town has little to do except peddle its past. The Victorian Festival erupts to that end every August, in order to fill the streets with urchins and bonnets, sepia photographers and inappropriate burger vans. But when was Llandrindod's heyday? During the lacy tide mark of high Victoriana or in Tom Norton's roaring twenties? Even earlier perhaps, in the mid eighteenth century, when the first hotel was built, a huge place that contained every last modish touch, but which was still located on a windswept Radnorshire common miles from the nearest road? The hotel's distance from fashionable Georgian society lent it a raffish, some would say seedy, air, and ideas have persisted ever since that the taking of the waters was little more than a front for brothels, opium dens, casinos and beyond-the-Pale licentiousness.

Years later Cooke's *Topography of Wales*, written in the 1830s, reminds its readers that the sulphurous water is a purgative of no mean order and "should on no account be taken in the afternoon". It would be the most malodorous of experiences, for the water already smells like the kind of bowel gas that you only ever emit when really quite poorly. It assaults your nostrils as you walk down

through Rock Park to fill your bottles at the chalybeate well. Try a sip though. It's not (quite) as bad as it smells. Like sucking a rusty nail – not that I ever have sucked a rusty nail, but this is what it would taste like.

The old pump rooms and spa buildings, opposite the well, are still seeking gainful employment. They're not the only ones: Llandrindod has the highest joblessness rate in Powys[13]. Like many seaside resorts with their ample supply of down-at-heel boarding houses, an old spa town is a useful dumping ground for local authorities' most persistently problematic clients. It's a policy that has ripped the thin fabric of civic pride to shreds, and mutterings about imported junkies and anti-social behaviour are the stuff of every shop counter. Then you go outside, and see bustling streets, handsome shops and folk chatting happily on every corner. The entrepreneurial chutzpah, the swaggering self-belief is still there, even if a couple of generations of tin gods have done their best to dent and squash it. Which is the mirage? Will the real Llandrindod please stand up?

PENYBONT

It's a quick blur through a wet windscreen on the A44, but Penybont hints at something much more substantial. There's still a railway station, if with precious few trains, and we're slap at the end of the runway of Llandegley International Airport. You've not flown from there? Oh, you should; it's a joyous experience, the antidote to the usual terminal tedium.

Where is it? As you'll see from the road sign on the A44 between Cross Gates and Penybont, you are just 2½ miles from terminals 1 and 3 of Llandegley International – but that is as near as you'll ever get, for it is an airport solely of the imagination. This gentle wheeze was dreamed up in 2002 by Nicholas Whitehead and friends, who wanted to place something that would stretch minds and alter horizons along this busy road. The sign disappeared in November 2009, but after some intensive lobbying, it reappeared in May 2010. I interviewed Nicholas about the airport for my TV series. He admonished me for daring to say that the airport wasn't 'real'. "It's real in the sense that Wednesdays and Christmas are real", was his unarguable response. At the time, John Lennon Airport at Liverpool had just adopted its motto from the lyric of 'Imagine':

"above us only sky"[14]. Does Llandegley have its own slogan? It does, Nicholas told me, and it's in verse:

> It's not all truth, this world of things,
> The soul can fly, the heart has wings.
> So find new worlds, defy the rational,
> Fly Llandegley International.

Signs of gigantism continue into Penybont. There's a vast wayside coaching inn[15] (where posters advertise a meeting next week at which farmers will be advised about the pros and cons of aborting sheep) and the inestimable Thomas Shop, a labyrinthine drapers and general store that has been there since 1805[16]. Massive hiring fairs took place here into the late 1940s, and until Foot and Mouth wiped it out in 2001, a huge livestock market sat just beyond the Severn Arms, with a branch of NatWest – now inevitably a private house named The Old Bank – opposite to stash the cash. Greatest of all Penybont's outsize features, however, is the trotting racecourse, fondly decreed by some zealous committee members in the 1920s to be the 'Wembley of Wales'. The name has stuck, if for no discernible reason beyond our need for aggrandisement by daft comparison.

It's race day. The indistinguishable announcements from the tannoy commentator are bouncing across the grey roofs of the village with the same randomness as the curtains of soft rain. Cars, horse boxes, vans, trucks, caravans and 4x4s are heading down to the course, over the sluggish waters of the River Ithon. Cool-boxes and thermos flasks are hauled out; dogs on short leads piss on tyres and size each other up.

I've only ever been here when there are no races on, when unhurried sheep occupy the stalwart little grandstand and lean-to bar, and quietly chew the racetrack itself. All change today. At the front of the grandstand is a small concrete dais, home throughout the afternoon to The Committee, all men of a certain age, a certain ruddiness and a certain shape. Leader of the pack is the Committee Member on the microphone, who, between puffs on his fag, regales us with the strange poetry of trotting: "And ladiesngennlemen, don't forget, on sale all the tack, harnesses and sulkies you could ever need", "it's Ynys Gwynfor from Saunders Playboy, though Ithon Ace is trying to break, ladies and gentlemen, and there goes Sunnyside Geoff, another from the Clarke Brecon stable, but – yes! – Saunders Playboy is powering through on the Blacksmiths' Bend, and IT'S SAUNDERS PLAYBOY ALL THE WAY TO THE LINE!".

Six bookies cluster in the centre of the course. Two have electronic boards on which to declare their odds, the others stick to marker pens and wipe-clean surfaces. There is much feverish comparison between the six about the odds that they are offering. Sometimes word sweeps round, and odds on a particular horse tumble like dominoes; the trick is to get in quick before they can wipe it clear of the old price. As I've never heard of any of the horses, riders or trainers, my only way of choosing is to seize on a name I like, or that they hail from somewhere I have connections with. As a result, I'm soon down eight pounds at two quid a flutter. At least my horses make it over the line. Last time I went racing, someone persuaded me to stick a tenner on a dead cert. They were half right: the poor beast had a fatal heart attack three-quarters of the way around the track and keeled over quite spectacularly, before being unceremoniously hauled off to the knackers on the back of a truck.

The big Penybont race day, the Wembley etc., is on the first Wednesday of August. This is the track's lesser event, the Llandrindod Wells meeting, traditionally held on the August Bank Holiday Monday that acts as the soggy chequered flag to the summer. Trotting, or harness, racing is a big deal in Mid Wales and the Borders[17]: a well-rehearsed roster of meets take place every year between Easter and September on farm fields throughout this green swathe of the country. Up close, it's impressive: horses in peak condition pulling their flimsy carriages at breakneck speed, their riders – by no means the tiny and svelte of normal horse-racing – hollering, tugging at the reins and lying flat on their backs to improve their aerodynamics. Penybont is the cathedral of trotting; the only course owned and managed by its race committee. No wonder they look so puffed-up and proud, crammed in on their little concrete platform. Most of the crowd look like regulars, for the sport has a diehard band of followers who traipse around the circuit in cheerful convoy.

Llandrindod Lions, the ones in the dayglo tabards, organise a plastic duck race on the Ithon during the interval, while we go and partake of the bar – a sheep shed for 363 days of the year. A neighbouring sweet stall offers a multitude of bright, sugary confections, laid tantalisingly out above a sign that informs us that 'WE ALSO SELL CIGARETTES'. There's something about the whole place, and the whole event, that is as if the nanny state obsessions of the twenty-first century had never arrived. Not only can you buy ciggies from her, but the sweets on sale look more suspiciously lurid

than anything I've seen since Woolies pic'n'mix in the seventies. We can walk right across the course, churned up by hooves and wheels, without anyone getting in a flap. Everyone looks both ways, as if crossing a busy road according to the rules of the Tufty Club, as they head over to the stand (a further pound on the five quid race-card and entry fee will get you a seat and a shelter from the squalls of rain). Last time I was here, the stand was wooden and lop-sided. It's now smart and concrete. Trotting is booming.

We're not, though. My partner is getting a headache from the incessant thump and screech of the loudspeakers, and neither of us can understand half of the terminology that is tumbling out of them at great volume. "One final flutter", I say, "before we go". I look at the bookies' boards. Someone is standing in the way of the horses' names and all I see is the word MAP. That'll do for me. It turns out to be a horse called Maple Star, or Map Le Star, as I prefer to think of it. Two quid on at 4/1. The odds are tumbling; I'm the third in a row to place money on it and the last before it is wiped clean to re-emerge at a far stingier 2/1. It's a fine-looking horse, and the jockey looks psyched up for victory at any cost. The horses flash past twice, nostrils dilating and hooves thundering. Map Le Star is out in front, and the man on the mike is getting so excited he's almost forgetting to smoke his fag. "And it's Maple Star coming off the last bend, romping home by a two horse lead. IT"S MAPLE STAR AT THE FINISH! WHAT A STAR! WHAT A MAPLE STAR!" Winning is wonderful. Adrenaline surges through my veins and I clutch my victory tenner as if it were an Olympic gold. For once in my life, I quit while I'm ahead.

RHAYADER

As the great green heart of Wales, Powys is undoubtedly home of the nation's crossroads. But exactly where shall we place it? There are, I think, four main candidates. Swayed slightly by localism, but also by a sense of occasion and by anchoring the country to its Welsher west, the clock tower at Machynlleth could stake its claim, where the trunk road from Aberystwyth to the north meets the main road through the Severn-Dyfi pass from the Marches.

For the more aesthetically-inclined, the seventeenth century market hall at Llanidloes, throttled by lorries but gracefully serene when left to itself, certainly fits the bill. Llanidloes claims to be at the geographical centre of Wales, so what better focal point than its own half-timbered hub around which the entire town whirls? Today's turbo-charged driver might perhaps opt instead for the more prosaic charm of the A470-A44 roundabout at Llangurig. Following the A470 signs that point to this tiny Montgomeryshire village from scores of miles away, unsuspecting motorists must be anticipating a settlement of some stature as they count down the distance to the Valhalla-in-the-hills, only to find that Llangurig vanishes as fast as it appeared, and best plough on to somewhere else.

Somewhere like Rhayader, for example. The A470 twists along a high bank above the Wye for the ten mile dash from Llangurig down to Rhaeadr Gwy, the waterfall on the Wye. Here is the nation's true automotive omphalos, at the stumpy clock tower where the A44 sweeps in from the plains to meet the A470 and the old mountain road to the coast. What a hallowed spot it is, and how fittingly it wears its crown as the national crossroads, for this is a junction of spectacular indecision, yet also sweet little outbreaks of politeness and consideration on a map whose arteries are becoming increasingly furred by road rage. No-one is ever quite sure of whose right of way it is, so all motorists hover uncertainly, juddering forward, pulling back, waving on and swearing quietly under their breath.

The scarred iron boulders standing guard around the clock bear witness to the many occasions when an artic has slightly misjudged its trajectory. Knowing full well that this is where the entire nation must meet, peer, hover, wave and slowly edge forward, the town has boldly, and baldly, named the four roads that radiate from it North, South, East and West Streets. The centre of the compass.

Crossroads are a dangerous place, a liminal spot beyond normal rules, and so it is with Rhayader. It lasted only a handful of years as one of the nominal capitals of the new entity of Radnorshire, before the murder of a judge there sent the whole imperial pageant scuttling as far east as it could go, to Presteigne. Since then (1542), the town has never shown any more enthusiasm for pulling up its socks and combing its unruly hair. With six toll gates surrounding the town on new turnpike roads, it was the epicentre in the 1840s for some of the most spectacular outbreaks of the Rebecca Riots, involving scores of local men dragging up in bonnets and frocks and going out gate-smashing most weekends for a year. A detachment of the 7th Fusiliers was sent to Rhayader, the Metropolitan police contingent increased to twelve constables and a Superintendent, but the locals closed ranks and few arrests were ever made. So intoxicated were the Rhayader Rebeccas by the experience that they carried on frocking up and causing chaos well into the twentieth century, long after the issue of the tolls and turnpikes had been settled. They turned their righteous ire towards the question of fishing rights on the rivers Wye and Ithon, poaching in large gangs. On the arrival of any authorities, the disguised men would form a solid square, one side of which was armed with spears.

Appropriately, Rhayader has spawned a latterday Rebecca, who wields spears as sharp as any of her predecessors. Rebbecca Ray exploded on to the literary scene in 1998, aged only eighteen, with her brilliant, scabrous, uncompromising (and wildly successful) novel, *A Certain Age*. Its opening words let you know exactly what you're in for: "I was about thirteen when I started letting boys feel me up. There was a whole bunch of them, four or five, and at lunchtime we'd all meet up; smoking a spliff out on the pitch if it was sunny, round their table in the library if it wasn't." She spent the next seven years working on the follow-up, *Newfoundland*, described by her agent as "a thousand page long love letter to Wales". It's no billet-doux of burbling sweet nothings, though: *Newfoundland* casts a harsh, unblinking eye on the dispossession and ennui of a mid Wales shunted out to the very edge of consciousness.

Having grown up on a ramshackle old farm near Rhayader, thanks to "dope smoking, goat-rearing, hippy artist parents"[18], Ray returned to the area in the mid 2000s and spent the next few years organising a festival, also named Newfoundland. Trying to harness the energy of the free party scene, which had been such a thrilling force in mid Wales, Newfoundland made great play about keeping its location secret up to the last minute, but as the years went by, the festival grew, it all became far more official, and the underground vibe became increasingly hard to maintain. Although the festival website promises another in the future, Rebbecca told me that she was knocking it on the head, and getting itchy feet about getting away from the area – again – altogether.

So it looks like the last Newfoundland, in 2009, was just that. I was there, and could see what a thankless task it was to organise. The location was superb, on a couple of fields by the Afon Elan, just up from its confluence with the Wye, and within easy sauntering distance of the very many, and very fine, pubs of Rhayader. But hippies and crusties are not the first to want to pay for anything, and there just weren't enough punters. Those of us reading on the Seren literature and spoken word stage had to compete with a neighbouring sound system which always seemed to boom in deep and bassy at just the moment you were trying to create a mood of maximum intensity or poignancy. Huge fun though: getting pissed and near-hysterical in a muddy field with the likes of Rebbecca, Tom Bullough, Samantha Wynne-Rhydderch, Deborah Kay Davies, Jasper Fforde and Tiffany Atkinson is a weekend I'd recommend to anyone, but the sparsely-filled dance tents, for all their coruscating breakbeats, organic techno and twisty psychedelic trance, seemed like pale imitations of the parties I remembered from ten, fifteen years earlier. Was it me getting old and crabby, or the whole scene? I still couldn't work it out as the farmer's tractor winched my camper van out of the mud two long days later, when all I could think about was a hot bath.

Oh god, growing up. It comes to us all. Rebbecca Ray once said, in answer to the question of what motivates her to write, that it was "an inbuilt desperation to prove myself, coupled with total unemployability". Yet the next time we meet, she's firmly employed at Carad (Community Arts Rhayader And District), the town's excellent arts organisation that runs a flexible performance space and lovely little community museum. I'm part of a theatre group touring a production of Alan Bennett's *The Lady in the Van* around mid Wales; Rhayader, and Rebbecca, make for one of the best stops of all. We retire to the pub after the play; it's gone closing time but

she knows which doors to knock on. She is on sizzling form, loving the town on nights like this, hating it at others and wanting to get away. Rhayader will always be there to return to, if needs be. We roar with laughter, both agreeing, and with only a modicum of embarrassment, that we'd far rather be drinking beer in a decent pub after a nice bit of middle-class theatre, than 'aving it large (and increasingly paranoid) in a wet field somewhere.

I think of Rebbecca again, when I'm back a month or so later on field duty, a mile out of town. No rave this time, but the orderly daily feeding of the red kites at Gigrin Farm, 2pm prompt (3pm BST). Watching the kites circle and plunge reminds me of the way she swoops and seizes on the meat of ideas and information, zooming in to pick them up in razor-sharp talons and spirit them away to who knows where. I shake over-laboured metaphors from my head, and just watch, in awe.

Binoculars quiver in the hides as, on the stroke of two, farmer Chris Powell bounces his tractor into the field. He emerges to pitchfork slabs of raw beef out on to the grass; Gigrin get through over a quarter of a ton of meat from the local abattoir every week. Until then, I'd only spotted a couple of circling kites, but suddenly the skies thicken as a host of birdlife swirl in for their afternoon snack. Kites are quite shy creatures, so it was up to the crows and ravens to make the first plunge, followed swiftly by the buzzards. Only then did the kites – dozens, then scores, then hundreds – begin to dive, with deadly precision. Unlike the other birds, kites will not linger on the ground, so they have to seize the flesh in mid-flight to earth, before a twitch of their rudder-like tail spins them back up into the air and aloft to a tree where they can safely enjoy their spoils. There were spats and even muggings between the birds, but everyone gets what they need. The kites have a well-ordered ranking for food: the older birds feed first, before making way for the younger members of the family.

The story of the red kite in Powys is well-rehearsed, but no less thrilling for that. Down to a dozen or so birds twenty-five years ago, careful breeding programmes and improved husbandry have seen the numbers climb steadily, spectacularly. Red kites have been introduced too into other parts of Britain, but they are imported Spanish hybrids; the Powys brethren are the only natives left. Standing at the crossroads, it all seems quietly hopeful[19], that this last redoubt can fly high too. There's something in the air. It might be a riot.

ELAN VALLEY

I'm getting a bad dose of topographic dislocation. Walking from Rhayader to the reservoirs of the Elan Valley, I slide out of an oak wood and into the Birmingham suburbs of my childhood. Specifically, into Bournville, that pub-free model village built by the Cadburys, full of fresh air, fruit trees and incy-wincy rusticity. My great-grandparents, Nan and Danty, had lived there, and Sunday afternoon visits were always enlivened by a bag of chocolate mis-shapes, dropped off by the rent collector. The Quaker Cadburys only started producing chocolate in a vain attempt to wean the working classes off beer and bad gin; so strong was their antipathy to alcohol that Danty had to take an empty violin case with him to the nearest pub, in order to smuggle a few bottles of beer back home. It all comes flooding back, and I then remember that I'm in Breconshire[20].

The scale model of Bournville, itself a model of the scale of Victorian philanthropic ambition, is the settlement known as Elan Village, built as part of the gargantuan reservoir scheme at the turn of the twentieth century. The solid stone village came at the end of the scheme, replacing a wood-and-zinc shanty town provided for the construction navvies and their families: in 1901, the population was over 1500. When new workers arrived for the first time, they were made to stay for one week in the 'Doss House' on the Radnorshire bank of the river, where they were kept in quarantine for a week, while being dipped and bathed like sheep, undergoing a medical examination and having all of their clothes and possessions disinfected. Should they pass all that, and get a job on the site, only then were they allowed across the bridge and into the village on the Breconshire bank. This one small suspension bridge was patrolled round-the-clock by Birmingham Corporation officials: only residents were allowed to cross, and they were frequently searched to ensure that they weren't doing a Danty. Suspicion of the demon drink was a major factor in the regime here too. The central canteen did serve beer, but only the weakest of brews, only in moderate quantities and only to men. Long lists of rules pasted to the walls ensured order. Number 12: "Amusements in the house are strictly prohibited. No music, singing, juggling, reciting, gambling, card playing, playing dice, dominoes, draughts, marbles, shovel-penny, or any game of either skill or chance, will be permitted in the house."

Once the tramps and navvies had left, the real village was built, brimful of Brummie municipal chutzpah[21]. They did their utmost to create a little patch of Midland suburbia in the alien hills; horse chestnut trees line a genteel walkway the length of a well-tamed stretch of river, pushing the gnarled rocks and mountains out of sight, out of mind. A hundred Welsh winters have battered the smart semis into a modicum of submission, but the houses, school, even the public toilet block, were built to last. Most importantly, they were built to stamp unambiguously their urban claim over this rural backwater.

The 71 square mile Elan Valley estate is an exclave of England's second city, Nagorno-Karabakh without the blood feuds. Mostly. There are nods to its actual locale, but they are few, token and entirely the product of more recent, more squeamish sensibilities. Lurking between the Visitor Centre and the bottom dam of the sequence is a huddle of jagged standing stones, which a plaque announces as Maesyfed 2000 Radnor, a millennial celebration of a county that had itself seen the waters close over its head. Each stone represents a different Radnorshire community, and they are grouped in the approximate representation of their place on the map, but even as you admire it, your eyes are drawn to the roaring wall of water behind that could overwhelm it in an instant.

There's a counter-point to the Radnorshire stones in Birmingham's Cannon Hill Park: a full scale model of the Elan Valley reservoirs in fifties concrete. The Welsh hills have been tamed into small grassy knolls, the sessile oak woods reduced to polite herbaceous borders and rockery plants, and the water sits foul and stagnant. For an episode of *Great Welsh Roads*, I decided to trace the route of the Elan Valley aqueduct from Brum back to Wales, and to start the programme at the Cannon Hill model. Getting permission to film involved a great deal of city council departments, line managers, official requests, phone calls and emails, but once the PR manager was on board, they couldn't do enough to help. Only latterly has anyone in Birmingham much thought about what was displaced by their epic water scheme, and in this age of guilt-tinged apologies for the strong-arm actions of earlier generations, the council wanted to be on their very best behaviour for a visiting Welsh TV crew. When we arrived, the water was clear and trickling, the grass looked as if it had been trimmed with nail scissors, brand new flowers shivered nervously in freshly-dug beds, and every dog turd and Coke can had been spirited away. I used to live just up the road, and there were always dog turds and Coke cans. A committee of cringing council managers and staff greeted us, thanked us profusely for our water, thanked us a bit more, photographed us for the municipal bulletin and invited us to stay awhile. Our cut-price schedule made that an impossibility, and it all seemed a little harsh to knock out a forty second piece to camera and then shoot off, Rhayader-bound, the welcome committee's overload of thanks still ringing in our ears[22].

In the early days, no-one thought to mourn what had been lost, or even to think that anything much had. Like the flow of the water itself, trickling down its 1:2300 gradient towards the east[23], it's all been a very one-way process. "The land in the Elan and Claerwen district being very poor, having but few inhabitants, but a large volume of pure water running in its streams, was admirably adapted for the gathering ground of the water required by a great city" boomed the Ward Lock guide of 1910, six years after the scheme had been opened by King Edward VII[24]. And the benefits were not only the obvious ones: "It is much softer than the water with which Birmingham was previously supplied", the guide continued to purr, "and when the scheme was under discussion it was calculated that the superior softness would effect a saving of one hundred and twenty thousand pounds in the collective soap bill of the citizens".

As also happened at Vyrnwy and Tryweryn, in military zones like Epynt and in the conifers of the Dyfi, Dyfnant or Hafren Forests, a paucity of people in great quantity was conflated into the idea that there was barely any community to disturb. The million gossamer threads binding rural, Welsh-speaking districts were never visible to those who could see only clanking, heavy-duty chains. The only eulogised loss at Elan Valley were the two houses in which Percy Bysshe Shelley briefly stayed, but in fact the reservoirs obliterated three manor houses, eighteen farms (all tenancies, so no compensation for the farmers), an assortment of cottages, a school and a church, and displaced hundreds of occupants of Radnorshire's last Welsh-speaking community. That this area had been such a tinder-box of the Rebecca Riots[25] surely only hastened its demise.

Elan Valley is where a Cymro-Brummie (Brumro?) feels at his most compromised. The hand-wringing guilt and apologies emerge waif-like and crusted from our lips, but are then blown away by a great fat fart of civic pride at the sheer bloody scale of the whole thing. Beginning at the bottom, by the Bournville manqué of Elan Village, gets the juices flowing nicely for starters, but they are soon cascading free as a mountain stream as we climb the grand staircase of reservoirs through ever more impressive twirls and swirls of a style that became pejoratively known as Birmingham Baroque (though true to form, most Brummies took it as a compliment). We gleefully point out the little redbrick valve houses that line the aqueduct's underground route along the road to Ludlow and beyond, and get a strange tingle of affection[26] at every glimpse of the four great pipes breaking cover and hurtling across a valley encased in stonework fit for the Romans. We remember that this soft, peaty water was probably the first we ever sipped, and that it brought new heart to our forebears, grinding out unimaginably tough lives in the foundries and grime of inner city Brum. By the time we reach the top reservoir, Craig Goch, we'd really quite like to see, as a counter-balance to the model in Cannon Hill Park, a miniature concrete Birmingham smiling down in gap-toothed wonder at the swollen hills that give it life.

RIVER WYE, SAFN-Y-COED

The Severn may grab the superlatives of size and significance, but its smaller twin, the Wye, got the looks. Both rivers rise within a few hundred yards of each other on the side of Pumlumon, and both topple wide and tidal into the Bristol Channel, seventy direct miles away[27]. Between their mutual alpha and omega, they grow apart in every possible way.

Having grown up by it, and gone to school on its flood plain (it was always a delight to see the monster rise and knock out games lessons), I'm far more familiar with the Severn. It has many idyllic stretches, but it is a working river of redbrick mills and factories, busy towns and freight traffic. The Wye, by contrast, flows past plump orchards and farms, half-timbered villages and lonely churches. Its most urban encounter is with Hereford, one of England's smaller, sleepier cathedral cities, and the definite junior of its Severnside siblings, Worcester and Gloucester.

The Wye, yr Afon Gwy, stays closer to Wales too. A few miles down from its Montgomeryshire source, it briefly forms the border with Radnorshire, before crossing the outstretched limb of the smaller county and, only six or seven miles south on the other side of Rhayader, becoming the divide between Radnorshire and Breconshire. Although the river meanders extensively, and proceeds to loop up on itself as it heads north towards Hay, it remains the county boundary throughout. It finally quits Radnorshire for Herefordshire at Rhydspence on the A438, returning again as the

England-Wales border in its final stretch from Monmouth to Chepstow.

Aesthetically, there's not a duff part of the Wye. You could argue for hours about which is its finest section: no two people would entirely agree, for there are far too many candidates for the prize. The river's broad beauty lights up even the humdrum experience of driving the A470, for sudden glimpses are caught regularly on the thirty-five mile drag between Llyswen and Llangurig, and they always thrill. This is the early-to-mid section of the Wye: from its rushing source, it has quickly established itself as wide, languid and pitted with fine, deep pools. It is in no hurry, and commands you to be the same.

On the Radnor side of the river, looking across at the southern tip of Montgomery a few miles downstream of Llangurig, is the farm of Safn-y-Coed, the throat of the wood, whose story is typical of many smallish sheep farms scattered across this deep green country. Derek Morgan's grandfather rented it off Radnorshire county council in 1946, and bought it soon after. Derek grew up there[28], and with his wife Veronica raised their children there. Nearing retirement age, they find that none of their offspring want to take on the place, a situation that is precisely replicated in four

adjoining farms. Derek doesn't much blame the youngsters, for a small set-up like theirs[29] is endless hard work and permanently hovering on the economic margins. "That's not what kids these days want," he says, with agrarian understatement.

It's a sharp winter's day, and I'm happy to drink tea, eat biscuits and chew the fat in their warm kitchen. For folk facing a daily battle to survive, they're resolutely cheerful and terrific company, happy to spell out to an agricultural ignoramus the changes they've witnessed in recent decades. "In the sixties and seventies," Derek tells me, "we were encouraged to produce food, and we did, extremely well and very efficiently. Britain was about eighty percent self-sufficient then; now it's fifty percent, and most of the emphasis on funding for farmers comes from us looking after the environment." This is not a mere moan however, for, he says, the Environmentally Sensitive Areas (ESA) scheme, in place for the last decade or so, has actually worked quite well. For instance, it's not been too much problem to change grazing regimes, allowing the heather to regenerate, and it has, he says, "kept a lot of locals here. Don't forget, hill farming has always been reliant on grants of some sort. There's an inherent high cost of production, and there always has been."

Schemes and subsidies come and go, however, according to the whims of politicians and civil servants in Brussels, London and, these last few years, Cardiff too. Devolution has been hugely beneficial, Derek says, for the concerns of Radnorshire hill farmers could never catch the distant eye. He's not so sure though, that "there's much joined-up thinking going on in any of the centres of government, and certainly not between them". He'd like to see as many decisions as possible taken in Wales.

The big development in the area lately is for franchised chicken sheds on an industrial scale. The farmer borrows enough cash to build the set up, which, along with the birds, the feed and the guaranteed market for pale chickens that go for three quid a pop in Tesco or Asda, is provided by the franchisers. Total start up costs are over half a million, but Derek has seen some of his neighbours recoup that in just a handful of years. "Had it come along a few years ago, I might well have tried it," he says. "It's a heck of a gamble though, because so many are doing it. There were around forty local planning applications just last year for chicken sheds. Those that got in there early will probably be fine, but is there enough for everyone? What if the market changes, or the price goes significantly up or down?"

Diversification has long been the buzzword thrown at farmers, but it's been an eternal reality for the smaller tenants and farmowners of mid Wales. The flatpack chicken sheds are the latest in a long line of crafty bits of income on the side. "When I left school," Derek tells me, "there were many jobs in the community that small farmers were able to fit in around their agricultural work. They'd be able to do a little work such as labouring or road-mending for the council, or planting and felling with the Forestry Commission. Those jobs just don't exist like that any more."

I take a tour round the farm, down to the geese by the Wye's edge, up to the horses and sheep in the fields. The scale is human, warm and should, by any rational analysis, be entirely viable. That it is not says far more about the way we have been run as a society than it does about the methods of Derek, his father and grandfather before him. "What will this place look like in fifty years, do you think?" I ask him. "Well, there's no real future for upland farming", he replies. "Someone will probably be running it, perhaps joined up with a few other nearby farms, or as a part-time concern. It's not difficult to separate the farmhouse from the fields: they'll probably have amalgamated the fields with other farms and have sold the house to people from away." He shrugs his shoulders.

'Away' is a word he returns to often. It's where his children went, and the children of many of his farming neighbours. It's where they find casual employees, on the rare occasions that they're needed. And it's where many of the area's newest inhabitants have originated. Retirees. Good Lifers. Folk who come on a sunny bank holiday weekend, and buy a dream on the back of it. Dream often turns to a nightmare, but there's always another set of starry-eyed hopefuls just behind. Away, away, far far away.

Derek is also one of twenty-eight commoners with rights to grazing and estovers[30] on Llandeuddwr Common, which runs up from behind Safn-y-Coed and over to the fringes of the Elan Valley reservoirs. The Elan Valley Trust gazumped the commoners when the freehold of the Common came up for sale[31], a fact that still rankles with Derek ("they're a charity – why would they stitch us up like that?"), but he's proud to be an active commoner, and enjoys the camaraderie and sense of historical continuity that it affords. Tradition is slipping away there too, the well-worn, hard-won instincts passed down in rock and water from one generation to the next. You can see them intricately mapped in the massive, shovel-like hands of both Derek and Veronica, hands that have

grafted endlessly, hands that I can't quite take my eyes off. The hands that matter now are those clutching their newly-acquired degrees from antiseptic classrooms, those of the over-qualified, under-experienced youngsters bearing down on them with this week's Good Idea. They seldom are.

LLANELWEDD

Ardent eisteddfodwyr may disagree, but the Royal Welsh is the nation's true cauldron. For four days in July, Wales' rural essence quietly elbows any Cymraeg puritanism out of the way, and everyone is invited. O Fôn i Fynwy[32] is a lovely, lofty ideal, but only here does it truly happen. Faces reveal the manifold tribes. Accents clipped, guttural and mellifluous combine into a Welsh Babel, while the Welsh and English languages collide and elide, slipping over one another like post-coital lovers. There is no sting.

Plenty of biting, bleating and shitting though. This is an agricultural show to its marrow; the Lifestyle Gurus won't have their wicked way here. The hot tubs and the hard-sell wine societies are there of course, but they are far outshone by the zing of new tractors lined up like Tonka toys in Hamleys, the banners promising cures for ovine adenomatosis, the starched white coats ushering gleaming beasts and the flat caps welded to weathered heads.

Past, present and future muck in enthusiastically together. Young farmers swagger in packs, like boisterous bullocks. My first Big Show, I settled in the front few rows of the shearing shed (Meirionnydd is its sponsor county), and was rewarded with a fine view of prime slices of Welsh manhood grappling their sheep into denuded submission. After a while, I noticed that most of my fellow front row audience were teenage girls, and that we all had much the same expression on our faces. The sheering competitions crescendo into a tumult of clapping, cheering, buzzing machinery, laughter and commentators goading each other on to ever higher plains of hyperbolic oratory.

The sponsor county idea is Wales at its sweetest. Every year, one of the old thirteen counties of Wales – Wales and Monmouthshire if we're going back that far and if we're feeling picky – takes on the task of being the major sponsor of the show. They get a little glory in return for a vast fundraising effort. It's a hark back to the days, pre-1963, when the show roved throughout Wales, as the Eisteddfod still does. Each county also sponsors a pavilion around the site, and there's often a tacit aptness between county and building. Montgomeryshire's pavilion is a substantial, if rather fusty, restaurant, members only, sat in plum position at the heart of the site: the best place from which to watch the world parade by. Glamorgan's is a sprawling, slightly tacky market. Tŷ Ynys Môn sits in gaunt isolation, a spiky little information booth that looks like an Eastern European border post. Pembrokeshire, of course, has built itself a Tower, a bold epithet for something all of two storeys high, and it's from there that the announcements for the main ring are barked out in commanding tones. And Meirionnydd, that wiry hill county, sponsors the shearing shed, perhaps the most fun place of all.

Not inappropriately, Radnorshire, the host county[33], is represented only by some backstage stock shed, visited by barely anyone. In fact, the entire site is the gift of Wales' least-populated county, for it was the Radnor Committee at the beginning of the 1960s who took it on themselves to find and buy a suitable permanent site, presenting it with quiet flourish to the Royal Welsh Agricultural Society. The society was broke; post-war shows had been hit by poor attendance and bad weather, and they had little option but to accept. Radnorshire's far-sighted graft and generosity of half a

century ago has paid handsome dividends, for every B&B, hotel, campsite and pub in the area bursts at the seams when things go on at the showground. And they do: the Royal Welsh is the event that brings the area to a shuddering halt, but there are numerous other festivals, from bikers' gatherings to a Christian holiday camp, to fill the beds and coffers.

Troi'r baw yn bres[34] promises one banner. It could be the motto for many of the stalls too, for seldom do you see so much tat so cheerfully – and ruthlessly – promoted, and always of course reduced from its original price. Guaranteed. Every year, there's one ubiquitous novelty toy or appliance, from Billy the Singing Fish fifteen years ago, through umpteen extendable window brushes to this year's squirting Crazy Daisy. I'm a sucker for the demonstration stalls, and always have to be restrained from buying the latest NASA-approved titanium pan set or magic dishcloth. One trim young lady invites me to feel her washboard stomach, all the result, she assures me, of the vibrating massage machine that she then runs up and down my back and bottom. It feels wonderful, though its tickling effect makes me shriek and giggle, and we soon draw a wide-eyed crowd.

The new food hall was the big story of 2010. It's light and a little blowsy, designed to strike a modernist Welsh pose amongst the age-old scene. Wood and slate try to make it look as if it has been grown from seed, but it's a chimera of Cymreictod, for the wood is Canadian and the slate Spanish. Inside, the narrow aisles are permanently clogged with punters checking out the free samples and making all the right noises about how they'll probably return and get some later, before sloping off to the next freebie. Like the building itself, the stall contents seem to be something of a pale imitation. Man can not live on bespoke ice-cream and artisan cheeses alone, even if it is washed down with a slug of Toffoc[35].

Wiping our mouths, we make our way past the forestry pole-climbers and the drenched kids water-bombing each other in kayaks to the comparative serenity of the Flower Tent. Every competitive part of the Royal Welsh is a celebration of human ingenuity and commitment, but this smells better than most. I get into a spirited discussion as to whether the winner of the Five Shallots on a Plate competition was merited: consensus seems to be that whoever won Third Prize was robbed. Shân Cothi bounces by in full piece-to-camera mode, her scarlet locks as iridescent as the nearby wall of fuchsias. One of the most enjoyable ways to spend quarter of an hour at the Royal Welsh is to strike an appreciative pose, all the better to eavesdrop, in front of the bespoke flower displays, those created according to themes such as 'Gwlad y Gân', 'America Celebrates', 'Our Industrial Heritage' or 'Cymru Wyllt'. If you manage to melt sufficiently into the background, you'll be rewarded by overhearing some of the most fantastically caustic comments ever uttered by respectable middle-aged ladies.

Normally, I loathe being forced to park'n'ride, but not here. The bus back to the car park, dusty and groaning with the weight of footsore punters and their new titanium pans, tinkles with chatter and laughter, everyone comparing their day and its many highlights. Grins crack the red faces, hands are shaken, alliances are forged and promises are made. Until next year, then. Tarra 'wan.

RHULEN

Is it real? Not entirely. Rhulen was the name given by Bruce Chatwin to his fictional town in *On the Black Hill*. It is the place to which the Jones twins, Lewis and Benjamin, and their parents before them, gravitate in times of need, excitement or crisis. It has a Broad Street, where Union Jacks fluttered with stiff pride in the victories of war, first, second and Boer. A Red Dragon inn, from whose smoky parlour the semi-feral Watkins clan are almost evicted as they clash antlers while circling predatorily around Jim's still-warm corpse. Unyielding, redbrick offices of land agents, solicitors and tractor merchants. Markets, fêtes, recruitment rallies, funerals and weddings. It is the town far beyond the Black Hill, where fashions ebb and flow, but rarely with enough force to skew the soul of the place. It is probably mostly Hay, though with a little bit of Presteigne, Kington and Knighton thrown in for good measure.

The opposite is true too. Rhulen is the embodiment of Otherness, a place apart, a looming backdrop that stays just out of focus, for the true place is a photographic negative of Chatwin's Rhulen. It is the real name not of a solid town of bricks, bars and gossip, but of possibly the most ethereal, gossamer parish in Radnorshire, itself the most insubstantial county in the land. Tucked in to the northern flank of the windy, wiry Begwns, the road to Rhulen across the hills from Painscastle and Clyro has only been driveable in anything less than a farm truck for the past decade or so. Prior to that, the only way in was from the deep green lane strung between Aberedw and Cregrina. The names sound as if they have been hauled up from the bottom of a dark, sweet well.

The parish is dissipated to the four winds[36]. A few farms, cattle chewing, rippling hills, the rush of unseen water, and you're there, at the whitewashed stone barn that is the thirteenth century parish church of St David[37]. In the sunlight, the glare of the walls bounces off a lapis lazuli sky and the scorching green of fields and trees; you'd be hard pressed to find a more intoxicating spot, or one at which you can breathe so deep and so heartily. David Barnes, in his *Companion Guide to Wales*, says that it has "a rare serenity somehow emblematic of the spirit of Radnorshire", and he is absolutely right. This is a county of wonderful churches in which you can happily lose days[38], but all the right ingredients collide at Rhulen.

Near perfect is the outside, the birdsong lane, the faded wooden

sign, the high-bank circular churchyard, the walls buckled by the weight of time and topped by a skewed wooden belfry. So perfect that you hesitate to go in, lest it should disappoint. It doesn't, of course. The massive wooden door, seventeenth century says Pevsner, swings open on vast hinges and you blink in the sudden gloom. There's something of a reverse Tardis effect going on, for the single cell room seems even tinier when you are in it than it looked from outside. The thickness of the walls makes some substantial difference, and you get a powerful idea of that from the recess in the east wall that houses the altar. The perfume of fresh(ish) flowers mingle with the must of antiquity, and just fleetingly, you contemplate the life of an anchorite, and find it appeals.

There's a book of services sat on one of the two window shelves, detailing every occasion (and how much was collected) in the church since 6th January, 1952, when the Reverend J.M. Evans gave twelve parishioners Holy Communion, and took the thirteen shillings and eightpence that they put into the plate. Congregations were never plentiful. The busiest service of 2009 was Lent 1 on St. David's Day, when there were a full eighteen worshippers, raising between them £47, though that may have been due to the fact that the ashes of Mrs Joyce Price were interred straight afterwards. The following weekend, Lent 2, four parishioners attended and gave, on

average, a pound each. Even the sole Christmas Day service, the 8am Holy Communion, saw only eight gather for worship. I can't think of anywhere I'd rather be as the first winter rays penetrate the royal depths of the biggest day of the year, and feel incredulous that anyone living within five miles of the place wouldn't think the same. Up on the Red Hill, and the Black Hill behind (yes, that Black Hill), no-one stirs, and no-one descends to the still-open church. They must all be in the other Rhulen, the one invented by Bruce Chatwin. Right now though, it's hard to say which one actually exists.

ABEREDW AND LLANSTEPHAN

I've asked novelist Tom Bullough[39] to take me to some of his favourite places. They will, I know, be in Radnorshire, despite the

CENTRAL

fact that Tom has been displaced for the last year or two down near Brecon. He is Radnor to the bone, telling me that he even gets a thrilling tingle when, in his travels, he comes across any lorry decorated with a declaration of its Radnorshire origins. "It doesn't happen very often," he says, "which only makes it all the more special". I guess not. There can't be many haulage companies in this green and empty part of the world.

The place that first sprang to Tom's mind was the valley of the Afon Edw between the villages of Aberedw and Llanbadarn-y-Garreg, somewhere I've never been before, despite whooshing past hundreds of times on the A470 just the other side of the Wye. It's July, but there's been a stack of rain lately, and the Wye is big and brown, fast and furious. There are lots of good swimming holes along this Builth-Llyswen stretch, but you wouldn't be chucking yourself in there today.

Aberedw has a bit of previous. There's a long-standing suspicion towards the village from amongst the Cymry, for this is where Prince Llywelyn, ein llyw olaf, hid out in his castle, and then in a cave before being betrayed and killed. Over seven centuries later, the wound still gapes. Perhaps that's the explanation for the village's slightly introverted atmosphere. Or maybe it's the stout physicality of the place: towering cliffs of rock everywhere, dripping with trees, ferns and mosses, the mouldering humps of both Llywelyn's castle and an earlier motte, the omnipresent rush of water. It manages to be both open and hemmed in at the same time. The contradictions continue: Tom tells me that for some significant part of the early middle ages, the English had taken land to the west of the Welsh, so that mottes and tumps seem to be fortified the wrong way around. It reminds me of the famous local legend that when Llywelyn attempted his last escape in the snow of December 1282, he had his horse shod back-to-front, so as to make it appear he had gone the other way. You can see the story illustrated on that lurid gable end mural at the main junction in Builth, surely the cause of a few gentle rear-end shunts.

Tom sets off at a gallop up the hill towards Llywelyn's Cave. I would never have found it alone. It is hidden behind a head-high forest of damp bracken that we have to hack through, which only makes the discovery of it all the more exciting. Tight clusters of beech trees pack the top of the cave, a slight gash in a wall of rock. You know it's the right one, though, because someone has painted Llywelyn's red-and-gold flag by the entrance, as if he is in residence. And maybe he is. There are more daubings inside the deceptively roomy cave: another flag, Llywelyn's crest, a Free Wales Army eagle, a freshly-painted slogan of Fe Godwn Ni Eto, We Shall Rise Again. It's all very respectful, if slightly odd, and Tom and I chat in reverential whispers as we squat on our haunches and peer around in the dank gloom.

We're off again. Tom's writing is muscular and sinewy, and so is he. He is also nearly a decade my junior and has managed to give up the fags, while I'm still hooked. It shows. He is off up the hill like a rabbit, while I huff along behind, rivulets of sweat starting to drip down into my eyes. We pass a derelict cottage, still full of the remnants of someone's life, that Tom has chosen to use as a location for a story he's written. Soon, we're out on the open heathland above, a desert of heather, whinberries, sheep, mawn pools and dazzling rock towers and platforms that demand to be climbed. The horizon is enormous, legendary: from the Camarthenshire Fan, through the Beacons and Black Mountains and right round to the distant humps of north Wales. My eye is continuously drawn to the more modest Mynydd Troed near Talgarth, the mountain with shoulder pads. I've been fascinated by it for years, but have never yet climbed it. I must.

We bounce along the hilltop ridge, on a springy grass track through the heather, scattering sheep and pheasants as we go. I want to sit on the grass and stuff my face with bright purple whinberries, but Tom is striding on, a proud shape atop the hills that he loves. We get to stop at Twm Tobacco's Grave, though. I find myself puzzling, for the umpteenth time, over the human tendency, when out in deep nature, to gravitate so unthinkingly towards anything manmade. In fact, the wilder the terrain, the more eagerly we seem to cling to evidence of ourselves, be it a signpost, a grave, an inscribed stone or a ruined bothy. The grave is a small mound of stones with a wooden sign telling us what it is. It doesn't tell us who Twm Tobacco was, though[40]. This is no-man's land, explicitly so, for a neighbouring boundary stone tells us that this lonely spot is the divide (or at least, it was in 1882) between the lands of two local bigwigs. Twm Tobacco straddles both, and neither.

Dropping down off the ridge, into a valley greener than a championship snooker table, we amble around the tiny, blank church of Llanbadarn-y-Garreg, before returning to Aberedw along the lane. The river thunders past, the colour of caramel, under yet more angular rock faces. This, Tom tells me, is the valley in

which he would like to end up, a place he can actually imagine settling. Such thoughts doubtless come to a man whose wife is seven months pregnant with their first child.

There's another nearby valley I'm keen to have him show me, the gorge of the Afon Bachawy, the 'Little Wye', a few miles south near the scattered village of Llanstephan. On the map, it looks steep, wooded and mysterious, an Iron Age hillfort perched high above the water on the middle of a meander. My interest is further piqued by reading in Kilvert's Diary his account of being told by some aged Clyro parishioner that this was the last place in Radnorshire where the fairies were seen. We talk rural hallucinogenics[41], fairies and Kilvert, whose diaries Tom has not read. The pantheon of Radnorshire writing may not be massive, but it is distinguished, the most famous product of recent times being Bruce Chatwin's *On The Black Hill*. To Tom, Chatwin's saga of the hillfarm is too fey: "you can't smell the muck and the mud in his writing", he says. Fair point. Muck, mud and amniotic fluids of all sorts flow gloopily through Tom's own great Radnorshire novel, *The Claude Glass*. Famously, hideously, the Culture Minister of the time[42] mistakenly announced *The Claude Glass* as the winner of the Wales Book of the Year for 2008, before correcting himself just as Tom arrived, apparently

victorious, at the stage under the harsh glare of the TV cameras. It should have won, for real.

Kilvert's words tinkling in my ears, I'm expecting something sylvan and elfin that we will probably skip our way down into. But of course, the Forestry Commission got here first. It's another sharp climb, with Tom bounding out ahead, me struggling to keep up, sweating, plastered in clouds of persistent flies. I have a slight ear infection, which they are drawn irresistibly to, and I spend an unhappy half hour slapping the side of my head to get the little bastards away from me. They retreat a few inches, and then divebomb me again. Flies and forestry, rather than elves and fairies. It's a crap swap.

Eventually, we are far above the gorge, looking down into it across a steep hillside of clear-felled timber. Paths on the map mean nothing, so we have to slide and bump our way down the hill. Below the clear-fell is a chasm of native broadleaf trees running along the gorge, too steep even for the Forestry Commission. Glimpses of sheer rock-face – where peregrines nest, Tom tells me – hint at the exotica of the hidden gorge, as does the roar of a waterfall somewhere down there. Somehow, it makes me think of the Raj. Tom came down here with a friend of his[43] who wrote a book about wild swimming, and the two of them clambered right down into the

gorge. His mate cheerily dived straight into the waterfall plunge pool. I'm well and truly beaten, though. The sides are getting scarily steep, my head is pounding, the flies are driving me insane, and I just can't go any further.

As we stroll back down to the cars, parked just above the splendidly scary wooden-slat suspension bridge over the Wye[44], we talk about the mixed identities of this area. Tom identifies as a Radnorshire writer, a Breconshire writer, a Powys writer, a Borders writer, Anglo-Welsh, British, sometimes Welsh, though that causes him dilemmas, as he grew up inches from the border and of Anglo-Scottish stock. He felt humiliated when he first read at the Hay Festival, for the chalk-board outside his event advertised him as 'a Local Writer', a phrase which does indeed have the ring of death to it, even if, as in this case, it is topographically accurate. "Yes, I am a local writer to Hay, but not when it's written down on a board by Peter Florence", he explains. "I take great pleasure in the tradition of place here, but in none of its inherently conservative elements". His contradictions are very much of this area, and he is spot on when he says that the great local divide is not between the English and the Welsh, but between those involved in manual and non-manual labour. "And it's always been that way", he asserts. Unusually amongst writers, Tom is a manual grafter too: he works often in a local saw-mill and is forever patching things up, both buildings and stuff mechanical. He is perhaps the only writer you'd call on in a real emergency, for most of us would be worse than useless. Somehow, that seems proper Radnorshire. He'll be back.

HEART OF WALES RAILWAY

6am, on the solitary platform of Sugar Loaf halt, "Britain's least-used railway station" (*The Independent*, 1 May 1999)[45]. Dawn is breaking on this far south-western edge of Powys, ripples of pink fire blazing over the hills. I'm breaking the rules by having a sneaky fag, hoping that it might deter the midges. It doesn't, and my head is swimming from nicotine. Three minutes early and the rumble of the train announces its appearance around the bend. Like hailing a cab, I stick my hand out, which seems slightly superfluous, but I want the driver to know I'm serious, that I'm not just here for the fun of it. I also want to catch his look of open-mouthed surprise. I'm not disappointed.

The train shrieks to an unexpected halt. The guard, caught off-guard, has to go and find his masterkey to unlock the doors and let me on. "This is a first!" he exclaims, as the door slides open. Not quite, it transpires, but not far off. When he comes to sell me my ticket, he tells me that in seven years of working up and down the Heart of Wales Railway, I'm only the third passenger he's ever picked up at Sugar Loaf Halt. According to the latest figures (2007-8) of the Office of Rail Regulation, 111 passengers used the station that year. That's two a week on average, at a station served by eight trains a day. I buy a return ticket so that I'll register twice in the stats, and take the pressure to perform off poor, eternally-threatened little Sugar Loaf for another week.

111 passengers a year might sound unbelievably light, but it's almost double the figure of two years earlier. Sugar Loaf could be on a bit of a roll, though it remains by far the most anachronistic, and least-used, station on the Welsh network. It makes Tonfanau or Roman Bridge look like Euston. And it's no surprise: you'd never even know it was there. This is one furtively anonymous spot, only a handful of yards off the A483 as it hammers between Llandovery and Llanwrtyd Wells, but completely unsigned from it, or anywhere else. A shattered tarmac track wanders off the main road to a little set of flaky white gates adorned with a few regulation railway

notices. A mildewed sign bans me from smoking in the still morning air (sorry). There used to be a phone box, but that's gone, though there is a shiny new information point with a button to press. A recorded announcement tells me that this is Gorsaf Pen-y-Fâl[46], and that the next train to Amwythig is at deg munud wedi chwech.

Prise open the gate and a set of steps drops you down to the track and the tiny platform. I pace its length and make it to be about twenty yards long. There's no name sign here either: someone's half-inched it. I imagine it sat in pride of place in some trainspotter's toilet, and feel insanely jealous that I didn't get there first. There used to be six railway workers' cottages next to the station, but those have long gone. Now there's just a couple of farms within any distance, and the only passengers at Sugar Loaf are walkers (and not many of them) and idiots like me who go there precisely because no-one else does, just to see.

Next stop up the line is Llanwrtyd Wells. It's a proper station with two platforms, flowers, a shelter, posters. Punters too, even at quarter past six in the morning. One passenger calmly eyes the arriving train and carries on smoking in an exaggeratedly leisurely way, just the right side of the line defining the forbidden *fangre*. He has the air of a regular, who knows that the train, despite its surprise halt to pick me up, is early and is timetabled anyway for a five minute wait here. As he gets on, the guard points me out – "he got on at Sugar Loaf, you know! Couldn't believe it when I heard the buzzer to stop!" I feel strangely special.

The Llanwrtyd smoker is off to work, at the Co-op in Llandrindod. Tesco opened in the town just three weeks earlier, and the Co-op emptied overnight. Staff, he tells me, are nervous about the future. Others get on at Cilmeri and Builth Road. It's obviously a regular commuting crowd, and the mood is bizarrely cheerful. Everyone says hello, especially when they're told where I got on ("Sugar Loaf! Wow!"). The first rays of buttery sunshine burst onto the greenery sliding seductively by.

After passing through the succession of tiny stations in quiet isolation, the redbrick cluster of Llandrindod is a shock, for it looks like a proper metropolis. This is the centre point of the line, where northbound and southbound trains are timetabled to pass each other. Just beyond the up platform, there's the massive new Tesco, a huge hangar surrounded by acres of fresh tarmac. The town's road system has been altered to their specifications: what Tesco wants, Tesco got. On the store's opening, the company donated five hundred quid each to two cancer charities, one of them based in the town, thus securing a slew of breathlessly positive stories in the local press. Not a bad return for 9.3 seconds worth of your annual profit[47].

If Llandrindod is as big as it gets along this line, the obvious question is how on earth did the whole operation survive Beeching? And not just the line, but each and every station – Sugar Loaf of course, but also the far-from-anywhere halts of Llanbister Road, Llangynllo, Cynghordy and Dolau? The southern end of the 121-mile line passes through the industrial towns of Ammanford, Llandybïe and Pontarddulais; it was carrying freight from here that helped secure it. The main impetus was purely political, however. The railway was earmarked for closure by Beeching, and recommended to shut by the Labour Transport Minister, Richard Marsh, but George Thomas, then Secretary of State for Wales, claimed to have reminded a cabinet meeting that the line ran through six marginal Labour constituencies. His intervention, Thomas believed with customary modesty, led to its reprieve.

Half of the thirty-four stations are request stops, necessitating a wave at the driver to get on, or a word with the guard to get off. It was easy to tell when we were approaching one, as the speed dropped just in case there was someone to pick up. On this first

train of the day, there weren't many, but when I return towards lunchtime, we stop nearly everywhere. Because the stations are so regularly spaced, it means that the train never picks up much pace: doing the full route from Swansea to Shrewsbury takes a stately 3 hours and 50 minutes, an average of 32mph. My 39-mile trek from one side of Powys (Sugar Loaf) to the other (Knighton) took exactly one hundred minutes, at a speed that entirely fitted this cautious countryside.

Most of the automatic stops are the larger settlements – Llandovery, Llanwrtyd, Llandrindod and Knighton, for instance – but all trains also call at one of the tiniest halts on the line, serving only a scattered community of a few farms and the village of Llanfihangel Rhydithon, a mile away. This is Dolau, known locally as 'Dolly', and dressed as one too; the mandatory stop is for us all to admire her pretty garb. For over a quarter of a century, the Dolau Station Action Group has been tending and tweaking floral displays on the station platforms, building ever more lavish towers of hanging baskets and proudly framing and displaying their numerous awards in the tidy little waiting room. A cross between the Flower Marquee at the Royal Welsh and a seaside prom in the middle of Radnorshire, there's not a privet out of place. It's the latest in a long line of genteel promotion, all the way back to the pioneer days of the 1860s, when the railway company added Wells to the names of Llanwrtyd, Llangammarch, Builth and Llandrindod, in a bid to bring in the tourists.

It is the brief stop at Dolau, regardless of customers, that best sums up the Heart of Wales line, for while it remains a useful piece of transport infrastructure, and provides a commuting option for those lucky enough to have work that fits the dreadful timetable, it is in its romantic, nostalgic and communitarian aspects that this railway truly comes into its own. Conversations are somehow easier to strike up on this little train; there is an unhurried assurance that we'll all get where we want to in the end, and not to worry in the meanwhile. Patchy mobile reception means that passengers can't spend the whole journey texting or jabbing their iPhone, immediately marking it out from practically every other railway journey in the land. And all against a slowly rolling backdrop of rounded valleys, crooked lanes, huts, barns, rivers, woods and sheep.

Provocative eavesdropping opportunities are legion too. On my return journey to Sugar Loaf, an excited, chaotic gang of mums and kids get on at Llandrindod, off on holiday to the Pembrokeshire seaside. As they bundle bags, cases and pushchairs onto the train, one mum suddenly shrieks "where's the cat?" A quick inventory of their ample luggage reveals that it isn't with them. "Oh God," the mum in question sighs. "We've not got the cat. I was that busy getting the kids ready…" Once the train moves off, one of the children pipes up: "what's going to happen with the cat?" Mum pulls a face and replies, "er, I'll do something…", which seems to suffice as an answer, at least as far as the kids are concerned. I'm intrigued, and full of silent questions. Will she alert someone with a key to her house to look after it in their absence? Ask someone to break in and rescue it? Or just make sure that she's first back in through the door when they return in a week's time, having parked the kids for an hour at the neighbours while she disposes of the evidence? And was the cat now cooped up in its travelling basket, mewing pitifully in an empty house?

In Knighton, I have two and a half hours before the next return train[48], so grab some almost inedible breakfast and have a good peer at the town's always entertaining shop windows (the prize for intrigue going to the charity shop displaying one of those dayglo stars usually advertising this week's special offer. It read 'Sorry We Are Unable to Accept Hardback Books'). Having apparently spread so much innocent joy by merely catching a train from a little-used

CENTRAL

station, I'm filled with the evangelistic zeal of bumping up statistics for worthy causes, so got some money out of the cashpoint yn Gymraeg at a bank only feet from the border. The town's station is actually in England, and when I got back to it, there were a full fifteen others waiting for the 0956 to Cardiff Central. Return to Sugar Loaf, please, via the nineteen fifties.

Notes

1. Between Wye and Severn.
2. Lee fervently believed the Welsh to be an inferior people to the English. He was behind the 1534 parliamentary statute (A Bill concerning Councils in Wales) designed to make the Court of the Council of Wales and the Marches the sole authority in the area, overturning centuries of dispensations to the Marcher Lords. Its opening words are very much his: "Forasmuch as the People of Wales and Marches of the same, not dreading the good and wholesom Laws and Statues of this Realm, have of long Time continued and persevered in Perpetration and Commission of divers and manifold Thefts, Murders, Rebellions, Wilful Burnings of Houses and other scelerous Deeds and abominable Malefacts…"
3. See the next entry on Llandrindod Wells for more details.
4. Otherwise known as the Radnor Basin.
5. There's not much more than a hilltop church and pub to Old Radnor, but both are well worth seeing. The church of St Stephen is a Norman and medieval masterpiece, containing what are believed to be the oldest font (eighth century) and oldest organ case (sixteenth century) in the UK. Across the way, and with great views into Wales, is the superb Harp Inn.
6. The charter was granted in 1562, and dissolved under the Corporations Act of 1883. During this time, the Radnorshire Boroughs, centred on New Radnor, elected their own MP separate to the county seat.
7. The miniature station building can still be seen on the south side of the A44 by-pass, now surrounded by a caravan park.
8. His blog, at ianmarchant.com, is always brilliant, and he writes a fine book too.
9. The town has two Holy Trinity churches: this original one has parts that date back to the thirteenth century. When the new town centre Holy Trinity was consecrated in 1871, the church authorities decided to discourage use of the old one, and the spired St Michael's church at nearby Cefnllys, by stripping both buildings of their roofs. It wasn't a popular decision, and before long, both old churches were rebuilt on their original spots. The work at the old Holy Trinity unearthed a superb example of a genital-splaying sheela-na-gig sculpture, which can be seen in the town's Radnorshire Museum.
10. Llandod is the name many people use for the town. It's not just laziness or Incomers' Cymraegphobia; there is some historical basis to the epithet, in that documents and maps from the early Middle Ages show the name 'Lando' hereabouts.
11. And in Welsh too: "ail-Fictorianeiddo", no less. I have rather over-used this plaque in writing and broadcasting, I admit, for it never ceases to amuse me. On my ITV Wales series, *Great Welsh Roads* (broadcast March 2008), I said in a piece to camera, "Why don't they go the whole hog [on re-Victorianisation] and introduce cholera into the town's water supply or send the kids up chimneys?" Local councillor Gary Price splashed his outrage all over the front of the *County Times*: "What kind of comments are these? To say

this could be dangerous," he fumed. "Imagine if someone listened to him and upset the watercourse."

12. And these truly were golden years; the town was a tourism beacon. In the 1920s, Ward Lock published four guides to the different parts of Wales. These were titled *A Guide to North Wales (Northern Section)*, *A Guide to North Wales (Southern Section)*, *A Guide to South Wales* and *A Guide to Llandrindod Wells*, which incorporated the area from Rhayader to Brecon.
13. In June 2010, Llandrindod East/Llandrindod West electoral division had the highest rate of claimants of unemployment benefit within Powys (7.9%), the 35th worst rate in Wales.
14. Which also lent us the joke that the airport's baggage handlers had appropriated a different lyric from the song as their bespoke motto: "imagine no possessions". More details of Llandegley can be found at the airport's website – http://pages.123-reg.co.uk/whitebeard-574512/llandegleyinternational/index.html – which is bang up to date with its security warning ("Please arrive two hours before departure to allow our staff to X-ray your wellies etc.").
15. The Severn Arms, named not after the river but after John Cheesement Severn, who came to Penybont in order to marry the wealthy local girl, Mary Price. Her fortune came from her father, John Price, who had taken over the village stores in 1734 at the age of eleven, on the death of his father. He became a famous entrepreneur, amassing a fortune from retail, property, an inn and in the fledgling banking sector, and went on to become High Sheriff of Radnorshire. Severn moved the village pub, the Fleece Inn, and rebuilt it in the florid style we see today in 1840.
16. Although the Thomas Shop closed as a drapers and general stores in 1958, it was reopened in 2003 as an excellent time capsule museum, complete with most of its original fittings and even stock, together with a shop for local crafts and a tea room.
17. See http://www.welsh-trotting.co.uk
18. Again, from the biography on her agent's website: http://www.lucyluck.com/authordetailpages.aspx?pgid=2&recid=52
19. Though there are, of course, warning signs of which to be aware. Rhayader is Wales' epicentre of support for the United Kingdom Independence Party, that ragtag ensemble of nostalgists, racists and Little Englanders that even sounds stupid as an acronym (UKIP).
20. Just. Although the Elan Valley reservoirs are firmly associated with Radnorshire, the Afon Elan flowing from their foot was the county border with Breconshire. Elan Village is on the Brecs side of the water.
21. This is, after all, the city with the civic motto of 'Forward!' Just the one word, and in good plain English – none of that poncey Latin nonsense for the second city. It must surely be the only municipal coat-of-arms motto that sounds best bellowed at volume.
22. And I hate to say it about my native accent, but there is something about the West Midlands twang that makes it sound forelock-tuggingly supercilious at the best of times. The best Brummie accent joke: "What's the difference between a buffalo and a bison?" "Down't be soft. Yow corn't wash yower 'ands in a buffalo."
23. No matter how many times you hear them, the statistics are staggering. The treatment plant at the bottom reservoir in Elan Valley is only 170 feet (52m) higher than the Frankley reservoir on the outskirts of Birmingham, 73 miles, many hills and river valleys to the east. Gravity alone gets the water to Brum. At the 1:2300 gradient, it travels at a stately two miles per hour, and takes a day and a half to get there.
24. The opening ceremony, on Thursday 21st July 1904, was as grand as the scheme itself. 750 guests of Birmingham City Corporation came by train from Brum; the king and queen travelled up by train from Swansea, where the royal yacht was moored. The Lord Mayor provided a banquet for them all, including dishes of caviar, quails and lamb cutlets. Local sensibilities were slightly pandered to as well: diners were serenaded by a harpist and a

male voice choir.
25. Gangs still calling themselves Merched Beca (Daughters of Rebecca) were operating in this part of Radnorshire well into the twentieth century, latterly targeting fishing rights on the River Wye, rather than toll-gates.
26. There is something faintly sinister about the sudden appearances of the pipeline too. You stumble across it in a wood, in fields, breaking free behind a farm or church; its stentorian utilitarianism seems at odds with the hazy countryside. The pipeline used to be marked on Ordnance Survey maps as a continual dashed line, labelled 'Elan Aqueduct (Birmingham Corporation Water Works)'. No more. In the febrile, post-Tryweryn, pre-Investiture atmosphere of the 1960s, members of Mudiad Amddiffyn Cymru (MAC, the Movement for the Defence of Wales) planted bombs on the Elan Valley pipeline at Crossgates, near Llandrindod (foiled in March 1967) and Hagley, near Birmingham (exploded on 2 December 1968, ripping a huge hole in a pipe and reducing the city's water supply by half). When researching my TV programme about tracing the route of the pipeline, I telephoned Severn Trent Water to see if they could provide a map of it. The press officer gasped and refused point blank, citing the 'War on Terror' as the reason.
27. The Severn takes 220 miles to cover this distance; the Wye 135 miles, making it the fifth longest river in Britain.
28. When I asked him if he'd lived here all his life, his response was "no. Not yet."
29. The farm is around 200 acres, most of which is hilly. Derek and Veronica have 300 sheep, a dozen cows and two horses.
30. Estovers are the necessaries allowed by law to be taken from common land by the commoners. In the case of Llandeuddwr Common, this means being allowed to cut peat and ferns.
31. The Lloyd-Lewis family of Rhayader were the historic freeholders of Llandeuddwr Common, but they too went Away and put the freehold up for sale.
32. O Fôn i Fynwy: "from Anglesey to Monmouthshire", i.e. the whole of Wales.
33. Radnorshire is indeed the host county, but only just: Breconshire starts just two hundred yards away, on the Wye Bridge into Builth.
34. *Troi'r Baw yn Bres*: turning manure into money (or crap into cash). Quite what the banner was designed to sell has escaped my memory, but it's wise counsel all the same.
35. Toffoc: In the food hall a couple of years ago, a petite lady sprang out in front of me with a cry of 'Do you want some Toffoc?' This, she told me, was a new Welsh product, a toffee vodka that was going down a storm on the clubbing scene. I pulled a face and bleated some pompous noises about the hideous corrupting influence of alcopops, but she pushed a small plastic thimbleful of the stuff into my hand anyway. It was delicious, like having a phial of gold injected straight into your bloodstream. I'll probably come back later and buy some, I promised her. I didn't of course, but I do make a beeline for their stall every year and claim my annual free thimbleful.
36. The population of Rhulen (Rhiwlen in Welsh) parish in 1847 was 129; in 1901 it was 59; it is something around thirty now.
37. On an eighth century foundation.
38. It truly is. There is no purer pleasure than a few days ambling these Radnorshire lanes, dipping in to musty churches and luscious graveyards. Disserth, Cefnllys, Llananno, Llanbister, Llansteffan, Llanddewi Fach, Llandeilo Graban, Colva, Glascwm, Cregrina, Pilleth, Casgob, Bleddfa, Discoed, Old Radnor and Llanbadarn-y-Garreg are some of my favourites.
39. Tom Bullough is the author of *A* (2002), *The Claude Glass* (2007) and *Konstantin* (2012).
40. Establishing the identity of Twm Tobacco is typically hazy. Three different stories: one has him as a local seventeenth century ne'er-do-well. Tinker, itinerant, drunkard, packman, sheep rustler, gadabout, tobacco salesman, Twm, perhaps unsurprisingly, died in mysterious circumstances on Llanbedr Hill. Another story has Twm Tobacco as a well loved 'packman'

buried either where he fell, or at his favourite spot. A packman was an early travelling salesman, and this Twm would in all likelihood have sold silk scarves, trinkets for the young girls, and of course tobacco. Yet another tale has him as a felon, hanged at the crossroads and buried here on unconsecrated ground.

41. Tom has made no bones about his history of magic mushroom use. In a BBC online interview, he states: "As a teenager in the Welsh borders, when you weren't allowed into pubs yet and the hills were covered in complimentary psychedelics... Well. Like everyone else I knew, I took mushrooms excessively. Have these experiences helped me as an artist? Yes, they have. They helped me to understand how people create their own reality, and if you're writing a character like Andrew in *The Claude Glass* – a borderline feral child, who lacks the mental structures that other people take for granted – that understanding is vital."

42. Rhodri Glyn Thomas, Methodist minister and Plaid Cymru AM for Carmarthen East and Dinefwr. His appalling cock-up at the Book of the Year ceremony in July 2008 became a huge hit on YouTube, and propelled poor Tom into an infamy lesser writers would have struggled to overcome. *The Claude Glass* was short-listed alongside two other brilliant books, both heart-rending memoirs of personal tragedies: Nia Wyn's *Blue Sky July* and Dannie Abse's *The Presence*. Abse was named as the real, and perhaps inevitable, winner.

43. Daniel Start, the author of *Wild Swimming* (Punk Publishing, 2008). As someone who, between about late April and October, is obsessed with hurling himself into lakes, rivers and pools, I've often snorted at the rash of books on wild swimming, aimed at people who vaguely want to be a little bit more adventurous, but need a book to tell them how. I did a reading of my own book, *Map Addict*, at the Stanford's store in Bristol, the week after Daniel had been there promoting his new book *Wild Swimming: Coast* ("or as we call it, going to the beach", I sniffily pronounced in the pre-amble to my talk). Hearing that he had made it to the bottom of the Llanstephan Gorge and hurled himself into the waterfall made me offer untold apologies for my cheap jibe. He is the real deal.

44. Llanstephan Bridge (at OS grid reference SO 113416) is the sole survivor of the narrow suspension bridges that first spanned this section of the Wye. Building this kind of bridge obviated the need to build piers in the river, but it has resulted in a crossing that is not for the faint-hearted. The bridge, built in 1922, was designed to be crossed by one vehicle weighing up to five tons and travelling at no more than 4 mph. The weight limit has since been cut to two tons, but don't overcompensate by roaring across at forty. You will regret it.

45. By 2006, it had crawled up the rankings to seventh least-used station, but that was only because most of the rest on the list had but one or two trains a week calling at them. Sugar Loaf has eight every day Monday to Saturday, and four on Sundays.

46. Pen-y-Fâl is the real name of the mountain above Abergavenny that is popularly known as the Sugar Loaf. The station here is named after a different Sugar Loaf: the conical hill, around which the A483 so tortuously weaves, a mile or so south-west of the station and just over the Carmarthenshire border. In Welsh, that's known as Dinas-y-Bwlch, not Pen-y-Fâl.

47. In April 2010, Tesco announced annual profits of £3.4 billion. This works out at just under £6500 a minute, or £107 a second.

48. The one after that is a full five hours later.

EAST
ENGLISH BORDER

OFFA'S DYKE

Offa's Dyke is what Google Earth was made for. Zoom in, pull out, jiggle it around, but there it goes, steady as you like, up hill, down dale, a crease across the landscape like a single line of bottle green corduroy. Sometimes it vanishes, occasionally it gets confused with an old railway line, but the staggering truth is that, thirteen hundred years after its construction, thirteen whole centuries of changing land use, the ebb and bloody flow of borderland politics, of agricultural and industrial revolutions, the dyke remains one of the most conspicuous features of the modern British landscape.

Coming across it, especially unexpectedly, is like meeting God himself. How can something be so old and yet still so distinct, so gnarled yet still such an accurate demarcation of different tribes? Offa's Dyke was not, we are told, built with any significant military purpose in mind. It was just a reminder, a line in the sand, an eighth century strip of leylandii (curiously enough, a plant first hybridised only yards from the Dyke, on the estate of Leighton Hall, near Welshpool). It wasn't razor wire or an electric fence, but it certainly wasn't a rose-clad gate on the latch either.

What it most reminds me of is a country house ha-ha, a ditch that acts as a very effective demarcation line, but that remains unseen from the ground until you are almost in it. Such a notion seems to fit too the cultural reality of the English-Welsh border, invisible to many, deep as a Pacific trench to those who can't keep out of it. Offa's Dyke looms far larger on the emotional horizon of the Welsh than it does the English, for although it acts as a proud reminder that our land border is long-established enough to be practically inviolate, it has also, as Emyr Humphreys pointed out in his cultural history *The Taliesin Tradition*, served to promulgate the eternal fortress and siege mentality that so bedevil Welsh progress. Fortress to some, neatly-defined play-pen to others: either way, it's perhaps less than helpful.

For all its lack of explicit warmongering, and all the fuzzy edges, the Dyke's creation helped precipitate the Kingdom of Powys into its lowest ebb. The fertile lands around Oswestry, Croesoswallt to the Welsh, the Severn plain as far as Wroxeter, near Shrewsbury, and around the Golden Valley in Herefordshire had all been part of the kingdom, but the new line pushed Powys back into the stern hills, where it has stayed ever since. The dream, fuelled by folk

memory, continued to flicker. Humphrey Lhuyd's famous map of 1573, *Cambriæ Typus*, so proudly adorning the cover of John Davies' magisterial *A History of Wales*, was the first to treat the country as a discrete unit, but it is splendidly overstated. Mapping the ambition that had died in the previous century with Owain Glyndŵr[1], Lhuyd draws the country's eastern boundary out to the Severn, so that only in the middle of Shrewsbury, Worcester and Gloucester does ANGLIAE PARS olim LHOEGRIA appellata ('Part of England, once called Lloegr') begin.

There's a path now all the way from one coast to the other. The Offa's Dyke National Trail was opened in 1971, hopping from one side of the modern border to the other twenty-seven times in its 177-mile schlep from Chepstow to Prestatyn. Most people do it that way, south to north, but that can't be right, for there can surely be no better definition of the phrase 'anti-climax' than Prestatyn prom. All the best bits are in the Powys stretch, of course. Nearly all of the bits that actually coincide with the eponymous earthwork too, for that matter[2]. Around Knighton, Tref-y-Clawdd, the town on the dyke; near Montgomery; in the Clun Forest; up towards Welshpool: the places to find the ditches at their most impressive and the bank-top oaks at their most elephantine. Here, suddenly, you feel your tracks dissolving into the footfall of centuries.

The finest section of all, looking like a flesh wound gouged across the plump, jelly-mould hills, runs from the River Clun, near Newcastle, around to the west of Llanfair Hill. This is the exact halfway point of the path and although in modern day Shropshire, it has all the hallmarks of deep Powys, numerous Welsh and Welsh-ish names included. Some local linguistic cross-overs including Pentiken, Llandinshop, Dingle-du Bank, Rhos Fiddle, Nether Skyborry[3], Monaughty Poeth[4], Rhespass, Gogin and Castle Idris, names all to lift the spirit and have you quietly working out daft limericks[5] as you pound up and down this part of the Trail. Up and down it is, for the stretch from here to Knighton is known in walker's circles as the Switchback, as both the Dyke and the trail thread their way across numerous tiny valleys and the swollen humps that divide them.

Despite the sheer physicality of the Dyke, and as the names more than suggest, the two lands slide easily enough over each other in many parts of the borderland. Even the official border, carved out in the 1536 Act of Union, shows signs of slippage hereabouts, particularly where it is formed by the lovely River Teme[6]. Look on the OS map and you'll see that the river and the border dance around each other like shy teenagers at a school disco, occasionally touching and then veering apart again. This goes on for more than fifteen miles between Felindre and Bucknell; many fields on the Welsh bank are in England, and vice versa, because the official boundary marks the line of the river in 1536. The border has not moved, but the river has, quite substantially.

I'll love Offa's Dyke always for giving me my favourite joke in the *Rough Guide to Wales*, not that there was much competition. The Lesbian and Gay Wales section (a couple of paragraphs, in truth) included mention of the monthly Sapphic social called Border Women, which is still going strong two decades later. Of course, I couldn't resist slipping in "who should surely have called themselves Offa's Dykes" in brackets after mentioning it. We got letters. Quite a few of them, in fact. Like Queen Victoria (who was said not to believe in lesbianism even as a theoretical concept), they were not amused. So no more puerile, predictable dyke gags.

Clare Balding came pedalling this way in her *Britain by Bike* TV series…no, I'll stop there. It's cheap, and it's nasty. Besides which, she's jumpy with the complaints[7]. She does the walking programme, *Ramblings*, on Radio 4 as well. Did Offa's Dyke in that too, as I recall. On a bike, and on a hike. What's not to like?

EAST

SYCARTH

No-one escapes from a Welsh-medium education without knowing about Sycarth. Mention the name and the Pavlovian response will almost certainly be a mechanical recitation of the famous poem by Iolo Goch. Not all of it though; just the totemic two lines that, damp-eyed, we all want to believe represents the soul of early medieval Wales:

> Na gwall, na newyn, na gwarth,
> Na syched fyth yn Sycarth.
>
> ("No want, no hunger, no shame
> no thirst ever in Sycarth")

It is almost certain that they won't, however, have been there. They may even assume that there is no longer such a place as Sycarth, that it is an inland Atlantis, more dream than substance, folklore not fact. Did this Shangri-la, described so lovingly (and, let's not forget, so dutifully) in Iolo Goch's panegyric hymn of praise, ever really exist? Or has it, like so many other aspects of the life and campaign of Owain Glyndŵr, evaporated into the mists of legend and fervent symbolism?

Sycarth exists. Rudely, brilliantly, absolutely so. It is perfectly possible – and eminently advisable – to go and see it in the green flesh, for it does not disappoint. It is there on the map, a double-circle of hatching in the valley of the little Cynllaith river. There you see it on Google Earth, a tumescent mound slumbering peaceably behind a farm. And there you see it as you sweep around the corner on the lane from the Green Inn by Llangedwyn – by far the best way of approaching. Even in the absence of a hall, its old mound commands the valley: it demands (and obtains) respect. Over six hundred years ago, a furious teenager, soon to be King Henry V, swept down this valley, brimful with the intention of razing Sycarth to the ground. Glyndŵr himself was long gone, folded secretly into the hills from where he was leading the English army – far superior numerically and in weapon-power – a merry ride. If Henry, fired up with an impotent rage, was unable to put to death Glyndŵr himself, then at least he could incinerate his birthplace. After the symbolic trashing, he needed more, and cantered off over the hills, his troops in hot pursuit, to Glyndyfrdwy, near Corwen, Glyndŵr's other

residence. That was torched too. Did the prince feel better after scalping these two homes? Or did that make the lack of a real scalp rage even hotter in his heart? You have to hope so.

The greatest irony (and isn't it so often the way, when the English have tried to crush the Welsh?) is that Henry's adolescent petulance has served Sycarth so well. Had any trace of Glyndŵr's palace survived, it would have been dug out and tidied up, fussed over by experts, packaged, parcelled and heritaged for visiting coach parties of bored *ysgol gynradd* kids and wide-eyed Americans on their Welsh Braveheart tour. The lack of a single interpretation board or even sign means that you have to do all of the work yourself. You need to feel the place, look at, around and through it, listen to it, run your fingers down the grooves of the bark of the vast oak trees, sit quietly in their roots, sniff the damp soil and taste the mossy air. Deliriously, deliciously, there is nothing to mediate between you and Glyndŵr himself: it is eyeball-to-eyeball across six centuries.

Lovely though it is to have been left this way, it is quite remarkable that this place of pilgrimage, the epicentre of Welsh history's most dazzling hour, has been so thoroughly ignored by the fat, feeble tourism industry. Entire heritage attractions, waymarked trails, visitor centres and interactive experiences have been conjured up on far flimsier foundations. Were they to try, I'd like to believe

EAST

that the Sycarth spirits – and my god, they're a fierce bunch – would dismantle the putative visitor centre every night as dusk fell and the builders had gone home, in the way that the construction of numerous churches was said to have been frustrated in the middle ages. Sycarth is just too big – as with its oaks, there's a hint of giganticism hanging in the ether – to be tamed by the tiny, tinny gods of modern tourism.

Borders have loomed large in Sycarth's recent history, as the Denbighshire-Montgomeryshire / Clwyd-Powys divide has shuffled around it: parochial tweaking by bureaucrats far away[8]. There's a small symmetry in Glyndŵr's Sycarth having come to rest – if only for now, perhaps – in Montgomeryshire. Far away on the other side of the county is the town that he chose, quite rightly, for his principal parliament; the place where the mountains of north Wales touch the rolling pastures of the south, where the hill farms of the east peer out over the sea of the west. Machynlleth, man Cynllaith, decided the man from the banks of another *Cynllaith*. If we're talking borders, however, there's a far bigger story just the other side of Mynydd-y-Bryn: England, just one small wood and five fields away, less than a mile. It seems almost impossible that this place that sweats Welshness from its every pore can be so very nearly on the wrong side of the tracks. In modern terms, only: the

Dyke is a safe three or four miles on the other side of the English border. Even so. It's one thing to wave the V-sign from a distant, perhaps unseen, mountain top, quite another to do it right in the flared nostrils of the enemy's rubicund face. Attaboy.

BRIDE OF THE BORDER

Of the eight seasonal Celtic calendar festivals, the two equinoxes and two solstices are impossible to ignore, for they are the principal spokes of the turning wheel, the pegs on which the entire year is hung. The cross-quarters take a little more work. Calan Mai (Beltane, May Day) the harbinger of summer, shouts for itself, a tumultuous roar of new greenery and frothing flowers, even if the bank holiday accorded it was chiselled out from the far sterner rock of international workers' solidarity and Soviet era parades of military hardware. Its opposite, Calan Gaeaf (Samhain, Hallowe'en) the *petit mort*[9] of the year, is equally strident, when the veils between the worlds are at their thinnest, and fog, fireworks and ghoulish tat mix gravity with glitter. The remaining two are far easier to forget: August's Lammas, or Lughnasadh, and its counter-point, Imbolc, or Candlemas, the first glimmer of spring at the onset of February, *y mis bach*. Both share a quiet demeanour, verging on shyness, for they are the early whispers of autumn and spring respectively and always overshadowed by the more full-throated equinoxes that follow six and a half weeks later.

Imbolc, pronounced 'im-molc', a corruption of 'ewe's milk', is the most tender and breakable of them all. Some years, I remember to run around the house and turn all the lights on for a few minutes, the blaze of bulbs supposed to celebrate and encourage the returning light, as well as chance to marvel at the speed of the rotating dial on the electricity meter. Turning on a few dozen lights in a Powys terrace is hardly Burning Man though, and one year, the urge to mark Imbolc properly, appropriately, crept up on me with a gentle determination. Yet again, it was to the map that I turned for inspiration.

St Bride, or Bridget, Santes Ffraed in Welsh, the Christianised version of a far older goddess figure[10], is the embodiment of Imbolc, her midwifery skills evident in the new-born lambs, her emblem of the snowdrop casting its ghostly blush across the landscape. These are, according to Julian Cope[11], the Bride-ish Isles, for she is central to our culture and clustered manifestations of her can be found all over: around St Bride's Bay in Pembrokeshire, where links with the local mother-goddess St Non are legion, in the gentle swells of the Yorkshire Wolds around Bridlington, Brigg and Brigham, where the Dorset rivers Bride and Brit meet near the Abbotsbury swannery (Bridget is a swan goddess too) and the settlements of Little Bredy and Bridport.

Cope also reminded me of somewhere nearer home: "far up the river Severn, [she] is revealed in Welsh form as the Breidden Hills... Here on the wide-open Severn flood-plain at her confluence with the river Vyrnwy, visible across the endless miles of border country, the three isolated and exhilarating Bridgit peaks of Breidden rear up eternal and significant". Across Wales, there are a number of villages too with Llansantffraed, or a version thereof, as part of their name, most of them in Powys. There's Llansantffraid-juxta-Usk to the east of Brecon; Llansantffraed-in-Elvel, in the Radnorshire hills, and Rhayader's lesser-known twin, Llansantffraid Cwmdeuddwr. Most famously, thanks to its giant-killing football team[12], is Llansantffraid-ym-Mechain, in the lee of the Breidden Hills. A route for my Imbolc pilgrimage was clear.

The Breidden Hills are the very last flourish of Wales before heading over the border into the Shropshire plains. Coming the other way – and this is by far my most frequent border crossing – the three whaleback humps beckon from miles away, calling me home. I don't even mind that it almost invariably begins to rain as I pass back into Wales, for the dramatic grey curtains sweeping across the soft hills are potent reminders that I have crossed not just a border on the map, but into a different dimension. The contours sharpen, the skies darken, the greens deepen and the crags grow ever sulkier, as they almost always seem to whenever, and wherever, you pass from England into Wales[13].

Hundreds of times have I gone this way, admiring the Breidden Hills from below, before finally escaping the main road and heading into them on that blustery February morning. Instantly, the ennui of the A458 vanished in favour of tiny lanes and unexpected views of the hills themselves, the monuments that top them and the masts of the Criggion radio transmitter station. The most conspicuous monument, a seemingly upended chimney known as Rodney's Pillar, crowns Breidden Hill itself, the northernmost of the three. The route up to it is furtively wooded, skirting around the gaping hole of a roadstone quarry, from which occasional explosions and

sudden volcanic upsurges of dust billow alarmingly.

Admiral Rodney (1719-1792) was still alive when his commemorative pillar was first erected. A naval hero of battles in the West Indies, the ships in which he was victorious had been built from his own fine Montgomeryshire oak. Despite his heroism and generosity, the government pension afforded him was miserly, and by 'a Subscription of the Gentlemen of Montgomeryshire', as the commemorative plaque on the pillar has it, the memorial was erected[14]. In this exposed spot over a thousand feet up, the pillar has needed frequent repair, and the accompanying plaques on its base tell an all-too-predictable tale of how civic largesse has progressed over the last two centuries. It was renewed in 1896 by subscription of the "gentlemen of the counties of Montgomery and Salop", and repaired in 1983-4 by Powys County Council, with subscriptions from the Secretary of State for Wales, Shropshire County Council, Montgomery District Council, Oswestry Borough Council, the Criggion Estate and the Amey Roadstone Corporation. Next time round, it will be spattered with the logos of numerous EU funding agencies, the National Assembly, Visit Wales, Cadw, Oswestry Rotarians and a clutch of rural enterprise boards.

This example of establishment prowess seems slightly at odds with the slumbering, secretive nature of Bride's igneous outcrops. Much more fitting is the far humbler column topping Moel y

Golfa, a mile to the south and the highest of the three hills. This commemorates a father-and-son, both Romany Chells, or Gypsy Kings. The first plaque remembers Ernest Burton, who died in 1960, the second his son Uriah, from 1986. Uriah, the plaque notes, was better known as Hughie or Big Just, and he is painted in inspirational tones: "Uriah was a fighter for the weak, good to the poor, teacher to the ignorant and a true legend in his time. He was known and respected by all Gypsies and creeds. He was never beaten in Fisty Cuffs from the age of five to sixty. A man who led his people into the twentieth century. He was a good husband, father and granddad, and was truly loved by all his family".

For a decade or so at the beginning of the nineteenth century, the hills were also home to meetings of an al fresco literary society, organised by naturalist, poet, pioneer ornithologist and chronicler of borderland fables, John Dovaston. Every summer would see a small festival gathering around Rodney's Pillar, with readings, plays and folk dancing. Activities would crescendo to the election of the Lady of the Hill, and then the Bard Ferniate, who was then crowned with a wreath of ferns. This is a world apart.

The outlawish feeling only continues down in Llansantffraid-ym-Mechain, though of an entirely different flavour. Breidden is a puckish otherworld; Llansantffraid a pure slab of borderland cowpoke. The long main street is tailor-made for a ten-steps-and-fire shootout, though I was trying to keep my mind on higher things, so made for the church of Santes Ffraed instead. It made me smile, so agreeably jumbled is the interior: part-Norman, part-medieval, part-Georgian, part-Victorian, all slipping unselfconsciously over each other. My quest for the day was to have and hold light, and the church seemed unusually full of it, though it was nothing on what awaited me outside. Walking around the graveyard at the back of the church, I fell into an ocean of snowdrops, and happily drowned. In the field behind a lamb bleated, and at the very moment that I looked up in its direction, a bonfire suddenly erupted on the hill above, its flames pulsing high and hot. Spring came, with a roaring fanfare.

CHURCHSTOKE

Sunday morning, and it's time for church. Churchstoke that is, home of the biggest car boot sale for miles, spread like a teenager's bedroom detritus over the car parks, yards and outhouses of Harry Tuffin's. It's a borderland legend, the independent supermarket chain that started life as a wayside couple of petrol pumps in the fifties, owned by Harry and Doris Tuffin. They moved from the centre of Churchstoke to a site on the edge of the village in 1972 and opened a 3,000 square foot supermarket alongside an expanded petrol station. Forty years on, the Churchstoke mothership is now 40,000 square feet, and around it are scattered a laundrette, post office, truck stop, mineral water extraction and bottling plant[15], garden centre, hairdressers, café, kids' play area, fifty acre country park and the massive weekly market. Under the management of Doris and Harry's grandchildren, Tuffin's has now spread to ten stores in mid Wales and the Marches. This is not your average village shop, struggling by on sales of *Daily Mail*s and curdling milk[16].

The first Sunday traders start setting up from half past six. By nine, it's in full swing and pretty much over by lunchtime. There's a stack of proper market stalls, mostly the same ones that you'll see in Newtown on a Tuesday or Machynlleth on a Wednesday, the regular pot pourri of army surplus gear, home-made bird boxes and people who promise to unlock any mobile phone, no questions asked. Spicing up this mid Wales mix are some boisterous arrivistes from the West Midlands, most audibly those vast refrigerated trucks with the entire side folded down to reveal a shrink-wrapped wall of cheap meat, overseen by a pink-faced Brummie flirting shamelessly into his lapel clip microphone. The sausage jokes are limitless.

To your devout car booter, the presence of stalls selling new stuff, whether it's AA batteries or half a hundredweight of burgers, is an unwelcome distraction. Car booting is a religion, and Tuffin's Churchstoke its cathedral. There's a respectful hush as people file past the piles of sandwich makers, games of Buckeroo and Ker-Plunk!, garden tools and old LPs, broken only by occasional bursts of intensive bartering. Everything must go; there are real bargains to be had, and no-one wants to be loading their Felicity Kendal Workout videos ("Never Used!") back into the car from whence they came just a few short hours ago. It's a regular crowd, and from a wide area – I always bump into neighbours from Machynlleth

here, and, in this, the last nodule of Wales, you'll hear hilltop Cymraeg stirred in with broad Yam-Yam[17] and the Brummie Banghra of Midland Asian.

You won't hear many cut-glass tones of the Ludlow set. Car booting may get its profile temporarily boosted by occasional austerity chic pieces in the weekend *Telegraph*, when some convent girl called Alicia squeaks excitedly about making forty-four quid out of her Cath Kidston duplicates and a stack of home-made flap-jacks, but not at Harry Tuffin's, thank you. From the parrot in its Perspex cage by the entrance to the abrasive strip lighting and special offers on Fray Bentos pies, Tuffin's knows – and loves – its audience, and it isn't the Shropshire gastro slow foodies, those who think that the word 'market' only comes after the word 'farmer's'. A few years ago, they stuck a fancy new automatic coffee machine in the Tuffin's Churchstoke café. Within weeks, they'd had to add a hand-written sign to its front: 'For Milky Coffee, press Cafe Latte'.

The hoity-toities are missing a trick. Tuffin's is the cheapest holiday going. There's the strange allure of a foreign supermarket about the place, and they are always so much more interesting than the ones at home. Yet look closely, and you'll see more local produce on sale here than in anywhere down the road charging three times the price. Encouragingly low food miles are marked on numerous products; food yards in some cases. Waste from the supermarket becomes the animal feed for the pigs in the country park, who, in turn, make the short hop to the shelves as sausages and bacon. Local sourcing has been company policy and practice since the seventies, even if it does turn up some excruciating puns (such as a local brewery providing an in-house bottled ale by the name of Special Offa).

My life is calibrated by Harry Tuffin's. Its eastern outpost is at Cleobury Mortimer in Shropshire, near where I grew up in Kidderminster. The westernmost branch is by the railway station in Machynlleth, my local town these past twelve years. Between the two lie branches in places that have been with me all my life: Bishop's Castle, Ludlow, Craven Arms, Knighton (which "boasts the first and only multi-storey car park in mid Wales", according to the company's own website). Independent, feisty, fun and unashamedly populist: I'm proud to have Tuffin's as my life writ large. I should ask to have my ashes scattered in the Fancy Goods aisle.

Churchstoke is in Wales (Yr Ystog, don't you know), but only just. Coming from Newtown, you are welcomed into England miles further back and then once more into Wales just as you come into the village. It sits in a protrusion of Wales shaped like a big toe, poking rudely into Shropshire's plump ribs, and with Corndon Hill its shapely bunion. Yet Tuffin's play their Welshness with quiet pride, even though only three of their ten stores are on our side of the border. Click on their website[18] and the words Croeso i Harry Tuffin's are the first to greet you. When they opened in Machynlleth in 2009, they surprised everyone with massive, glossy monolingual Welsh hoardings filling every plate glass window, inveigling punters in for their *diodydd, ffrwythau* and *papurau newydd* (no mention of the *pasteiod porc* or *pryd ar glud am un*[19]). I once interviewed Paul Delves, current MD and grandson of Harry and Doris, and he told me that this enthusiasm for Cymreictod came from his son, who was then starting his career in the family firm by shelf-stacking, and who is now a junior manager. The lad had taken his dad the previous year to the National Eisteddfod, which they'd both much enjoyed, though Paul couldn't help but notice "that nearly all of the folk there seemed to be working in the public sector. Didn't look like they'd done a proper day's graft, most of them".

HAY-ON-WYE

Tuffin's is proper graft, constant and unrelenting, and against the almighty cartel of the supermarket big boys. Who can blame them if they get a little Wild West at times, in everything from gargantuan biker's breakfasts to elastic interpretation of the planning regulations? What else would you expect hereabouts? Often in the Marches, you feel that you are in neither England nor Wales, but somewhere that looks like both yet neither. It is the Third Way, long before Tony Blair fastened on the idea; the calm, unchanging eye in the middle of the storm; the lawless enclave that we all so need to believe in. It is the OK Corral, and Harry Tuffin its sheriff in a big gold star badge. Aisle four, £1.99 for a pack of three.

HAY-ON-WYE

Arthur Miller, when asked to come to the festival: "Hay-on-Wye? Is that some kind of sandwich?"

> Yes. It is.
> Fresh, locally-sourced, organic.
> Hand-carved, home-baked, artisan-crafted.
> Drizzled, pampered, plumped.
> Blasus, tasty, scrummy.
> Though the price will make you wince for a week,
> And it'll drown the fire in your tummy.

★

1977; I'm ten years old. On the news, in the 'and finally…' bit at the end when the newscaster raises their eyebrow in arch mock-amusement, comes a story that a town on the Welsh-English border has declared independence from the rest of the UK. Footage shows a crowd of cheering bumpkins with flaming pitchforks, gathered before a home-made stage upon which sits a gawky, bespectacled man. The King of Hay, Richard Booth, holds the sceptre and orb of the new nation, fashioned out of a ballcock and some copper piping. Punk is exploding, but that's of no interest yet. The UDI of Hay-on-Wye though electrifies me. I nag and beg to be taken there, to be a witness to this rural revolution. Look, I say to my dad, brandishing the Ordnance Survey map at him, it's only at the other side of our new county[20]; we could be there within a couple of

hours. He pats me on the head, wearily it has to be said, and suggests I go out to find some friends to play with. I stay in with my maps.

Although these pronouncements of independence for villages, islands in rivers, old military forts in the sea, even individual houses and flats are two-a-penny these days (Lonely Planet has gone so far as to publish a guidebook to the world's *soi disant* micronations), Hay was one of the first, and definitely the best, the one you could most believe in. Independence fits it like a gauntlet. Geographically, it already straddles a national border; you need to tweak that only slightly and there's your lumpen British Liechtenstein or Andorra emerging into the sunlight. Historically, it was already a place apart: a Norman enclosure, La Haie, The Hay (that definite article has a lot to answer for. And it's only augmented in Welsh, for Hay is Y Gelli[21], The Grove). Temperamentally, it defers to no-one or nowhere, far enough from any major population centre to plough its own red furrow with insouciant style and yokel wit. Even etymologically, it all fits. Limitless puns and meaty alliteration present themselves: Make Hay Not War, Hay Days, Way-on-High, the Battle of Haystings, Haybraham Lincoln, Hay Fever, Home Rule for Hay. Only the *Daily Mail* struggled to find either fun or word

play in the shenanigans: 'Storm Clouds of Belfast Loom Over Hay' it portentously proclaimed after Hay's declaration of UDI.

Behind the japes, the passports, stamps and car bumper stickers, the publicity and grandiose titles[22], there were some deathly serious politics rumbling. Richard Booth railed against the ignorance and indifference of government to rural problems, and the fat-cattery of new quangoes such as the Wales Tourist Board and the Development Board for Rural Wales (the latter, according to Booth's autobiography *My Kingdom of Books*, had only "encouraged foreign imports and subsidized London property deals"). To Booth, the answer to rural depopulation and isolation was the spirited uptake of unusual local specialisms, and he was proving its worth in Hay, having turned a remote town of one and a half thousand people into the world capital of second-hand books.

Booth's monarchy was anarchy, a creed that sat well in Hay. "My Cabinet was picked in five minutes in the pub," he stated in his autobiography. "Most were wearing jeans and there was a high proportion of lorry drivers. The advantage of Hay's small population of 1,500 was that I could give everyone a top government post. Mackendrick, a Scottish stone-mason, was appointed Minister of Scottish Affairs on account of his accent. The Welsh Office was occupied by a vaguely nationalist telephone engineer. There was a unanimous veto on having a Minister of Arts for fear of encouraging ponces. Norman Radcliffe had had so much to drink he could not remember whether he was supposed to be Prime Minister or Minister of Defence. 'Just like real government,' someone remarked." Fantasy and fact merged even more intimately with thorny questions at Cabinet being referred to the Hay Decision-Maker, a spinning wheel that would randomly settle on a choice of eight potential solutions: Have a Drink, Try Bribery, Spin Again, Appoint a New Committee, Get a Rural Development Grant, Forget It, Do it Yourself, Defer to Next Session. Rumours that it now resides in a locked committee room in Llandrindod Wells are, of course, entirely unfounded.

Without Richard Booth and his egomaniacal flair, there would be no booktown[23], no Hay Festival, no Florence père et fils, no queue of politicians and quangocrats eager to cash in on the reflected glory. There would be precious few tourists, boutique cafes, artisan gift shops and gastropubs either. Although the townsfolk rather tired of his increasingly belligerent rants, even going so far as to vote against him when he stood for the County Council, their success is all down to his initial, bonkers vision. Twenty-seven years after watching King Richard's coronation on the *Nine O'Clock News*, I was thrilled to be coming to Hay to interview him for my TV series. Properly thrilled, more so than for any other interviewee I can remember. Although much diminished by a series of strokes, he didn't disappoint. It was a little like interviewing a very loud juke box. I'd punch in the buttons – J4 for the festival, F11 for the rural economy, P12 for the publishing industry, A9 for devolution, Q5 for the internet – and he was off, the speech slightly slurred, but each well-worn record delivered with such unshakeable force and self-assurance that all I could do was wallow in the waterfall of trenchant opinion, wait for the very occasional pause and thank my lucky stars that I wasn't going to be the one stuck in an edit suite trying to dice it all into palatable nuggets of Thursday evening telly, just after *Emmerdale*.

Around us in his office in the Castle sat the remnant paraphernalia of Hay's independence adventure, all a little dusty and rusted, looking like memorabilia from a long-forgotten Rag Week, but it was treasure to my eyes. And then came the zenith of the interview, my being knighted into Hay nobility. The strokes had left him a little shaky, and I was frankly nervous when he made me kneel, and started to brandish a sword around my shoulders and neck in order to anoint me as Sir Michael. The ceremony passed without major mishap, though I did have to stop him trying to knight my dog, Lady Patsy as she was to become. She was eyeing him very warily, and would have had his arm off had he gone too close with that tottering sabre.

Months later, the phone rang. "Hello, it's the Castle here," said a female voice. "The Castle?" I replied. "Hay Castle," she snapped, sounding incredulous that I hadn't worked it out. "Did you get your knighthood certificate?" I hadn't, and when a cardboard tube, addressed to Sir Michael, Lord of Ceinws, arrived a few days later, the postman knocked and handed it over with only the slightest of smirks. It's a thing of great beauty, wax seal and everything, and it sits framed by my desk, my only honour. King Richard went on to amass a few more. He was crowned Emperor of the Book Towns of the World, which is starting to get distinctly Bokassa-esque, and given the MBE in 2004 for his "services to the tourism industry in Powys". Just in case you think that the old git's sold out for good, he also formed an unlikely alliance with Arthur Scargill and stood for his Socialist Labour Party in the inaugural National Assembly elections of 1999, and for the Welsh seat at the European elections ten years later[24]. God save the King.

CLYRO

Ideas. May. Blossom. Ideas May Blossom. Ideasmayblossom. Especially with its accompanying close-up photo of the first soft pink flowers of the cherry tree, the slogan of the Hay literature festival is undeniably cute, but over-exposure to it is starting to curdle my brain. I can't manage another day of self-delighted twinkling in a Breconshire field, so I hook up with poet Damian Walford Davies for a springtime amble out of the playpen and into Kilvert Country. Damian's a fan of Kilvert[25], slightly to my surprise. I'd been dimly aware of the parson-diarist, and conscious that he had a devoted following, but had never read any of his works, rather assuming that such books will come into my life with the carpet slippers and the *People's Friend*. As we walk alongside the main road from Hay to Clyro, Chelsea Tractors whooshing up the dust into our faces, Damian will have none of my cynicism. Kilvert, he assures me, was one of the finest nature writers ever, his evocation of the turning wheel of the year in the borderlands of the 1870s a deserved classic that should, he believed, never go out of fashion. He is passionate and persuasive, and I resolve to try the *Diaries*. Damian tells me how they were not published until sixty years after Kilvert's death, at the onset of the Second World War. It was the timing that propelled them into immediate success. At times of war, we inevitably turn to a yearned-for past, a place and a time for which it is worth fighting. Kilvert, with his vivid prose and winsome mid-Victorian sensibilities, fitted the bill perfectly. As did the *Diaries*' physical location principally in Herefordshire and Radnorshire[26].

This intrigues me. The idea of the recent past, just slipping out of first-hand memory, as a repository of our dreams and hopes is nothing new (although just how predictable and unyielding this force remains down the ages is something that never ceases to surprise), but I had never particularly thought that there was a geographical equivalent, a particular place that we can trace on the map, one that holds the nub of our romantic displacement. Yet it is perfectly possible to see that Kilvert Country is just that: a land beyond now, a place that straddles borders both literal and metaphysical.

Just as it was the tales of Victorian Radnorshire that calmed the jagged nerves of Britain as the Luftwaffe strafed the skies, so it was other nostalgic writing from the Marches that acted as the collective Rescue Remedy in the previous war. In 1896, A.E. Housman had been unable to find an initial publisher for his collection, *A Shropshire Lad*, so had self-published it to a lukewarm reaction. The Boer War and then the Great War had changed its fortunes entirely, and this evocation of a lost England, of stout country towns, muscular lads and intense comradeship was found in many a breast-pocket of the beautiful corpses in the trenches. Some such copies, it is claimed, even stopped bullets.

Does this idea that the Welsh-English borderlands are some kind of inherent locus for our national hiraeth, to be invoked at times of emergency and greatest need, continue in to our own era? Indubitably. Shropshire, Herefordshire and Radnorshire, with bits of the counties of Montgomery and Brecon, are inevitably presented in the popular media, if they are presented at all, as a balm and poultice against the nasty modern world, a place that city-slickers need to believe in, even if they never come here. This is Narnia, fairyland and the physical embodiment of our half-remembered golden childhoods. Hay has made a fortune flogging the

dream, and Kilvert has been enthusiastically co-opted as a cheerleader.

Clyro church is cool and welcome[27], and plays its Kilvert connections with quiet pride. Damian is delighted finally to have seen it, and, even more importantly, the wisteria-covered house over the road, Ashbrook, where the man himself lodged. "It's exactly as he describes it; same trees, everything", he hisses excitedly. After imbibing a bottle of pop each from the fusty little village store, we set off up the hill past the church, not quite sure where we're heading, but determined to get there anyway. It's all very much in the spirit of Kilvert, I'm assured, who tramped miles in these hills, popping in on parishioners as he went: 'villaging', he called it in the diaries. I wonder out loud whether we could call Housman's version 'cottaging'. I think so.

We chatter our way uphill, on to the lower slopes of the Begwns, that little-known ridge of hills that runs east-west across the jowls of Radnorshire. Damian's exuberance is beginning to pay off, and I'm truly thrilled at the prospect of my imminent loss of literary virginity to the Reverend Frank Kilvert. It is a golden spring day, larks trill on the wind as tiny, fluffy clouds drift coquettishly through a china blue sky. Across the Wye valley, Hay Bluff and the Black Mountains command the entire scene with dark gravitas. Distant engines thrum, sunlight dances on the Wye, fields and hedgerows light up and go out; it is difficult not to sing at the sheer clichéd loveliness of it all. If Kilvert can conjure up just a fraction of this beauty, then he will be a much valued companion.

He does. I fall for him completely, and devour the three volumes of his diaries, covering a period from 1870 to 1879, the year he died, aged just thirty-eight. Kilvert's world is so vividly woven, particularly in the early years at Clyro. Even his seasons – baking hot summers, snowy winters, spring and autumn that sweep their changes with perfect precision – seem larger and brighter than any we know now. In each season, upon each landscape, Kilvert gives voice to the joy of nature's flawlessness.

Kilvert arrived in Clyro as the village curate in 1865, just a few months after the railway had reached nearby Hay-on-Wye, and the heady excitement of the early railways infuses his accounts. He is forever striding across the fields to catch the 9.4 to Three Cocks Junction (change for Builth and Rhayader), or the up-train to Whitney and Hereford. He gives us a picture of rural Britain at the exact point that it is opening up for the very first time, offering an intoxicating world of possibility. Up to that point, most people in the countryside would barely have gone further than a dozen miles from their birthplace throughout their entire life. Kilvert records a revolution in progress from an unlikely front line.

It's not – as I think I'd probably expected – all sunshine and lollipops in Kilvert's world. The black dog of poor health, physical and mental, stalks him, and the poverty and misery he confronts while villaging makes for sometimes uncomfortable reading. Suicides pepper the account with monotonous frequency: farmers do away with themselves in remote barns, while for young servant girls, the other main suicidal constituency, it's a desperate dash into the River Wye until the waters close over their broken souls[28]. Damian and I walk back along the river from Llowes to Hay, through big fields and wide skies. Polite festival-going children wave to us from their kayaks and canoes, dogs and a few hardy swimmers splash around on the big curve of water at the Warren, on the edge of town. The Wye is wearing its brightest smile on this idyllic late-spring day; it's hard to see it as a place of pitch darkness in which to drown. Ideas Have Blossomed. In May. But out of Hay.

EAST

Notes

1. Had Glyndŵr's Tripartite Indenture of 1405 succeeded, whereupon plans were drawn up to divide Britain into three between himself, Roger Mortimer and Percy, the Earl of Northumberland, the Welsh border would have been the River Severn from northern Shropshire all the way down to the Bristol Channel.
2. By 'the Powys stretch', I mean also the bits in the neighbouring English counties of Herefordshire and Shropshire. The southernmost section of the Trail, near Chepstow, follows extant stretches of an earthwork that is most probably Offa's Dyke, but apart from that, they are all in the stretch between near Presteigne and Chirk.
3. From ysgubor, a barn.
4. From Mynach-dŷ, the house of monks, or monastery. Poeth means hot.
5. *A surly old maid of Rhos Fiddle,*
   Had a feline companion named Tiddles,
   'Twas time to be rid of the cat,
   When it shat on the mat
   And put out her fire with its piddle.
   Your turn now.
6. The 81-mile Teme (Afon Tefeidiad in Welsh) is one of the sweetest, yet least eulogised, rivers in Britain. It rises on the mini-Pumlumon of Cilfaesty Hill near Newtown (source also of the Mule and the Ithon), and flows eastwards towards England, watering the agricultural citadels of Knighton, Leintwardine, Ludlow and Tenbury Wells, before joining the Severn just south of Worcester.
7. See www.guardian.co.uk/media/2010/sep/17/pcc-aa-gill
8. Until the county reorganisation of 1974, Sycarth, part of the parish of Llansilin, was in the far south of Denbighshire. Upon the creation of the new counties, the border was moved slightly, so that Sycarth became part of the district of Montgomeryshire in the county of Powys, rather than Denbighshire's short-lived replacement, Clwyd. When the 1974 counties were abolished in 1996, the parish remained in Powys, even though Denbighshire was reinstated at the time. Although technically a recent liberty, therefore, to allow the inclusion of Sycarth in a work about Powys, it has long looked to a Montgomeryshire hinterland of the Tanat, Cain and Vyrnwy valleys.
9. 'The little death' in French, also a euphemism for an orgasm. Many cultures mark this time of year as a variation on the theme of a festival for the dead.
10. St Bridget is "an old heathen goddess of fertility, disguised in a threadbare Christian cloak" (Sir James George Frazer, *The Golden Bough*)
11. Julian Cope, the former singer with the Teardrop Explodes, has become an unlikely expert in megalithic history. *The Modern Antiquarian* (Thorsons, 1998), his effusive gazetteer of pre-Christian sites of significance in the British, or Bride-ish, Isles has become a staple of the genre. My quotations here are from this book.
12. Llansantffraid FC burst into the national consciousness in 1996, when, as winners of the Welsh Cup, they qualified for the UEFA Cup Winners' Cup. The Cinderella tale of a tiny Welsh village football side taking on the giants of Europe made headlines around the world. They've qualified a few times since, coming up against opposition as mighty as Manchester City, Liverpool, CSKA Sofia and Anderlecht. Following their initial European adventure, Oswestry computer firm Total Network Solutions stepped in as sponsors, and in 1997, the team was rechristened after them, becoming the first club in the UK to be named solely after their sponsors (and leading to Jeff Stelling's regular retort, when reading the football results on Sky Sports, "they'll be dancing in the streets of Total Network Solutions tonight!"). In 2003, TNS merged with Oswestry Town FC who, despite being over the border in England, also played in the League of Wales. Following Total Network

Solutions' buyout by BT, new sponsors and a new name were needed, and the club is now called The New Saints, handily keeping the old abbreviation.
13. The most celebrated local border crossing was across the counter of the Lion Hotel in Llanymynech. Two bars in England, one in Wales (or, as a regular put it to me there once, "I like to sup my pint in Wales and piss it out in England"). The oft-quoted story that, when Welsh Sundays were dry, you could drink in the English bars, but not the Welsh one, is not strictly true: on those far-off Sundays, the front door (in Montgomeryshire) was locked, and drinkers had to come in through the back (in Shropshire). The Lion is a sad sight now, having been closed for years and still awaiting redevelopment.
14. Though it's a moot point as to how much use a commemorative pillar is when you're hungry.
15. This is where Montgomery Spring and Celtic Spring bottled waters are extracted.
16. I felt that I'd been accepted into my home village on the other side of Montgomeryshire when, a few months after moving there, I went in to the shop to buy some milk. The elderly lady proprietor bent down to the fridge below the counter, drew out a two pint of full fat and peered at the Sell By date. "Ooh," she wheezed, "it's nearly out. I'll keep that for the caravan park." She put it back and got me a fresher one from behind.
17. Yam-Yam is the name for the dialect of the Black Country, the area around the sprawl of industrial towns that merge together on the western flank of Birmingham.
18. www.harrytuffin.co.uk. It's a great read.
19. Drinks, fruit and newspapers, but not the pork pies or ready-meals for one.
20. I'm probably one of the few people to remember the 1974 reorganisation of British counties with any fondness. I was seven years old and deliriously excited by the fact that, without moving an inch, I had ceased to be a child of industrial north Worcestershire, but was now a proud resident of Hereford & Worcester, the Sonny'n'Cher of English counties. The fact that I was suddenly in a border county was even more thrilling.
21. Or fully Y Gelli Gandryll, the shattered grove. Even better.
22. King Richard ennobled anyone who either played their part with gusto, or paid the going rate (exactly the same way other honours are generally bestowed). April Ashley, Britain's first post-op transsexual, lived in the town for a decade from 1975 and became the Duchess of Hay and Offa's Dyke.
23. Other booktowns, modelled on Hay, have sprung up worldwide. Blaenafon, not far down the road, tried it for a while, but it didn't last too long.
24. He stood too, for his own Rural Revival Party, in the Brecon and Radnor seat at the 1983 general election, coming last with 278 votes (0.73%).
25. The Reverend Robert Francis Kilvert (1840-1879), always known as Francis, or Frank, was born in Wiltshire, son of the Reverend Robert Kilvert, Rector of Langley Burrell. He came as curate to Clyro in 1865, leaving in 1872. His first parish as priest was also in Radnorshire: St Harmon's for just a year (1876-7), before he was appointed to the rectory of Bredwardine, back near Hay, but over the border in Herefordshire. True to the fashions of the mid-Victorian age, Kilvert was an incurable romantic, falling in love with (and swooning over) girls on a near daily basis. His famous diaries come to an abrupt end in March 1879. In August of that year, he married Elizabeth Rowland, but died shortly after they had returned from honeymoon in Scotland.
26. The *Diaries* take us also to Wiltshire, and the family home near Chippenham, London, Bath, Worcester, Oxford, the Isle of Wight, and on a tour through mid and north Wales. There were doubtless other trips unguessed at, for the *Diaries* were savagely filleted by Kilvert's widow, for reasons never quite established.
27. Even if the Pevsner volume on Powys loftily denounces it as "dull".
28. And doubtless pregnant bellies in all too many cases.

SOUTH
Breconshire

COUNTY TOWN

Unlike its northerly siblings, there has never been any ambiguity as to the county capital of Breconshire. Since the era of the kingdom of Brycheiniog[1], all roads, all thoughts and all privileges have converged on Brecon, lying serene and self-assured in the lovely Vale of Usk.

The best way into town is to march up the middle of The Watton, preferably in combat fatigues. You wouldn't be the first. With the possible exception of the King Edward VII Avenue in Cardiff's Cathays Park, this is Wales' most military thoroughfare, its generous width designed to allow marching regiments and full accompanying oompah, its precisely lopped and spaced lime trees looking like green busbies standing sentinel at the side. All lines of this handsome boulevard are drawn to the church tower at its apogee, below which soars the colonnaded entrance of the old Brecknock Shire Hall[2]. Sergeant Major, Reverend and Alderman in perfect alignment: Brecon's Holy Trinity.

The squaddie mood is mobilised as soon as you loop off the by-pass roundabout at the town's eastern end. To the right is Dering Lines, the much modernised barracks and home of both the Infantry Battle School and a division of the Gurkha rifles[3]. The entrance is guarded by a bronze statue of an infantryman, bulging with kit, a rifle hung low in his right hand, his left pointing the way forward into enemy territory. It's an evocative image, even if you can't help but wonder just how useful the frond of metallic ivy on his helmet would really be as camouflage. The town's older barracks, now used mainly for administrative purposes and as the occasional film location, is a little further up The Watton. A thumping fist of a building, the Victorian castellated gatehouse fronts the street and leaves no doubt as to who's boss. In the barracks' old arsenal building, the South Wales Borderers Museum is, as you'd expect, chock full of medals, guns, banners, flags, drums, paintings, all being quietly cooed over by neat, greying gentlemen. The old regiment's finest hour, the 1879 defence of Rorke's Drift from the Zulus, is lavishly explored and lovingly eulogised. Replicas of the eleven Victoria Crosses awarded that day, the single largest haul ever awarded, take pride of place.

Quick march, up, up towards The Bulwark, Brecon's handsome central square, crowned by a florid statue of Wellington and the

impressive parish church of St Mary. Even that is a military *trompe l'oeil*, for the solid, lofty sixteenth century tower reveals itself to be semi-detached from the body of the church; it was built in fact as a look-out post for soldiers. There's further confusion, for many visitors assume that this is the town's cathedral and are puzzled when told otherwise. You can't blame them: the real cathedral is low-slung and squat, half-hidden in the trees to the north of the town centre. Built initially as a far-flung outpost of Battle Abbey in Sussex[4], it grew into a significant Benedictine priory, and on the Dissolution of the Monasteries, became the town's parish church. Cathedral status came in 1923, following the disestablishment of the Church in Wales and the creation of its new dioceses. Proving that ecclesiastical politics is no less of a minefield than the secular variety, the counties of Brecon and Radnor were hived off the diocese of St David's, along with a dogleg of land along the Swansea valley and down to Swansea itself and Gower. Brecon's old priory became the cathedral church of the new, and bizarrely-shaped, diocese, though the town has still not been upgraded to city status. But then neither has it asked for it (unlike places such as Wrexham, presenting themselves with monotonous dependability at every municipal beauty contest with a prize of city status). It is a two-way misconception that anywhere with an Anglican cathedral automatically becomes a city, or that a city must have a cathedral. Brecon is one of nine towns in England and Wales (St Asaph is another) that has a cathedral, while there are sixteen cities with no cathedral. One such place is Swansea, which gained city status in 1969 as a present from the newly invested Prince Charles, so the diocese now has a city and a cathedral, albeit 44 miles apart.

With its battlements and air of solid impregnability, its regimental chapel and their threadbare battle colours, the cathedral only continues the militaristic theme. More battlements just below too, in the walls of the castle wrecked by the townspeople themselves in the Civil War, thus, they hoped, lessening the appeal to either side of storming the town. Just across the Usk bridge, the chapel and gothic turrets of Christ College, the second oldest school in Wales[5], soar haughtily over the town roofs. Around a fifth of its 325 pupils come from forces families and 65% are boarders, who pay an annual fee of £21,465. CCB did score one notable debut in Wales, as the home of the country's first school cadet force. Junior square-bashing, which began in 1894, has turned out a moderately illustrious roll-call of sportsmen and minor theologians, as well as the BBC's genial Jamie Owen and veteran Liberal Democrat MP, Simon Hughes.

At ease! Enough of the marching; it's time to saunter and take in the town's flourishing flip side. Religious first: the Plough chapel, its exuberant interior hiding behind a nondescript frontage, dazzles more than the cathedral will ever manage. Rarely do chapels feel like much fun, but this is one with light, theatricality and nature sunk into its bones; appropriate that this was where Roland Mathias[6] came to worship. The poet and pacifist would never have fitted in amongst the heavily militarised Anglican congregation of Brecon. Even here though, there's not much sting left in church versus chapel, for the battle lines have had to be redrawn: God versus Mammon is the one that matters. For where there are squaddies, public school kids, clerics and tourists, there will be pubs, late-night drinking dens and parties aplenty. From a picnic by the old Usk bridge to an increasingly woozy pub crawl through the narrow streets, Brecon is a machine well oiled in getting you the same way. Within two hundred yards, you can top up at the Bull's Head, the Boar's Head, the Wellington, the Wheatsheaf, the Old Cognac, the Puzzle Tree, the Punch Bowl, the Gremlin, the George, the Clarence and the Camden Arms. Finish with an appropriately

theatrical flourish at the Sarah Siddons: the eighteenth century 'Queen of Drury Lane' was born here in 1755[7] when her father's troupe of travelling actors was in residence.

The town's biggest whoopee of the year comes in early August, and the arrival of the annual Brecon Jazz Festival, started in 1984 on a budget of a hundred pounds. Against all expectations, conservative little Brecon and hot, smoky jazz seem made for each other, a doe-eyed affair that has lasted longer than anyone could have imagined. Even for those of us who remain determinedly agnostic about the joys of jazz, the weekend always throws up plenty of choice moments and unanticipated musical epiphanies. Better still, it gives ample opportunity to ponder the strange syncopation of black, rootsy American rhythms and white, beardy British pedantry. I can't imagine ever getting aggressively shushed in New Orleans at an outdoor street jam, but it sure happened in Brecon.

Periodically, organisers have had to pin the celebrations back a little in order to calm the well-worn nerves of the town's highly vocal anti brigade. In 2006, this came to a head when the festival was forced to take performers off the streets, a feature that had been blamed for encouraging drunkenness and disorder. Dark whispers in shops and bars laid the fault firmly at the feet of the hordes who bussed it up to Brecon from the Valleys, revealing an ever-present fault line between the town and its reluctantly-acknowledged hinterland. The 1969 *Shell Guide to Wales* calls it "an English-speaking town with the sense of being an English cathedral city", and they're right. In Brecon's mind, the town shares a stage with Salisbury or Worcester or Hereford, and not the far more proximate Merthyr, Ebbw Vale or Cardiff.

Try as they might, the mental elasticity of geography cannot quite overcome its topographic reality, however. Brecon has always been the great Cardiff or Valleys day out, a bottle of pop and an ice cream in the Beacons, topped with a few pints and a shuffle around the town's rather swankier shops. In his recollections of 1946 National Service in Brecon, Cardiffian Glyn Williams recalls how "we learned to smoke and we drank. At weekends the girls came from Merthyr and went to the pubs. If we, and they, drank enough we could be found sitting on one another's laps, but the NCOs were wrong; by our reckoning there were lots of virgins in Brecon, including most of the 18-year-old soldiers."[8]

The journey in the other direction, from Brecon to Merthyr, was generally less leisurely and bristled with far greater menace. It is Brecon's proximity to the Valleys that spurred on its military growth: while the hottest flames of the industrial revolution seared the sky fifteen or twenty miles to the south, the militia of Brecon were on permanent red alert, ready to be called out whenever the seething cauldron boiled over. In these devolutionary days, when we see the slight tweaking of the mental map to place Wales as the primary, discrete unit of consideration, the relationship between these mismatched siblings is probably less strained now than it ever has been. Age has brought some mellowing, but it's still not a meeting of equals. Not now, and not ever.

BEACONS

The Brecon Beacons National Park: 520 square miles, created in 1957, the tenth in Britain. Of the three in Wales, it's the least visited, the middle in terms of size, and the most populated[9]. You could be forgiven for assuming that it was more or less coterminous with Breconshire, but in truth, only 66% of the BBNP lies in Powys. There are bits of the park under the jurisdiction of nine local authorities[10], although for two of them (Caerphilly and Neath-Port

SOUTH

Talbot) it's just a couple of their most peripheral acres on distant moors.

It's a three way split, left to right. To the west, the Black Mountain and the Fforest Fawr. The Beacons proper in the middle, and the Black Mountains, plural you see, towards the English border in the east. The bit in the middle gets the lion's share of the attention and the visitors, for here are the eponymous Beacons themselves, the scalloped heights of Pen-y-Fan and Corn Du, just a shade under three thousand feet. Nowhere truly mountainous, nowhere really wild, but all lovely and shapely enough, a tidy machine to extract the cash of those who dash down the M4 for their muddy weekend fix. Visitor centres, car parks, gastropubs, waymarked walks, bikers' haunts, picnic areas, pony trekking, ice cream and burger vans, barn conversions, flower baskets, red rocks, scorched earth, Cymru Lite, nature trails, GoreTex one-upmanship, kiddies' fun parks, gentle streams, brown signs.

If you catch a whiff of disdain or ennui in my description, you'd be right. The National Park is the slab of red meat thrown to the wolves, the ritual sacrifice on the altar to the gods of tourism. It'll show you anything for the right price, especially in this middle belt. As always, the best bits are to be found away from the over-subscribed centre, so to that end, here are a couple of postcards

from the edge of the park, the splendid melancholy of the Black Mountains.

*

Capel-y-ffin, the 'chapel on the border' seems self-explanatory enough, for the national boundary runs high above the tiny settlement on a ridge of the Black Mountains. It's not the only divide to be found on the local map, and it isn't even the one being set in the stone of its name. There are other borders at work here: the most pertinent for a church is that this is where three Anglican dioceses meet, Monmouth (formerly Llandaff), Swansea & Brecon (formerly St David's) and Hereford. For our purposes here, it is also where the eastern border of Powys finally leaves the side of England and heads into Wales, as Monmouthshire takes over the role as Border County.

None of these exist, except on the map and in our overheated cultural constructs. I'm not so sure that Capel-y-ffin does either. It's there right enough every time I've inched my way down Bwlch-yr-Efengel, the Gospel Pass, from Hay, the tiny church and the chapels and the tumbledown Victorian monastery, but I'm sure they vaporize as soon as no-one's looking. Inevitably, this green cathedral of a valley has lured in a steady stream of artists, visionaries and bombasts: the wandering Kilvert of course, who met mad Father Ignatius here, the Wordsworths, Bruce Chatwin, David Jones, J.M.W. Turner, Jan Morris, John Piper, Paul Sandby, Gerallt Cymro, Joshua Thomas, Walter Savage Landor, even the Virgin Mary, twice[11]. It's possibly just as well that neither of her visits coincided with Eric Gill's sexually incontinent retreat in the valley; if children and dogs weren't off limits, then it's hard to imagine that a shimmering apparition of heavenly perfection would have stood a chance.

★

"Let the industrial-capitalist disease do its worst – the Black Mountains of Brecon will remain untouched and their green valleys lead nowhere," Gill wrote, many years after he'd left the area. Over the ridge of Tarren yr Esgob is the going nowhere valley of the Grwyne Fawr, a very special place. I take a day's walk around it, climbing to the church of Partrishow, lost in all time. It's much eulogised now (Simon Jenkins gives it a rare maximum four stars in his book on Welsh churches and houses), and there are lesser-known, but equally powerful, isolated churches throughout Breconshire[12], though St Issui's has an atmosphere of such contented charm that it deserves the praise. The exquisite oaken lace of its fifteenth century rood screen is what brings most people here, though the medieval memento mori, the skeletal figure of Time with his scythe, shovel and hourglass, always holds my gaze for longer.

Down the lane is St Issui's well, repaired, it tells us, by a troupe of Boy Scouts in 2005, when "the water started flowing once again". It's not flowing today. Instead, it is dark and damp, surrounded by votive offerings, flowers and home-made crosses out of twigs. I mutter curses at the plastic tat that some have left, and the crosses seem unnecessarily strident and only semi-relevant to this green gloom, for its power is far older than Jesus or Issui, but I let it pass, and throw a couple of plump sacrificial blackberries, picked on the lane, into the dank interior. I feast on many more on the path down to the Grwyne Fawr, a mottle of pale rocks and sheep fleece on thorn bushes, vivid against the red ochre of the earth. The sandstone soil is the same colour as the Partrishow *memento mori*, that of drying blood.

In the valley, the Grwyne Fawr babbles by, clear and fast. Dark shadows of fish dart through, and a car sweeps over the little bridge. It parks, and I see the occupant getting out and carrying a box towards a chapel opposite. In such a remote, and scarcely populated, spot as this, I'd first assumed that the chapel was long abandoned, probably a holiday home by now. But there's noise coming from it, laughter and the always lovely sound of tinkling crockery, and I have to investigate. All eyes turn towards me as I enter. It's a gang of six or so, decorating the place for the harvest festival service this coming weekend. There's a line of apples along the organ top, an artistic pyramid of carrots, swedes and turnips on the altar, crowned by an oversized marrow, mounds of damsons, grapes and tomatoes on the sills, flowers in the gallery, mis-shapen potatoes everywhere, and even two great lumps of coal ("that's a harvest too", they tell me). It looks wonderful.

I forget the chapels sometimes. Maybe it's one of the most stubborn (even snobbish) redoubts of my Englishness, but I'll always presume that there's more interest in an old Anglican church than a chapel, even if – as is the rule, rather than the exception, in Powys – the church was extensively, if not entirely, rebuilt by the ever-zealous Victorians. Partrishow church had been as serene as ever, but like the *memento mori*, there was no life and little prospect of any. Here in the Tabernacl that countless Partrishow pilgrims must have passed with barely a second glance, there was salt, community, laughter and kindness. Beauty too: the simple interior, a wooden gallery on three sides around a central well only eight pews deep, was polished to a shine and clearly loved.

I wasn't allowed to leave without being given a drink and a chocolate bar. They even offered me an apple off the top of the organ, but that would have felt like nicking the church plate. The regular congregation here is six strong, of whom three are organists, but they were hopeful of tipping into double figures for the harvest service. We chat about growing fruit and veg, and I confess my antipathy towards marrows, of which I have a glut at home. They're just too big and watery for my tastes, and there really is only so much marrow chutney you can give as Christmas presents. One old boy carefully talks me through how to make rum, involving dripping sugar through the marrow and a pair of tights. "Got a great taste, and a hell of a kick," he tells me. I hadn't expected to learn that in chapel.

Someone new arrives with a big box of onions and cabbages to add to the display. I've been clocked, or at least my van has. "Is that you parked down in the cwm?" she asks. It is, I tell her (she's the second person to ask). "I thought it might be a magic mushroom van," she shrieks, and everyone joins in with the laughter. There's a lot of them around at this time of year apparently; the Black Mountains are a legendary tripper's paradise. I take my leave, a real spring in my autumn step, and offer up my thanks for all our harvests. They're a fine reminder that there's plenty of life before Time sharpens his scythe.

CRICKHOWELL

"Goodness me, no, we wouldn't like *that* at all." A tinkle of laughter and the ladies behind the desk[13] all bob their heads in unison, like a toy you might get at the garage free with five gallons of unleaded. I've only asked them a simple question: wouldn't Crickhowell be happier in Monmouthshire? Once I've passed the fortress of Tretower guarding the passes up into the hills, and am skimming across the Vale of Usk below, I always feel that I'm more or less in Abergavenny, in the Land of (Waitrose) Milk and Honey.

Crickhowell doesn't dent the illusion in the slightest, and it's always a shock to remember that I'm still in Powys.

Everyone says the same, in response to my question. I'm surprised. Reasons are many and varied, but one that keeps cropping up is that Powys, Breconshire, is proper Wales, but Monmouthshire really isn't. It's not a theory I imagine they've road-tested around the steep streets of Tredegar or Abertillery, but I can see their point. It was only in 1974 that Monmouthshire was finally, officially tied in to Wales, and there are many there who still haven't noticed. Breconshire – this part of it, anyway – might have lost the language, might have wavered towards Marcher lords over Powys princes, but there's still no mistaking which side of the border you're on. The hills have that sculptured menace; neither Table Mountain nor Sugar Loaf[14] could be anywhere else but here, in the bottom right corner of the Brecon Beacons National Park, and the bottom right of Powys.

Maybe that's part of the answer too. In these islands, the money and the power almost invariably slide down to the bottom right, the south-east. Doesn't matter what constituent unit you take – Britain, Wales, Powys, even Brecs, Monts or Rads – the influence and the cash are all down there↘ ? Same with Scotland, Ireland (North and Republic), England too. Crickhowell punches above its weight in the south-eastern corner of Powys, makes it look even smarter by comparison. It might struggle in the top left corner of Munmuthshuh, against Abergavenny, Monmouth, Tintern or Usk.

Last time I had so many people assuring me how happy they were in Powys, and how much they wanted to stay there, it was in Ystradgynlais, in the other bottom corner of Breconshire. There the similarity ends. Crickhowell is Powys at its most dapper. It is calm, urbane, well-spoken, well-dressed and well-coiffed; an old-school Tory with a roguish twinkle in its eye. You can try to dislike it, but there's no point; it'll charm the pants off you in the end. Google Crickhowell and one of the first things that comes up is a shaky YouTube video of Prince Harry attending his former equerry's 2010 wedding in the town's parish church. Harry and Crick (for that's what they call it) do make a lovely couple.

There's form there too. Princes Harry and William's first nanny, Tiggy Legge-Bourke, is a Crick girl. She's the daughter of Shân Legge-Bourke, Lord Lieutenant of Powys, Lady of Glanusk and splendidly no-nonsense blueblood, blessed with a voice like crunchy country house gravel. In a BBC series a few years ago all about the Legge-Bourkes[15], Shân told the story of how, shortly after the war, her mother had got so vexed by the maintenance problems of the big house[16] that she went out one morning "and blew it up". No nonsense, no sentiment, just get rid of the bloody thing. Since then, the family has lived in the dower house, Penmyarth, over the private castellated bridge on the other side of the Usk, though it's hardly slumming it.

No-one's missed the big house. It was a Victorian Gothic monster, a Hammer House of tat, and far, far too much of a visual reminder that it was built by new money, blood money. Genuine aristos would never have built something so ostentatiously vulgar, but what else would you expect from Joseph Bailey, Shân's great-great-great-grandfather, Nantyglo ironmaster and cousin of Merthyr overlords, the Crawshays? Joseph's previous architectural experiment was rather more spartan: the roundhouses at Nantyglo, with walls four feet thick and musket holes in the iron doors, where he and his brother Crawshay (really) planned to hole up in the event of a workers' uprising. The fact that they had just, yet again, cut their workers' wages only made such an occurrence more likely. No negotiation, no room for manoeuvre, just a pair of fortified artillery towers rammed in their faces.

It's a bit of a sore subject. In a 2003 *Western Mail* profile, Shân Legge-Bourke told Mario Basini how her mother and grandmother had been reluctant to talk about the family's industrial past, and how her mother had refused to discuss Alexander Cordell's novel *Rape of the Fair Country*, much of which is set in Nantyglo, on the grounds that it had nothing to do with her branch of the family. "You did not mention Cyfarthfa or Nantyglo to Granny," said Shân. "You just didn't talk about it." But the current Lady of Glanusk has done all she can in reparation. The survival instinct of the upper classes is powerful, and they know how to adapt. Shân is *primus unter pares* of the new breed of Welsh gentry happy to embrace, and even embody, the devolutionary age. Like the food being piled into wicker baskets and hessian bags in nearby Crickhowell, she prides herself on being locally-sourced and practically organic, and is a one-woman ambassador-cum-charity roadshow for all manner of Welsh, Powys and Breconshire organisations.

Tiggy and her family are just up the lane, running a B&B at Tŷ'r Chanter. A mad, braying mêlée of children, chickens, ducks, dogs (Havoc, Rocky, Jambo and Baffle), fishing, wellies, whisky and free range eggs on the Aga, it gets rave reviews, though everyone's too polite to write what must surely be uppermost in their minds: "Bloody Hell! It's that Tiggy Leggy-Thingy, she made my breakfast! The one that everyone thought was, y'know, with Charles. That's worth a five star review any day." She's not shy to use her infamy as a marketing tool either; the website has a whole section called The Tiggy Experience, which is what you are promised, and it's definitely her that wrote it all, unless some website designer geek has perfected the voice of a gregarious, galumphing posh girl ("Cheques or Cash only please. Cards to [sic] technical!! Sorry").

Once upon a time, I'd have been waiting with my box of matches at the barricades, but now I look at the Legge-Bourkes and can only admire their drive and commitment to their small, but lovely, patch of Breconshire, its place in the wider country beyond and their single-minded determination to ensure its future. The estate seems superbly well-run, at least on the two occasions that I've been allowed on it, namely for the Green Man festival. The setting is sublime; almost up there with Glastonbury. I remember watching bewitching American harpist-songstress Joanna Newsom there one night, the pure bubbles of her voice and harp ricocheting off the dome of Pen Cerrig Calch behind. During Newsom's extraordinary

set, the sun went down and the mountain throbbed from fiery red to a deep black. I cried. Cried like a Crick girl whose pony had gone to that great knacker's yard in the starry heaven.

PENWYLLT

Powys, Texas. Dust, rubble, growling hills, industrial scars, rickety lines of telegraph poles wheezing into the russet yonder. You wouldn't bat an eyelid to find some toothless old crone chewing baccy on her verandah up here in the Breconshire boondocks. Take a wander, and the sound of a rustily plucked Jew's-harp floats in the ether. Strain hard, and you might catch a twang of banjo. Yet here, at the end of the pitted, dead-end lane, lay a miniaturised fantasy palace, built for a homecoming queen.

It all goes a little odd as soon as you leave the main road[17] and the valley floor. Skeletal clumps of limestone and inexplicable hollows and holes pock the landscape, giving it the surly demeanour of a teenager's face. On the map too. Take a look at this area on the Ordnance Survey 1:25 000 Explorer, and the rash of shake holes, sink holes, swallow holes, pot holes, cairns, tumps and caves really does look like a bad outbreak of topographical acne. As the lane grinds up towards the plateau above, you might just notice a dark aperture gaping under a large shelf of limestone to one side. It doesn't look like it could amount to much, but this is an entrance to one of Britain's most extensive and labyrinthine caving systems, Ogof Ffynnon Ddu, over thirty miles of passage going over a thousand feet underground. Climbing higher, the green moonscape becomes ever stranger, until the lane coughs its last in a dustbowl of old quarries, derelict shacks and, slashing through them, the chiselled-out cuttings of the long-gone Neath and Brecon Railway. And there lies Adelina Patti's private station, Penwyllt for Craig-y-Nos, the most improbably-placed bauble of grandeur in Wales.

Madam Patti (1843-1919), the superstar diva of her day, was lured to Wales by her friend Lord Swansea. She fell in love with this grand, soulful valley of the Upper Tawe and, in 1878, bought the mansion of Craig-y-Nos, the Rock of the Night, far below Penwyllt. It was her much-needed refuge from the world tours, the pressures of global celebrity, the intense interest in her colourful private life (she married three times: to a French marquis, a French tenor and a Swedish baron, the last when she was 56 and he 30). Her castle was remodelled with the latest in creature comforts: central heating, an ice-making plant, a gasometer and its own generating system that made it the first house in Wales to be lit by electric light. Power was even used to work an electric organ in the billiards room. Alterations gave rein to the full excess of her thespian tastes, with mock-Scottish baronial turrets and towers, fountains and flags, a conservatory, a Winter Garden[18], guest suites for visiting European royalty[19] and, as the lavish encore to it all, a faithfully miniaturised version of the Theatre Royal in Drury Lane, whose stage curtain portrayed Adelina herself in her favourite opera role, Rossini's Semiramis charging by in a chariot. In order to make the theatre a suitable space for dancing, an activity she loved only slightly less than singing and flirting, the entire auditorium floor could be raised by a system of hydraulics. The Liliputian opera house has been lovingly patched-up, and houses concerts again, but no amount of latterday musical histrionics by south Walian enthusiasts can come close to the opulent, operatic splendour of Adelina's era.

Taking the castle's architectural cue from muscular Scots baronialism was no idle whimsy. This upper reach of the Tawe does ring of a Highland glen, its juxtaposition of grandiose bleakness, ample fishing, wooded seclusion and even a particularly virulent strain of midge making it feel as if has come fully-formed from the picture on a souvenir tin of shortbread. Romance is in the air – not the continental *dolce vita* of Adelina Patti's upbringing[20] and grand tours, but the cosy, companionable romance of a roaring hearth, a tartan rug and a crystal glass of golden malt. Fittingly, and so very romantically, the valley even has its own landscape guardian keeping eternal watch, the whaleback hump of the Cribarth, which, from the road beyond Abercraf, offers a fleeting optical illusion of a recumbent figure, easily earning its nickname of the Sleeping Giant.

Small wonder that Adelina Patti, whose life was showered in gold and roses[21], fell for this place. The late Victorian age was awash with saccharine sentimentality, the inevitable counter-balance to the brutal, smoky zenith of Empire and Industry, and none more necessary than in Wales. The Land of Song had been a precious creation of the nineteenth century; the mutual admiration between singer and country was of huge benefit to both. Miners and quarrymen were invited to hear her sing, for free, at the castle. They, in return, thronged the roads and formed guards of honour when she returned to Penwyllt from her travels. In 1889, the love affair reached its climax when she appeared at the National Eisteddfod in Brecon, and soared out 'Hen Wlad Fy Nhadau' to an adoring throng.

Since her death nearly a century ago, Craig-y-Nos has limped along in a succession of guises: a tuberculosis sanatorium, a geriatric hospital, a youth hostel, the headquarters of a contract cleaning company, a conference centre, a hotel pitched firmly at the wedding market. It seems always to be playing a distant catch-up, condemned forever to fall far short of its stratospheric heights under the chirruping Baroness Cederström, as her third marriage made her. Mementoes of her era are draped all around the castle, and the tiny theatre still cranks into action on special occasions, but the life – such extravagant, sumptuous chutzpah – has been draining away incxorably for decades, and it won't be coming back. The lavish gardens are now a country park, where waymarked trails and stern warnings keep the great unwashed out of its more magical corners. Almost opposite are the national showcaves of Dan-yr-Ogof[22], now far eclipsing the castle in their appeal to passing visitors.

The lingering decline of Craig-y-Nos makes it an overly wistful place to ponder Madam Patti's stellar career and her position as an honorary *Cymraes*. Even the promise of her ghost is thrown into the marketing. For a far better spectre, take the lane already described

up to Penwyllt. The road itself was created especially for Adelina, to connect her castle with her railway station. Penwyllt for Craig-y-nos, on the Brecon and Neath line, was her very own: a suite of brocaded rooms was built for her sole use and the railway companies even agreed to tack her private coach on to any train she fancied. The Brecon and Neath knew its market: there were private halts too at Abercamlais and Penpont, for the grand Uskside estates in Wales' Loire valley towards Brecon. Not so many exclusive stops in the other direction.

Amidst the rubble and the splendid dereliction of Penwyllt, a landscape made for cameo roles in *Dr Who* and *Torchwood*, the little station still stands quiet and lonely. Madam Patti's private rooms have long since collapsed down the social scale, being stripped of their finery, turned over to the hoi polloi and finally sold off when the line closed in the sixties. Now a dingy holiday let, the windows look out blankly onto deserted platforms, for a train that never comes. Vast blocks of stone have been placed across the old track to deter joyriders tanking it up and down the line. Far below, the castle tries perpetually to regain just a fraction of its former glitz, a battle almost certainly beyond possibility. Up here, there is no cheap re-gilding of the lily, just the dust of a dead celebrity, a perfect shrine for the twenty-first century.

EPYNT

"Egg beans, egg beans", sang my sister along with the forceful chorus of Gruff Rhys' 'Epynt'[23], which consists of him chanting the name repeatedly, like a battle cry. In her mind, it was a joyous song about the pleasures of a full cooked breakfast. Half an hour later, we'd shattered the illusion, given her a crash course in the forcible depopulation of the Welsh uplands for soldiers, forests and water, and managed to ensure that she'd never listen to it again without feeling properly sad, the Welsh way[24].

Of all Powys' evacuated landscapes, Epynt is the gloomiest. You can look at Vyrnwy or Elan Valley and appreciate that the "watercolour's appeal / To the mass", as R.S. Thomas had it in his poem 'Reservoirs', is undeniably strong. Even the massive conifer forests have their surprising corners and unexpectedly lovely moments (after a heavy snowfall, they're magical), while the wind farms, looking grand enough in a certain light, are, or perhaps were, tolerated through gritted teeth for their supposed efficacy and forward-thinking. There is little to soften the blow with a military range, and so it is with Epynt[25]. Water and wood and wind, even at their most industrial, can keep up the pretence. Barracks, bombs and red flags cannot.

The first time I came this way was twenty years ago, researching the inaugural *Rough Guide*. On the back road between Brecon and Builth, over the Epynt and past the blank stare of the old Drovers Arms, I stopped to make some notes. Within a minute, an army Land Rover had appeared, lights flashing. Two squaddies emerged, rifles slung casually over their shoulders, and proceeded to interrogate me as to who I was, what I was doing there, why I was writing things down in a notebook, and then order me on my way and not to stop until I'd cleared the range. The PR strategy has been buffed to a glossier sheen these days, but it's a gruesome illusion, masking a brutalised landscape.

The limited niceties of clearance for a forest or a reservoir count for nothing when it comes to the military. Within weeks of the Second World War breaking out in September 1939, an army captain was touring the farmsteads of Epynt and warning the tenants that there might be need to evict them for a military range. Nothing was heard again until registered letters arrived on every doormat in early March of 1940, giving everyone up to the end of

April to get out. Protest was muted and starkly split by language: the English-speaking Welsh press saw nothing untoward, but the gwasg Cymraeg cried foul. No-one heard. Two hundred and nineteen people turfed from their homes, whose names, shapes and field boundaries appear still on the OS map, pale and ghostly, all colour and life drained away. The roll-call of names echoes in the long-gone schoolroom:

> Ynys Hir, Waen-fawr, Cwm Car, Tir-bach, Tir-cyd, Crofte, Cwmffrengig, Berth-ddu, Pwll Du, Llwyn Coll, Ysgubor Newydd, Nant-y-Main, Neuadd Fach –
> *The National Interest!*
>
> Gelli-gaeth, Bwlch Gwyn, Gythane, Glan-y-rhyd, Gors Fach, Y Graig, Pen Gawse, Gwibedog –
> *The Greater Good!*
>
> Pant-y-Blodau, Blaentalar, Cefncyrnog, Ffos-y-hwyaid, Abercriban, Beili Richard, Cefn y Fedw, Rhyd-y-Maen, Tyn-y-cwm, Cefn Bryn, Maerdy, Carnau, Yscir Fawr, Ffynnon-las –
> *State of Emergency!*

Clawdd Brythonig, Bryn tŷ mawr, Llawr-y-dolau, Llawr Llamarch, Cae'r Llyn, Llwyn-on, Blaenegnant, Fedwen, Pantllefrith-fâch – *We'll be finished when the war is over, and then you may perhaps return!*

They never did.

It is possible to get a glimpse of the vanished community in the spirit of the surviving hamlets and farmsteads that bunch around the range's southern skirts. This is Breconshire at its least showy, a tangle of slumbering lanes (many now artificially truncated dead ends), darting sheepdogs, tractor tyre marks squished into the red mud, and even a few barns that still function as intended, rather than having been converted into pony paddocks or holiday lets. As with the now vanished community on Epynt, the population is scattered hereabouts, but there are numerous places to gather and commune, and plenty do. One of my fondest-remembered pub nights anywhere was in the Shoemakers Arms, Tafarn y Crydd, at Pentrebach, just before Christmas one year. There were fifteen or so of us, mainly gogs, staying down the lane, and by the time we were on our second pint, the singing had begun, and continued to crescendo for hours. Songs from south and north of the country were enthusiastically swapped in a cheery, beery haze that seemed the perfect echo of the long dead drovers' inns above on the heights of Epynt. The Shoemakers is one of the most successful community-run pubs in Wales, brought back from the dead a decade ago. Every village should have one.

Once a year, a pilgrimage of pacifists, nationalists and descendants of the former residents is allowed on to the Epynt to mourn its loss, gathering in the graveyard of the now vanished Capel y Babell[26]. It's the price that the army have to pay, and to be seen to pay, but it is far eclipsed by the price that they can extract for access for the rest of the year. For *Great Welsh Roads*, I wanted to cross the Epynt range on the road[27] that climbs over Mynydd Bwlch-y-Groes, from the village of Llywel on the A40 to Tirabad, né Llandulas, near Llangammarch Wells. The Defence Training Estates, a semi-privatised executive arm of the Ministry of Defence[28], wanted twelve hundred quid for us to film my lumbering old camper van – which had only cost me twice that much to buy – crossing their turf. ITV Wales budgets didn't stretch to that, and we managed to knock them down to five hundred, but it wasn't easy. And it was still way too bloody much.

You pay, you get the Epynt, a landscape not so much militarised,

as entirely privatised. Squeezed in around the army manoeuvres are all manner of money-making ventures, most notably the huge car rallies that the area hosts every year. Epynt is legendary amongst petrolheads; take a look at the numerous shaky videos on YouTube of souped-up Escorts roaring over the concrete military roads, careering into the grasses and copses, flipping over, crashing and even thwacking sheep at over a hundred miles an hour. All part of the MoD's much-promoted, multi award-winning conservation work on their estates; read all about it in their glossy magazine, *Sanctuary*. No, really.

As for Epynt, so it is for all of Powys' evacuated landscapes. The statist midset that established them has long gone, replaced by an opaque patchwork of stakeholders, bureaucrats and profiteers who are increasingly looking far, far beyond the original purpose for which the land was seized. Rallies, races, film sets, tourist trails, outward bound centres, rehab schemes, nature reserves and visitor experiences slot all too easily into a landscape stripped of its people and its context. So does the dirty stuff, as dirty as it gets. Powys forests have been fingered as potential nuclear waste dumps; Epynt housed one of the largest disposal sites of dead animals during 2001's Foot and Mouth outbreak. Eighteen thousand sheep and cattle were buried on top of Mynydd Bwlch-y-Groes, but as fears grew about contamination of the watercourse, Assembly Environment Minister Carwyn Jones[29] ordered them to be exhumed and burned instead. The toxic pyre of animals, coal and railway sleepers[30] burned for five months. That didn't make it into *Sanctuary* either.

Oh, but it's not all gloom. You may not be much fussed about a car rally, and the bad smell still lingers from F&M, but SENTA has been aiming a little higher of late, and even perhaps learning a little irony. Universally recognised as the highlight of the National Theatre of Wales' debut year was their 2010 production of Aeschylus' *The Persians*, played out against the backdrop of the military range's mock village[31]. This ancient play shied away from the prevailing glorification of war and instead spun in on the brutal agony of its reality. The juxtaposition of the uncompromising text and the savage bleakness of this raped mountain was extraordinary, and it haunted me for weeks. As the coach took the audience back to Sennybridge afterwards, a stunned silence hanging heavy over us all, a gang of roadside Gurkhas waiting to start night manoeuvres grinned and waved frantically at us. We waved back, like children on a train. Evacuees, perhaps.

THE WELLS

The Breconshire Wells towns – Llanwrtyd, Llangammarch and Builth – are the most non-identical of triplets (they show little family resemblance either to their Radnorshire cousin, Llandrindod). You'd barely even think that they were related. Llangammarch is the runt of the litter: a shy little soul, peeking out from beneath her fringe of exuberant ash and oak, but forever oppressed by the gloomy wall of the Epynt leering above. Nothing much stirs in Llangammarch, for everything seems to move at the stately pace of the Afon Irfon as it sidles past fishermen and ramblers. Skittish dragonflies and the occasional flash of a kingfisher provide the only real sense of momentum.

The 1910 Ward Lock *Guide* states firmly that "the Lake and Pump House Hotel practically is Llangammarch", and so it remains, for the tiniest of the Wells towns is home to the finest of their hotels. The Lake is almost a settlement in itself, an imperial hill station straight out of the Raj, dripping in moist green promise, with verandahs and lakes, chintz and chandeliers, terraces and tea rooms, picturesque rambles and roaring fires. Famously, Kaiser Bill himself came here for a barium treatment in 1912, as the storm clouds hunkered down over Europe. This was the resort's heyday, when trains on the Heart of Wales brought a steady stream of invalids in and whisked out tons of bottled water and even spa-branded cigarettes to all corners of the hypochondriac kingdom.

On the opposite bank of the river, disconnected from the hotel since a footbridge was demolished, lies the ruined barium chloride pump room, hissing quietly in a forgotten field. The fashion for spas, though, has gone full circle. Where businessmen and Edwardian gentlewomen once grimly ingested the waters on the principle that if it tastes bad, it's probably good for you, today's hen parties and honeymooning couples book in for a weekend of indulgent, candle-lit pampering in the shiny new Kingfisher Spa suite. It's popular: ranked "#1 of 1 Hotels in Llangammarch Wells" on Trip Advisor, which perhaps isn't saying much, but most folk seem to have had a wonderful time here, especially the girls who use lots of exclamation marks and smiley emoticons, for whom everything seemed to be fab!! or to die for!!! I've sampled it myself, and was filmed[32] having my face slathered in some green goo, which left a definite tingle, and only the slightest trace of shame.

In Llangammarch churchyard lies one of the village's more colourful priests, Theophilus Evans (1693-1767), usually credited as the man who first discovered the healing properties of the water in neighbouring Llanwrtyd Wells, one stop down the line or a short glide down the Ithon. The story has taken on the smooth patina of over-telling, but it's worth it. There had long been, behind the town's Dol-y-Coed Inn, a powerful spring known as the Ffynnon Drewllyd, the stinking well. People believed the sulphurous water to be poisonous, but Evans once spent some time observing frogs in the rudest of health bouncing around in it, enough to convince him that it might help his scurvy. He bathed in and drank the water for a number of weeks, and, wouldn't you know, his scurvy healed and he had never felt in ruder health. Llanwrtyd, most definitely a senior sibling to Llangammarch, developed its sulphur spring, and found saline and chalybeate wells too. The visitors started to arrive, and they still are.

When visiting Llanwrtyd, I always make a little pilgrimage to the abandoned sulphur spring at Dol-y-Coed. There's something compelling about the combination of clear riverside air and the

smell of a rusty fart emanating from the bowels of the earth[33]. Over the years, I've watched the old spa buildings, in their peeling red-and-white livery straight from the end of the pier, moulder away little by little as another window goes, another doorway boarded up and then broken into. On my last trip, I was amazed to see them done up, repainted bright as buttons and evidently lived in. Not such good news round the back, from where the familiar pong of sulphur was rising: the old domed pump house was half-demolished. A small planning notice cable tied to the fence announced that it was due to be completely bulldozed. I stood on a breezeblock and craned my neck to see inside, and in particular, to see the ornate Victorian wellhead, a circular mosaic platform studded with copper taps for dispensing the water. Having only seen it on old postcards, it was strangely thrilling to get a glimpse, but sad to see it in such terminal decrepitude. Miserable Old Fart. Put it out of its misery.

The opening up of the various springs, and the arrival of the railway, turned a small Ithon-side hamlet named Pont-Rhyd-y-Fferrau[34] into Llanwrtyd Wells[35]. Wells was a classy suffix for any town, a fine piece of subconscious advertising, and the railway company sprinkled it around their new timetable with gusto, adding it to the names of Builth, Llandrindod and Llangammarch as well.

Explorations were going on into the water at Garth, on the line between Builth and Llangammarch, and a pump room was hastily built, but came to nothing. On the other side of Llandrindod, Llandegley – just near Penybont station – was also a spa, but on the wane. Had they been added to the list, six out of seven stations in a row could have been appended with the word Wells, which would surely have been overkill. Or rather overcure.

Llanwrtyd was always my favourite of the Wells towns, for there really did seem to be something in the water. It's a proud, self-contained little place, even taking a tilt at the crown of Hay in developing oddball specialisms to boost both its profile and economy. For more than thirty years now, it has been home of wacky events, dreamed up by Gordon Green, the former landlord of the Neuadd Arms in the main square. Bog snorkelling, a race between men and horses[36], a drovers' pub crawl and mountain bike charioteering have all been pioneered here, as were pony trekking holidays thirty years before them. Compared with most places dependent on the whims and fashions of tourism, Llanwrtyd has always been pretty good at insuring itself by spotting the next trend and going wholeheartedly for it. Yet, and yet… something was amiss this time. There was a rotting, faintly malodorous air hanging over the place, and I don't think it was the sulphur.

If my favourite Wells town has fallen away, then what used to be my least favourite has rocketed up the rankings, and perhaps for the same reason. Builth, more than anywhere, makes me so happy to have jettisoned all responsibility for the *Rough Guide to Wales*, for I'm no longer interested – and no longer have to be interested – in the tourist board or guide book version of the country (the version that Llanwrtyd does so well). I co-wrote five editions of the book, between 1993 and 2006, but that was enough. It was a great grounding exercise in getting to know the basics of the country, but the gap between the intense, textured Wales that I was now part of and the sanitised, anglicised, deracinated portrait of the Rough Guide eventually grew just too wide. When I first came to Builth all those years ago on *Rough Guide* duty, I wasn't impressed. In fact, if I check that first edition from those distant pre-internet days, I find that I airily dismissed it as "an earthy agricultural town that has little to detain you". Worse, when writing about nearby Llandrindod Wells, I stated that "after faintly gloomy Builth, the town can seem like a salty breath of fresh air". Salty? Patchouli, with faint opiate top notes more like, but we'll leave that for now.

SOUTH

Truth is, Builth frightened me back then. All those pick-ups, burly farmers and Ifor Williams trailers full of noisy livestock made me feel as if I'd landed on another planet. I must have shuddered at it, climbed back into my hire car and sped away, desperately searching for a gastropub full of nice, familiar *Guardian* readers. For all of the same reasons that I once feared it, it's now one of my favourite towns in mid Wales. It is not a museum piece, nor a playground for smooth-talking down-shifters. Tourists are welcome, but the whole town doesn't have to bend in their direction. It has great, largely local, shops, steamy caffs, proper pubs and some ribald characters. Best of all (and none more so than during the week of the Royal Welsh[37]), it is still boisterous, beery and lairy enough to scare a snotty English guide book writer.

A470, ERWOOD: SAVE OUR TOILETS

The Welsh M1 (if the M1 careered like a drunkard and shrunk to a single carriageway every so often) is 186 miles long, from the prom at Llandudno to the appropriately teardrop-shaped gyratory just short of the Wales Millennium Centre in Cardiff. Great Orme Head to the Pierhead, as Jon Gower had it. And wouldn't you know, exactly half – 93 miles – is in Powys, from the grimy lay-by between the Llwyn-On reservoir and the Nant Ddu Lodge hotel on the cusp of the Beacons, to the edge of Mallwyd on the cusp of a rather loftier National Park, Snowdonia.

In between, there's plenty of time to admire the scenery, rolling greenly (and often wetly) past the window. In the spirit of those *I-Spy* books, where you got points and badges for spotting Edward VII post boxes or the Belgian flag, here's my *I-Spy* game for the Powys stretch of the A470. Tick them when you see them. How the journey will fly by!

Things to get stuck behind for fifteen miles or half-an-hour, whichever is longer:
* a Spar delivery lorry [2 pts].
* a tractor jettisoning straw and mud (I hope it's mud) on to the road and your bonnet [3 pts].
* a nervous tourist who hardly ever hits thirty but still brakes extravagantly for every slight kink in the road [3 pts].
* a 4x4 tugging an Ifor Williams horsebox, affording you a long, lingering look up a horse's arse [5 pts].
* a caravan with a collection of Celtic nation stickers on its swaying backside [5 pts; bonus 30 if the caravan actually uncouples from its car at any stage].
* either Ian Botham on a charity walk or the bloke who wheels a large cross along main roads in Wales most Easters [50 pts].

Places to be overtaken by the apoplectic driver who's been tailgating you for ten miles:
* the long straight stretch past the garage and café at Doldowlod, south of Rhayader [1 pt].
* coming off the roundabout at Llangurig [3 pts].
* by the many 'Pant Cudd – Hidden Dip' signs between Cwmllinau and Mallwyd [5 pts]
* on the blind bends in the middle of the Beacons [5 pts. Bonus 10 pts and considerable *schadenfreude* if there's a speed patrol lurking in the lay-bay just afterwards].
* on the Brecon by-pass [lose 5 pts].

Things that make you stop completely, one point per minute's wait:
* the traffic lights on the bridge at Newbridge-on-Wye, that myste-

SOUTH

riously change from green to red as you approach them, and return to green many minutes later, nothing having come through the other way. Will be a much-missed part of the journey when the new road opens.
* any set of temporary lights on the stretch above the Wye between Rhayader and Llangurig. Bonus 5 points if there are more than three in a row or any of them remain in place for longer than a year.
* the level crossing at the Caersws turn. There can't be another train, for god's sake, it's single-track for miles.
* Not knowing whose right of way it is in the middle of Rhayader.
* a lorry that has got wedged in the double right angle bends on the bridges at Llanbrynmair or Commins Coch [bonus 20 pts, 40 pts for the same but with a static caravan transporter; either way, you've got a long wait].

Did I just see...?
* a still open petrol station? (n.b. does not apply in Builth)[38] [5 pts]
* a ghostly remnant of the branch railway line to Llangurig, that only ever had one train run on it? [3 pts]
* Clap Coch, Clatter: the best address in Powys? [2 pts]
* a car in front scrape its hubcaps on the metalled pavement going

on to the bridge in Builth? [3 pts]
* dogging? (n.b. does not apply in the car park just before the Storey Arms; that's a given) [5 pts]

Can I NOT see (however hard I look in any direction)...?
* a red kite? [5 pts]
* a windfarm? [25 pts]
* a LibDem election poster in a hedge? [2 pts]

The highway of loss #1: a closed...
* school? [3 pts]
* railway station? [5 pts]
* asylum / workhouse? [5 pts]
* petrol station? [2 pts]
* shop? [1 pt]
* pub? [½ pt]

The highway of loss #2: banners demanding to Save Our...
* school? [3 pts]
* hospital? [2 pts]
* bus service? [5 pts]
* way of life? [10 pts]
* fieldsports? [10 pts]
* toilets? [25 pts][39]

CILMERI

Many places have their brief moment – sought or surprise – in the full-beam headlight of history. Rarely is it as prescriptive or unyielding as in Cilmeri, a place that you barely even register as you pass through on the main road west of Builth. Its split-second moment of destiny came over seven centuries ago, and still the quiet village reels from it. For it was here in 1282 that an escaping Prince Llywelyn, ein Llyw Olaf[40], was cornered by the army of English king Edward I, and butchered, beheaded. Since the once formal, and nominally equal, relationship between the two royal houses had disintegrated, Edward's encroachment on Llywelyn's lands and subjects had become more frequent and more deadly. After leading the English army a merry dance, Llywelyn retreated into the cantref of Builth, his totemic power base. Travelling from Aberedw (see the

account in Radnorshire), it's said that he was murdered as he drank from the well below Cilmeri, and by a soldier who failed initially to realise who he had killed. Llywelyn's decapitated head went to London, his body, perhaps, to Abbey Cwmhir, a few miles north; the grand cathedral that Llywelyn Fawr had planned to be the ecclesiastical capital of his principality.

Every year, on the weekend nearest the anniversary of Llywelyn's death, an assortment of patriots, flag-wavers and hangers-on gather for activities to commemorate Wales' darkest hour. This being in early December, it is often a bitterly cold or wet endurance test for the super-keen only. It's been something I've long idly contemplated seeing, and the dawn of a bright, sunny winter weekend finally has the desired effect in propelling me towards Cilmeri.

First event is a mass and service of sorts in the church of St Llyr at Llanynys, just across the Afon Ithon. It's not a village I've heard of before, and before leaving home, I do the obligatory Google and it quickly becomes apparent why, for there is no village of Llanynys. A clutch of scattered farms look towards the tiny, whitewashed church, sat in haughty isolation in the middle of fields, with the Afon Ithon burbling happily behind. Having consulted the map, and noticed it marked as a right of way, I'd intended to cross to the church by a ford across the river, but one look at the fast-flowing reality of it convinces me otherwise, and my partner drops me in Cilmeri village as people huff, puff and stamp their feet in the pub car park, packing flags and banners into the backs of cars, ready for the seven mile drive through the back lanes to reach Llanynys, about half a mile distant over the river.

Once at the church, the promised priest fails to show up. No explanation is proffered, but the organisers get on with it, conducting the service themselves. Very well, too. There is a bit of singing from a be-robed choir, a bit from us too, some sonorous readings and poetry that bounce magically off the stone walls, a superb oration about the place of Llywelyn in the hierarchies of medieval Europe and a stirring rendition of 'Hen Wlad Fy Nhadau' to round it all off. My pew is by a window on the river side of the church, and at one point, while the choir is giving it their all with a Sanctus, I look out to see sheep grazing contentedly on the riverbank in the winter sunshine. It is such a timeless image, and a pulse of warmth and love stabs my heart, for here, for now, for then, for Wales, for us. The sheep seem to be smiling back.

The farmer is not, however. We emerge from the thick little church to find him waving his stick and shouting about idiots leaving gates open and letting all his flock into this field. No wonder they looked so bloody happy.

By the time we get back to Cilmeri village, the forty well-wrapped souls in church has swollen to a far bouncier hundred or so in the Prince Llywelyn pub. It is heaving. Beer, food and warming tots of whisky are vanishing down gullets, boozy breath is vaporising in the sharp air. Conversations in Welsh and English jostle along together in a motley medley of accents, flags and banners pile up in the car park, the atmosphere is proud, swaggering. It's a strange sight to see so many people in a Breconshire village pub, on a pre-Christmas Saturday lunchtime, sporting the insignia of the Free Wales Army (FWA), but it's cosy more than bellicose: the stylised symbol of the white eagle reproduced as cloth patches on fleeces and badges on tweed caps, pulled firmly down over wisps of grey hair.

By the time we take off for the Llywelyn memorial down the road, the crowd has topped out at about 200, the biggest gathering since the seven hundredth anniversary in 1982. One lady from Neath, with her grandson in tow, tells me that this is her favourite weekend of the year, and I can see why. There is an enviable camaraderie flowing, something real and spontaneous, a world away from the sterile, stage-managed proceedings that characterise mainstream politics and all of its participants these days. Barely any of those here come from the (party) political classes, save for the local LibDem MP, Roger Williams, and his predecessor Lord (Richard) Livsey[41], who both give speeches at the memorial when we finally make it there. It's surreal, seeing the juxtaposition of a sitting Liberal MP, a ruddy faced scion of Breconshire farming stock, with the banners and flags of insurrection and revolution fluttering angrily around him. Even odder is when he starts to clap a fellow speaker coming to the end of his passionate rant, and can't quite stop in time when the orator punches his fist into the air and hollers "F!W!A!" into the microphone. A couple of cars roll past, people craning in the back seat to see what on earth is happening on a cold December day. Perhaps Williams is a relatively typical attendee: the FWA and other fringe Welsh separatist groups have always drawn their membership from amongst farmers and workers, and there's no change today. Most of the participants seem to have come up from the Valleys.

Speeches are plentiful, variable and mostly dignified. Again, our two languages rub along together, slip and tinkle over each other, with no-one making a big deal either way: it's refreshing and too much of a rarity in any Welsh gathering, let alone one so explicitly nationalist. There's a bit of music, some poetry. A couple of big, bearded lads near me toke urgently on spliffs. Boots are stamped into the mud and hands rubbed to keep warm next to braziers flaming. As the low winter sun, almost at its nadir of the calendar, starts to dip and blaze into its sunset colours away behind a line of skeletal trees, I try to take a photo of it illuminating a flag of Llywelyn[42] from behind. "D'ye like my flag?" asks a man in a beige anorak. I do, I tell him, especially against the backdrop of a sky on fire and shrieking crows in gaunt winter trees. He transpires to be from near where I grew up in Kidderminster, and it is his one man mission in life to educate the world about Owain Glyndŵr's 1405 stand-off with Henry IV on two adjoining Worcestershire hills[43]. "Welsh history doesn't just stop at the modern border," he enthuses, and he's right. But growing up there, it was an incident that was never mentioned in my schooling, and one of which I remained utterly ignorant until moving to Wales in my thirties.

With the PA system finally silenced, the speeches over and the sun about to disappear in a blaze of glory, I turn my attention to the Llywelyn memorial itself, its granite blade thrusting sharp and chilly out of its green mound. It's a monument I've always been quite moved by, so unexpectedly does it appear on the outskirts of a very ordinary village, alongside a very ordinary main road. That way went Llywelyn's head, transported to London and pride of place over the gates of the Tower. That way too went the unified nation. Look hard towards the horizon; there might be something stirring. Or is it just a trick of the dying winter light?

LLANAFAN FAWR

Sullen, swollen hills, a church, a pub, a sprinkling of farms: the sum total of Llanafan Fawr. Yet its name can be seen on hand-painted wayside signs for miles around, threaded in the hedges on every main road, and all of them encouraging the weary traveller to beat a path to "the oldest pub in Powys", the Red Lion. Is it? Perhaps. Probably not: proof is singularly impossible either way, and truth and beer are rarely the most reliable of bedfellows. In some references, its aged status has been upgraded to become "the oldest pub in Wales". On the ITV Wales programme *Great Pubs of Wales*[44], the commentary declares it to be "the oldest in Wales, if not the British Isles," – but chucks a 'reputedly' in beforehand, so that's OK.

Dig deep enough and it seems to be a dose of the old Beddgelerts, a little bit of invented history to lure in the tourist buck. The only given proof of the pub's antiquity is the oft-quoted fact that Gerallt Cymro stayed at an inn in Llanafan Fawr, so as to pay homage at the shrine of St Afan in the church, on his marathon route through Wales in 1188. I've scoured books old and new, dozens of them, and can find no references to this event in anything prior to about fifteen years ago. Indeed, there's precious little reference to Llanafan at all in the books I've consulted. In recent years, the combination of saint's tomb (even an almost entirely unknown saint), impressive church, older archaeological fragments and self-declared 'oldest pub in anything from Powys to the known cosmos' have combined to propel it into every guide and tract, but there is nothing at all in books as venerable and exhaustive as the *Shell Guide to Wales*, the *Blue Guide to Wales*, the *Companion Guide to Wales*, the Ward Lock series, the *AA Touring Guide to Wales*, Peter Sager's *Pallas Wales*, *The Matter of Wales* by Jan Morris, John Davies' *A History of Wales*, William Condry's *Exploring Wales* or Simon Jenkins' *Wales*. Neither does it feature in Gerallt's own painstaking account, *Itinerarium Kambriae* (The Journey through Wales), save for a mention in an aside in which he tells the story of a steward of Radnor Castle who came to Llanafan Fawr to pay homage, slept in the church with his dogs and woke up blind, a presumed slap from the Almighty for his bad manners. Gerallt talks of visiting another Llanafan (in Ceredigion), and staying in the nearby mother parish of Llanbadarn Fawr; perhaps some obfuscation of these, accidental or otherwise, resulted in the claim.

Of course, it doesn't much matter. 'Oldest pub in Powys' it says on the inn sign (a suitably geriatric red lion in specs and a cardy, leaning on a walking stick), and stating it often enough makes it as near true as anything in this shifting, hazy landscape, these "bitter parishes / Of the buzzard striking from lonely circles", as local boy T. Harri Jones[45] had it in his poem 'Llanafan Unrevisited'. He moved to the far ends of the earth, from old south Wales[46] to New South Wales in Australia, but could not escape: "and I am / Still a member of a narrow chapel, and a boy / From a hungry parish, a spoiled preacher, / Greedily taking the surplus of your sunshine, / And still afraid of hell because I've been there."

It's a bloody fine pub, all the same, and there's sufficient genuine antiquity, both in the building and its development over the years, to reward a visit. The food and beer aren't bad either, and there's a handy field next door where you can camp, or just kip under the stars, whichever comes first. Until the early 1990s, the Red Lion was one of the last remaining farmhouse cwrwau bach, parlour pubs, in Wales, a tiny slate-floored bar at the end of a fifteenth century cruck-beamed farm, regular horse sales out in the yard. When landlady Dolly Jones retired in 1994, her sons Rhys and Roy decided to employ a tenant manager instead of taking it on themselves, and they expanded it into a proper pub, with a full (if possibly semi-fictitious) history. In 2004, the brothers decided to sell up and concentrate on their farms, and the Red Lion was on the market for the first time in over three hundred years.

In their mam's day, the bar was usually known simply as Dolly's. There's very few of these parlour pubs left now, beer in foaming

jugs, barrels on a slate floor, a food menu restricted to pickled onions and the occasional aged ham bap. They were usually known more readily by the name of the landlord – or, more frequently, landlady – than by the name on the sign. In Powys, there was the incomparable Lucy's in Hay-on-Wye, officially the Three Tuns. "Inside her pub, cats still thread through chair legs in the half light, embers hiss in the grate and Lucy's bright eyes peer over the bar like a country mouse" wrote the King of Hay, Richard Booth, in his gloriously bonkers autobiography. Lucy had been born in the Three Tuns, and ran it well into her eighties, until a fire engulfed it in February 2005 and drew her long era to a sad end. First time I ever went there, early nineties, I had two and a half pints of the local scrumpy and then passed out in a field, hallucinating. I learned to pace myself better on subsequent visits, and savoured every moment of chatting with the birdlike Lucy and her loyal tribe of oddballs and regulars. It's revamped and gastro now, of course (8oz Grilled Fillet Steak with Peppercorn Sauce, Chips, Roasted Flat Mushroom and Cherry Vine Tomatoes – £22.95; sandwiches a mere seven quid) and Lucy doesn't so much as scrape a mention in their publicity, even though the old sign, with her name on it, is still over the front door. Heritage chic, sweetie; who was she again? I can't go in there, mind. It would break my heart.

My own local in Esgairgeiliog is still, seven years after she retired, known as Nora's[47]. It was another of this dying breed, where you were effectively having a beer in someone's front room. Scattered throughout were Nora's personal artefacts, from piles of paperwork on the bar to cardigans hanging by the dart board. It doubled up as our community centre, polling station and shop, with tins of Kit-e-Kat jostling the tonic waters and boxes of sweets that the village kids would run in for when they got off the school bus. She opened to sell the morning papers (spread over the pool table, alongside the jazz mags pre-ordered by various villagers), and stayed open through the day. Unlike many in far bigger towns, we were able to buy a pint of beer or milk, a newspaper or a can of beans, at any time between about six in the morning and midnight. We were spoiled rotten.

Dolly's, Lucy's, Nora's (as well as Flossie's over the border in Leintwardine, Herefordshire[48], and the legendary Bessie's[49] in Cwm Gwaun, near Fishguard): these homely bars dominated by a garrulous matriarch had an atmosphere unlike any other pubs. In Nora's, my local, if I popped down there on a late summer's afternoon, many of the village mums would be in with their kids, each group nattering, laughing or having a few games of pool. Sometimes I'd find myself the only bloke in there, the normal rules of pub-going nicely up-ended.

Country pubs are going down like drunkards in a storm, but there are still some corkers tucked down the lanes of Powys. The Goat, in Llanfihangel-yng-Ngwynfa, is the nearest thing to a parlour bar left in the county, a flush of red faces and gentle Maldwyn lilts around the fire. Tŷ Brith, in Carno, only lets you know that it is a pub with one tiny, old-fashioned Ansells sign facing the road. A few miles further west, the Dovey Valley Hotel at Glantwymyn/Cemmaes Road is almost as furtive in announcing itself: the place was open only when the light over the side door was on, and woe betide anyone who tried the door when it was dark. Mr Davies, the landlord[50], was no slave to opening hours, nor to conventional business planning. When the 1981 National Eisteddfod was held in the riverside fields below, making the Dovey Valley by far the nearest pub to the still-dry maes, Mr Davies closed for the week as he didn't fancy the bother.

Still in Montgomeryshire, there's the labyrinthine Cann Office at Llangadfan, whose sign states boldly that it dates from 1310. In a

Radio Cymru interview, bard Twm Morys said that this was his favourite part of the world in which to go and recharge his batteries, and that the pub was the best equivalent in Wales of a proper Breton tavern, the kind that spills over with music, poetry and laughter. On a good night, you might also find the same in the Star Inn, lost in the scars of the old Dylife lead mines and at 1300 feet up, Powys' highest pub (though not, as often claimed, the highest in Wales). Playing pool in there one dark autumn night, we were interrupted suddenly by the door crashing open and a dazed man in a blood-spattered suit staggering through. His car had hit a patch of black ice on the lonely road, and had somersaulted down an embankment. Landlady Sue was utterly unfazed: "see it all the time", she muttered as she dialled the ambulance.

Radnorshire's finest drinking outposts include the happy Happy Union, lost down the lanes at Abbey Cwmhir: its name supposedly inspired by the union between England and Wales, and its sign showing a portly Welshman, complete with leek in hat, a plate of cheese and a foaming tankard of ale, riding a goat. The goat's nationality isn't specified, but you can have a good guess. The Severn Arms at Penybont manages to maintain its coaching inn swagger in much reduced times, the Harp at Old Radnor oozes terrific grandeur from an unbeatable vantage point, while the most exciting game of darts in the county is at the Triangle in Cwmdeuddwr, where players have to open a trap door and stand in a pit, to avoid any risk of spearing the low seventeenth century beams. It's a good hopping off point too for the most entertaining pub crawl in Powys, around Cwmdeuddwr and Rhayader, staring bleary-eyed at each other across the Wye. This is a place that likes a good drink, loves it in truth, and doesn't seem give a toss about the surefire hangover in the morning. Although Rhayader does shade it as the best pub crawl in Powys, it's a close run thing; dishonourable mentions should also go to Llanidloes, Presteigne, Brecon, Welshpool and Hay.

Heading southward into Breconshire, back towards the Red Lion and the thin scatter of Llanafan Fawr, many of the most quirky old bars have either gone under or been forced into sharp suits and reborn as gastropubs. The leader of the pack, and the one that seemed to compel everyone else into a game of catch-up, is the Griffin at Felinfach, just to the north of Brecon. Darling of the dining pages in the weekend supplements, the Griffin is fantasy Wales for wealthy Londoners, a Bwrdd Croeso advert come hideously to life. Just down the road is the real deal, at less than half the cost. The Star Inn, by the canal in the middle of Talybont-on-Usk, has 'proper pub' stamped into every fibre of its cheery soul. Tafarn y Crydd, the Shoemakers Arms, in Pentrebach (see the Epynt account above) is the best community pub in Powys, and the other Griffin, by the junction in Llyswen, avoids all gimmickry in sticking to its longstanding formula of superb food in cosy, traditional surroundings. With one exception (I'll leave you to work it out), I've loved every trip to all of these pubs, and many more – more than I will ever remember – of the couple of hundred others, and falling, across Powys. Pubs are "universal places, like churches, hallowed meeting places of all mankind" (Iris Murdoch); in rural mid Wales they are the glue that binds us together.

Notes

1. Traditionally believed to have been founded in the fifth century AD, the small kingdom of Brycheiniog has long acted as a buffer zone between the grander Welsh kingdoms of Deheubarth and Morgannwg, and the lands of the English to the east. It was founded by, and named after, Brychan, an Irish chieftain who married into the local uchelwyr. He is said to have fathered an astounding number of children (anything up to 63, says the *Oxford Dictionary of Saints*) from this and two further marriages, with many of his progeny gaining the status of saints in the Celtic church.
2. The Shire Hall was built in the early days of Queen Victoria's reign, in the Greek Revival style. Originally serving as a court house and seat of the Assizes, it became the county HQ on the establishment of the county councils in 1889. When Brecknockshire was abolished in 1974, the Brecknock Museum, established in 1928 in a nearby former chapel, moved in, keeping the original Victorian court room as a central exhibit. The name of Brecknock has been used coterminously with Brecon, particularly as the name of the former county (Daniel Defoe wrote that it would be better named 'Breakneckshire'). Brecknock is an anglicisation of the Welsh name Brycheiniog, the ancient kingdom of Brychan, though the town of Brecon is known in Welsh as Aberhonddu.
3. The Gurkha Company (Mandalay) is its official title. The Gurkhas have been in Brecon since 1973, and in 1985 were made Honorary Citizens of the town.
4. The village of Battle, a couple of miles to the north-west of Brecon, commemorates the link.
5. Christ College Brecon was founded in 1541. Only Ruthin School in Denbighshire is older, as its tendentious slogan ("focusing on the individual since 1284") makes clear.
6. Roland Mathias (1915-2007) returned to Brecon after decades of teaching. With Raymond Garlick, he founded the literary periodical *Dock Leaves*, which grew into the *Anglo-Welsh Review* (now the *New Welsh Review*). His own poetry dug deep into the Breconshire soil, especially in collections such as *The Flooded Valley* (1960), inspired by his native Glyn Collwn, flooded in his youth to create the Talybont reservoir.
7. The pub was known as the Shoulder of Mutton when Sarah Siddons was born there.
8. Glyn Williams' recollections of his National Service in Brecon can be found at

www.bbc.co.uk/wales/mid/sites/history/pages/brecon_virgin. It's no saccharine-coated nostalgia: he details the bullying, the bragging, the racism and sexism of the officers, and the sheer nerves of the raw recruits in their temporary new home. The brutal sexualisation of the recruits is a major theme, and the extract quoted refers back to one poor kid, named Virgin, mercilessly ribbed by an officer on discovering his name. His inevitable punchline was "You must be the only virgin in Brecon, lad."

9. The population of the National Park was 32,654 at the 2001 census, of whom eight thousand are in Brecon itself.
10. In order of their proportion of the park: Powys, Carmarthenshire, Monmouthshire, Rhondda Cynon Taf, Merthyr Tydful, Blaenau Gwent, Torfaen, Caerphilly and Neath-Port Talbot.
11. The Vision Farm, just down the lane, is a reference to the latter of the Virgin Mary's appearances, in 1880. Bruce Chatwin used the name in *On the Black Hill,* but changed its location.
12. My favourites are Llaneleu, above Talgarth; Llangasty-Talyllyn on the reedy shore of Llangorse Lake; Llanfilo and Llandefalle, either side of the A470 between Llyswen and Brecon.
13. In the superb gallery upstairs at the Crickhowell Resource & Information Centre (Cric). Highlight for me are the two massive patchworks depicting both sides of the High Street. At first, they look slightly twee, but then you start to notice intriguing little details and touches of sparkling wit, and find yourself becoming hopelessly charmed by the whole thing. Much like Crickhowell as a whole, really.
14. Otherwise known as Crug Hywel, which gives the town its name, and Pen-y-Fâl.
15. *The Lady of Glanusk,* a four-part BBC Wales series shown in 2007.
16. Glanusk House had been left in a pitiful state after being requisitioned by the Army in World War Two. A fire hadn't helped things either.
17. The atmospheric, and scenic A4067 from Sennybridge to Abercraf and Ystradgynlais, which follows the upper reaches of the Afon Tawe.
18. The centrepiece of the Winter Garden being the huge glasshouse, which Madam Patti donated to the town of Swansea after her death. It was reconstructed in the town's Victoria Park, by the Guildhall, and rechristened the Patti Pavilion.
19. Queen Victoria's dyspeptic son, known as Bertie, and who eventually became the short-lived Edward VII on his mother's death in 1901, was a guest at Craig-y-Nos.
20. Patti was born in Madrid, her father a Sicilian tenor, her mother an Italian soprano. She largely grew up in New York.
21. Quite literally: in St Petersburg, she was carried from the concert hall to her hotel suite in a seat made of flowers, while a brass band accompanied the procession. In Boston, Massachusetts, she was paid five thousand gold dollars for one performance of *La Traviata.*
22. Dan-yr-ogof has been an unqualified Welsh tourism success over the last thirty years; in 2005, it topped a *Radio Times* poll to find Britain's 'finest natural wonder'. It is easy, too easy perhaps, to sneer at the plastic dinosaurs scattered through the park, the more mawkish son-et-lumière tableaux in some of the caves or the endless coach parties going exactly where they are told, but the sheer heft of the underground complex itself swats away any cynicism and leaves you gasping. And even that is only a small fragment of the whole. Since being first discovered by local brothers Jeff and Tommy Morgan in 1912, ongoing exploration has revealed that the Dan-yr-ogof complex is enormous: eleven miles discovered so far, but with many more to come.
23. From his first solo album, *Yr Atal Genhedlaeth* (2005).
24. Or as Gruff himself puts it in the song, "Wyt ti isho dyfodol / Neu ddim ond gorffenol?" (Do you want a future / Or only a past?). The essence of Epynt, and its many dead siblings, in eight words.
25. The Epynt range is more properly known as the Sennybridge Training Area, or SENTA. It

is the third largest military range in the UK, covering approximately 37,000 acres (about 150 square kilometres), just over eight percent of the total area of Breconshire.
26. A plaque in the ruins quotes the Book of Isaiah chapter 2, verse 4: "...and they shall beat their swords into plowshares, and their spears into pruning hooks: nation shall not lift up sword against nation, neither shall they learn war any more". You can read it as the shells detonate in the distance.
27. The road is public, and is marked as such on OS maps, though it is controlled by the military and frequently closed. Flags, barriers and lights are used to that end. At its southern end, by Llywel, the road is perhaps the oddest dual carriageway in Britain; two parallel, single-file country lanes, divided by an earth bank and occasional hedges.
28. As of April 2011, they are now part of the Defence Infrastructure Organisation (DIO), whose mission statement is "to deliver estate solutions to defence needs". As well as overseeing ranges like Epynt, the DIO are the ultimate managers of the defence forces' housing stock, much of which was sold off to property developers Annington Homes for £1.6 billion in 1996. In 2007, DIO pledged £5 billion worth of improvements, of which £2 billion went straight back to Annington Homes as rent. Part of the portfolio of venture capitalists Terra Firma, Annington has been the subject of repeated controversy. One in four homeless people are ex-servicemen.
29. First Minister of Wales since December 2009.
30. It was estimated that about 500 tons of coal would be needed to incinerate the animals. In the end, over 4,000 tons were used. Railway sleepers often contain arsenic. The pyre was more than 400 metres long.
31. The village is known as FIBUA, which stands for Fighting in Built-Up Areas, and it was built as a practice ground for soldiers engaged in urban street fighting (within some army circles, such places are nicknamed Fish & Chips: Fighting In Someone's House, and Causing Havoc In Peoples' Streets). Conceived in the early 1980s, the Breconshire FIBUA was given the appearance of an East German settlement, the presumed most likely forthcoming battleground of the time. It opened in 1989, just as the Berlin Wall fell and the Cold War thawed.
32. For an episode of *Great Welsh Roads*. The journey had started in a sweaty, windowless boxing club in Merthyr and had progressed across the army ranges of the Epynt. After all that machismo, I needed a suitably fluffy counterpoint to end the programme; a facial and dainty cream tea at the Lake did the job beautifully.
33. Alternatively spelled Dolecoed and Dolcoed.
34. The bridge over the ankle-deep ford.
35. The original settlement of Llanwrtyd, from which it took its name, is a little over a mile upstream along the Ithon. It's not much more than a church.
36. In 31 years, a man has beaten the horse only twice, in 2004 and 2007.
37. See the account for Llanelwedd, in Radnorshire (the Wye bridge at Builth is the county border).
38. On this 93 miles stretch of Wales' main spine road, there are only four petrol stations, and two of those are opposite each other in Builth.
39. There's only one example of this that I know of, at Erwood. SAVE OUR TOILETS daubed on an old bedsheet and strung across the roof of the malodorous little bogs in the village lay-by. The banner was up there for years, its plea getting fainter with every downpour. At the time of writing, the banner's gone but the toilets are still open. Chances are it'll be the other way round by the time you read this.
40. 'Our last leader' or Prince.
41. Brecon and Radnorshire is a strange constituency. Although usually thought of as a fairly safe Liberal bastion, it has elected MPs of all three main UK parties over the past forty years. Despite being the most rural constituency south of the Scottish highlands, Labour

held it until 1979 and came a very close second in the 1985 by-election. Then, the Conservatives were relegated to third place, having won it in 1979 and 1983. They won it back in 1992, but for one term only. The Liberals first won it at the by-election, when Richard Livsey was elected. He was re-elected in 1997, before passing the seat on to Roger Williams in 2001. It has been a stronger seat for the LibDems at Assembly elections, and has been represented from the outset by Kirsty Williams, now the LibDem leader in the Assembly. She even survived the LibDem rout of 2011, remaining their only constituency-elected member in the new Senedd (the party losing their other two seats in Montgomeryshire and Cardiff Central that night).

42. Llywelyn's flag, or Royal Standard as it is sometimes known, is divided into quarters: two red and two yellow, with rampant lions of the opposite colour on each quarter.
43. This non-battle came at the height of Glyndŵr's uprising. Henry IV led his troops to the top of Abberley Hill, Glyndŵr camped his out on the top of neighbouring Woodbury Hill. And there they stayed, staring eyeball-to-eyeball, for eight long days, before Glyndŵr slunk away. There had been the odd fracas, but no substantial battle ever took place.
44. This was a strange series. Comedian John Sparkes, so brilliant as Barry Welsh and his Fishguard cohorts, was the affable, if faintly bemused, host. He spent a full half-hour on a different pub in every episode, which rather proved that there really are only so many shots of beer pumps, and stories of pub ghosts and drunken farmers, to go round. The episode about the Red Lion was broadcast in August 2008.
45. T(homas) H(enry) Jones (1921-65) only became the more poetically Welsh T. Harri Jones posthumously, following his death by drowning in his adopted home city of Newcastle, NSW, Australia.
46. Breconshire: south or mid Wales? It depends on who you talk to. When I've asked people in the Valleys or Cardiff if they've ever been to north Wales, the answer has often been some variation on the theme of "yeah. Been to Brecon." From my position further up the map, the county looks fair southerly to me, even if this upper lump of Breconshire, the old kingdom of Buallt (Builth) rather than that of Brycheiniog, is probably best classed as mid Wales. Plenty will disagree.
47. Officially, it's the Tafarn Dwynant. It's been sold twice since Nora retired: the first time fairly disastrously, the second two years later with great results. When it was for sale the second time, I sent a round robin email to friends, asking them to forward it on. I wanted to alert them not just to the business opportunity of a comparatively cheap village pub in such a great spot, but also to the chance of doing something concrete and positive for a marginal Welsh community. No-one was much interested in buying the place, but quite a few people who work in TV got in touch asking if I thought the imminent loss of our village pub would make a good insert, or perhaps even a whole programme or series of its own? Making telly while Rome burns, I think it's called.
48. Officially the Sun Inn, one of the finest old parlour pubs in Britain. Flossie (Florence) Lane followed in her father's footsteps as landlord, and ran it for 74 years, until her death, aged 94, in 2009.
49. Officially the Dyffryn Arms. Still going strong, with octogenarian Bessie Davies at the helm.
50. Who sadly died in May 2011.

WEST

Ffin Cymru Cymraeg

YSTRADGYNLAIS

Yes, it is in Powys. Assuredly so: everyone I ask about the matter is fierce in their loyalty to the county, and its predecessor, Breconshire. "We get noticed in Powys; we'd be invisible if we weren't", one lady tells me in a charity shop full of people drinking coffee and laughing. "I remember once when there was a fire on Mynydd y Drum[1]," she continues, "I rang the fire brigade, and their first question was 'which side?' 'What do you mean, which side?' I asked. 'Ours or theirs?' they said". She beamed proudly.

This bottom-left corner of Powys, an ostensibly homogenous area along the top edge of the south Wales coalfield, has long been divided by the oddest county borders in Wales. Head up the A4068 the six or so miles to Brynaman, and you'll be skitting uncertainly between three counties and then back again. In the car park of the George IV pub at Cwm Twrch Uchaf, the three actually meet. The confusion doesn't stop there; the institutional dithering of the last few decades has only darkened the already muddy waters. Forty years ago, it was Glamorgan, Breconshire and Carmarthenshire that collided. Twenty years ago, we had West Glamorgan, Powys and Dyfed. Now it's Neath-Port Talbot, Powys and Carmarthenshire. You wouldn't risk much on betting that it will stay that way for very long.

Until the first big county reorganisation of 1974, Breconshire contained a number of communities that would more traditionally be thought of as part of the Valleys, that catch-all name for the south Walian towns – valley floor and windswept hillside alike – that grew up in the nineteenth century around the pits that produced the fuel of an empire. Cefn-Coed-y-Cymer, Pontsticill and Faenor (Vaynor) went into Mid Glamorgan (and then the County Borough of Merthyr Tydfil), Brynmawr, the largest, was transferred into Gwent, but Ystradgynlais, at the top of the Swansea valley, stayed put. The town gives Powys its only real sooty fringe, as well as a regular supply of the Lesser Spotted Labour Councillor. More surprisingly perhaps, it is also home to the highest proportion of Welsh speakers in the county, at around sixty percent, three times the Powys average. We are on another border, after all: *Pobol y Cwm* territory.

Like many other former industrial towns of the region, Ystradgynlais likes to wear its heart, and its leftist internationalist politics, on its sleeve. There are proud tales of miners marching off to the Spanish Civil War, fondly recalled moments with Paul Robeson, well-worn anecdotes from the General Strike of 1926 and Scargill's battle with Thatcher. Almost everywhere in the Valleys will say the same, but Ystradgynlais has two entirely unique arrows of solidarity in its quiver. In 1942, just months after the Nazi SS has razed the Czech mining community of Lidice to the ground, and summarily executed 173 of its men and boys against a chapel wall, the Crown Film Unit recreated the horrific episode in their movie, *The Silent Valley*. Filmed in neighbouring Cwmgiedd, all the parts were played and improvised by locals, although it is remembered that the appearance of so many people in Nazi uniforms caused untold kerfuffle in the area. The film, still watched as a classic piece of wartime reportage-cum-propaganda, had massive impact.

Even more proudly, Ystradgynlais became the home for eleven years of one of Britain's most celebrated escapees from the Nazi regime, the Polish Jewish artist Josef Herman (1911-2000). Invited to visit the town by writer-miner Dai Williams, he got off the bus in the summer of 1944 and was instantly hooked. "I vividly recall the heat of that afternoon and how deeply I was struck by the quiet of the village around me," he later recalled. "There was hardly a soul to be seen. In the distance, low hills like sleeping dogs and above the hills a copper-coloured sky – how often I later returned to the colour and mood of the sky!". The silence was suddenly broken by the clatter of a group of miners leaving their shift, and his muse was born. "Their heads appeared against the full body of the sun… the image of the miners on the bridge against that glowing sky mystified me for years with its mixture of sadness and grandeur, and it became the source of my work for years to come."

During Herman's sojourn on the banks of the Tawe, he became a cult figure in the art world. Metropolitan art journals twittered excitedly about this exotic creature so immersed in the painting of people they understood even less. His meaty portraits of miners both thrilled and challenged, and he readily acknowledged that it took him years to appreciate too the backdrop against which they worked. Comparing it to the soot-black mining communities that he knew in Silesia, he said "but Ystradgynlais is colourful and green. Only the men are black".

Here where the deep seams of the Valleys coalfield rise to the surface before they dissolve into the limestone belt at the bottom of the Beacons and the Fforest Fawr, the airiness and brightness of the

villages and towns along the cusp still surprise. Open cast operations continue to pick out anthracite, the coal that burns brightest and hottest, blazing into the copper-coloured sky. It is a heritage to savour, though breakfast in an Ystradgynlais café soon exploded the myth that such philanthropic internationalism was a permanent edifice. Six men, accents creamily local, while away a workless weekday morning over mugs of tea. Their conversation, largely about 'smacking Pakis', is delivered at such unapologetic full volume that eventually the lady manager is forced to ask them to tone it down. They grumble a little, and then head outside instead to continue. I catch another punter's eye, but there is only cold, hard steel to be seen, glittering with trepidation.

The iron works went first, then the pits, and then the doomed attempts to plug the gap with subsidised schemes like the Tic Toc, a watch and clock factory set up in the run-down mansion of Ynyscedwyn. Unemployment amongst men is well over twice the Powys average, and three times more than amongst local women. It was horribly obvious in my overheard breakfast conversation that it was the men of around forty, men of my age, men who had never known secure or fulfilling employment, who were the angriest. The older fellas tried to smooth them down, challenge them even when they thought they were taking it too far, but the younger men were not having it. In a BBC interview, Josef Herman talked of the men of the town in the most reverential of terms: "I am struck not only by their heroic appearance, but by the similarity of their troubles and joys, and their concerns in each other's lives. You hear them say quite often, 'Men must give each other a hand'." I hoped that a twenty-first century Herman, getting off the bus in Ystradgynlais, would still be moved by the brightness of the coppery sky and the shining ambition of the men he met, but the awful fear wouldn't shift that the coppery taste of his own blood in the back of his throat might get there first.

THE DEVIL'S STAIRCASE

Nudity might not seem like the most obvious association with the damp, midgey air of the Abergwesyn Pass, but it's worked out that way for me. Not every time, of course, but enough to make me occasionally go a little out of my way, just for the pleasure of a beautiful drive and the accompanying frisson of some tingling memories.

This old drovers' route is a staggering drive, straight out of the golden age of motoring, scarves in the wind and a picnic hamper in the boot. The thin ribbon of tarmac rises and falls along the Irfon valley, crossing the river five times before climbing a vertiginous 1:4 series of hairpin bends known as the Devils' Staircase and up on to the conifer-clad moor above. A couple of years ago, a pensioners' excursion coach came this way, despite the signs warning that it's unsuitable for caravans, which you'd think might also apply to a 54-seater bus. The vehicle got wedged fast on one of the bends, its front end threatening to teeter over the edge. *The Italian Job* in wet Welsh firs. The Pass continued as a drovers' route well into the modern age. Beasts from Cardiganshire were herded along its contours on the route from Tregaron, heading to the railway at Llanwrtyd and onward by train to the markets of southern England. It was only fully tarmaced in the 1960s, and has become a popular rallying route since.

But back to the nudity. There was that big free rave at the bottom of the Devil's Staircase, must have been about 1998, perhaps '99. Most of the mates I travelled with from Birmingham had never been up the Abergwesyn Pass, so I was on proud host duty and relishing their wonder as we ground our way from Llanwrtyd, alongside the swirling Irfon, through the hanging oak woods and then out into the wide bowl of the valley. Deep in the growing gloom, lazers were strafing the sky, while an illuminated projection of a red dragon filled a hillside. Dirty beats thumped out, ricocheting off the overhanging rocks. Crowds of silhouettes were already bouncing in time. My heart soared. It promised to be a good one.

A couple of beers and a cup of mushroom tea later, I was dancing under the stars, drinking in the projections that flashed up on to the hills above. A few familiar faces from the local party circuit loomed out of the crowd, winked and grinned manically, their teeth and eyes glowing skeletal under the UV lanterns. Drum'n'bass beats collided with techno, while reggae and ska throbbed somewhere in the corner. Hours thundered by, the DJs spinning us up into successive frenzies of hot delirium and shirtless ecstasy. Spliffs and water were passed, sound and light fused into one pure hammerbeam of pleasure.

No matter what I have, or haven't, taken, a cup of tea always goes nicely with it. If I can get a *paned* at a party or club, it'll prolong me for hours, its sugary uplift the best boost I know. Sipping happily by the counter of one of the tea stalls run by young crusties, I fell into chatting with a group of locals. "Having a good time mate?", they asked, as you always did. I leered happily back that yes, I was. And then it just got better. Chatting away with them, the handsomest of them all lingered by my side. He was a big lad, strapping you'd call him. Huge hands, a rug of hair poking out of the top of his shirt. Glittering eyes. Fit as. "Hope you don't mind me asking, mate", he started, "but…but, are you, y'know…are you a Friend of Dorothy?"

Bursting into laughter probably wasn't the reaction he was expecting, for it was the sweetest, quaintest way I'd ever been asked That Question, and it deserved a courtly eyelash flutter rather than a ribald belly laugh. I did get asked it a lot though, if not usually with quite such unexpected delicacy. When I first moved to mid Wales, I was in my local village pub one night, and kept meeting the same farm lad at the bar every time I went to buy a fresh pint. It was about the third meeting when he asked, "no offence me asking, like, but are you… you know… are you, er, that way inclined? Not that it's a problem or nothing." I congratulated him on his detective skills, confirmed that they were right, and he shuffled off, perhaps to collect his winnings from a bet on the matter, I decided. That had happened before too. When I next went up to get a pint, he was

there again. As the barman filled my glass, he leaned into me and sidemouthed quietly, "er, do you want to come out to the car park and have a look at my tattoos?" To my eternal regret, I didn't.

The offer was even more explicit that night in the Abergwesyn Pass, and before long, we were pounding up the Devil's Staircase – and that's not a euphemism – looking for a suitable spot in the conifer forest above. My hairy paramour with a perfect Maldwyn accent turned out to be a lumberjack, and it felt as if I'd landed in a seventies porn flick. Albeit for a highly specialist market that would get its kicks by watching us scampering around, butt naked and screaming, after inadvertently disturbing an ants' nest half-way through.

Sunrise came soon after, and the day dawned hard and hot. No-one felt like driving, so we lounged by the river, drinking tea, listening to music and talking bollocks. Someone offered to show us the Camddwr Bleiddiad[2], just down the valley. The best river swim in Wales, he said. For a few hundred yards, the Afon Irfon funnels into a narrow stone chasm, in which a number of small waterfalls tumble. At the bottom, the fissured wall of rock gives way to a peaty brown pool. This is where you get in, and you can then slide through the rock gateway and swim up the channel, under mossy rock faces, ferns and flowers. We stripped off and fell in, squealing deliriously and stirring the residue of the previous night's excess into unexpected reprise. The odd car trundled past, too far away to see whether the staring faces were thrilled, or appalled, by the sight of a few naked hippies shrieking in the river far below. Some went very slowly indeed. I've swum it a few times since, as sober as a Tuesday morning, and it was just as magical.

If this sounds an overly licentious way to think of Wales' most impressive old drovers' pass, my only answer is that, if it's good enough for Gwynfor, it's good enough for me. In his autobiography, *For the Sake of Wales*, the late Plaid Cymru stalwart Gwynfor Evans[3] talks of his fondness for naked swimming, especially in this lonely valley. "I liked to feel the wind and the sun's warmth on my body," he wrote. "After selling tomatoes at Llanwrtyd, I would sometimes go through Abergwesyn to Cwm Irfon, before cars could go that way or any bridge was built over the river, and wander the mountain tops with nothing on, or lie in the river with my body streaming with water from the Irfon falls." Vote for skinny-dipping! Makes a welcome change from Change.

PUMLUMON

Pick out any map of Wales from before the nineteenth century. In that pre-theodolite, pre-contour world, altitude was necessarily vague and usually depicted by the use of crude molehills scattered across the land. On most early maps, Snowdon is depicted correctly as the highest peak, though its nearest rival on every sheet is Pumlumon[4], that great upland sponge that squats like a fat toad at the centre of Wales. On the all-Wales map in John Speed's definitive Tudor atlas, *Theatrum Imperii Magnæ Britanniæ*[5], Pumlumon shades Snowdon and seems to be the highest of all.

Yet Pumlumon is only the forty-ninth highest peak in Wales. At the mnemonical height of 2468 feet, it is almost 1100 shorter than Yr Wyddfa, Snowdon. Its cartographic enhancement seems odd,

but what is being mapped was not its size, but its reputation. Pumlumon is notoriously disorienting, prone to sudden mists and blanket cloud. Barely anywhere is the land stable or dry enough to cross it with a decent track. And as its name implies, it is a massif of five peaks, and none very distinguishable.

Its exaggeration on English maps is a stark, simple warning to invaders not to come this way, for no good will come of it. In June 1401, despite being heavily outnumbered by English and Flemish troops, the army of Owain Glyndŵr won their first great battle here, thanks almost entirely to their superior knowledge of the terrain. It was this victory that transformed a collection of localised grudges into a powerful national uprising. It transformed too the dark renown of the mountain.

Perhaps it is Pumlumon's hostility to invaders that put me off climbing it for so long, although in truth, it was more to do with the fact that whenever I fancied a mountain climb, there were always others that appealed more. When I was moving to mid Wales, in the first few months of 2000, I undertook a pilgrimage to the source of the Severn, the river I'd grown up next to, hoping that it would point me in the right direction. Even amidst the tight competition found elsewhere on the mountain, the official source of Britain's longest river sits on one of Pumlumon's bleakest moors. Flagstones now guide you to the spot across the oleaginous sump, but back then, the path was precarious and disheartening, any step likely to plunge you knee-deep into the black gloop. Finally reaching the post that declared a particular set of greasy puddles to be where the Severn begins, I noticed the cairns of one of Pumlumon's peaks[6] on a near horizon, but getting there looked nigh on impossible. It'll wait, I thought.

It did: almost ten and a half years later I was finally looking the other way, down from Pumlumon Arwystli on to the plateau that is said to give birth to the Severn[7]. In the intervening decade, I'd skirted around all sides of the mountain, had viewed it in all lights and from all angles. Not that there is a great deal to see: only from Nant-y-Moch reservoir, on the seaward side, is there a view that makes Pumlumon look even remotely precipitous, like a proper mountain. It was from that side that I decided to climb the monster, although the path that I started following soon vanished, and I had to trek wearily through unmarked heather and wet sphagnum, trying not to twist an ankle in the plod up to the summit.

Just as there is no real view of Pumlumon, often there's not much of a one from it either. A true mountain soars in gaunt isolation; Pumlumon squats on its wet haunches, its surrounding barren landscape billowing out like a succession of grubby clouds. It's gruff and impressive, without ever being especially moving. It was hard to disagree with George Borrow in *Wild Wales*, who stood on the same summit and noted that "no signs of life or cultivation were to be discovered, and the eye might search in vain for a grove or even a single tree. The scene would have been cheerless in the extreme had not a bright sun lighted up the landscape".

Not much sun today, but at least the grey miasma oozing out of the slopes had successfully blotted out most of the two hundred plus wind turbines that now encircle Pumlumon. On a clear day, you can see over ten per cent of Britain's turbines from here; the updated version of those fabled viewpoints over six or eight counties. There will be more. In 1973, the Cambrian Mountains, whose high point this is, made history as the first hitherto dead cert candidate for National Park status to fall at the final hurdle. Since then, it's failed even to make the grade as a lesser AONB (Area of Outstanding National Beauty), a status accorded to the coast of Ynys Môn and the Clwyd Hills. As a result, this boggy backbone of Wales has seen breakneck development of wind farms, and has been confirmed, under the Assembly government's TAN 8 guidelines, as one of the main parts of Wales where future windpower developments will be concentrated. Seven areas have been identified; three of them surround Pumlumon, a series of ever-whirling *chevaux-de-frise*[8].

Whether all such developments finally come to fruition must be open to some doubt. 2011 has been an excitable year for mid Wales windfarms, with the proposals to build substations and massive power lines in the east of Montgomeryshire provoking the largest protest ever seen at the Senedd in Cardiff Bay. Few of us know many hard facts about the turbines, but we're all prepared nonetheless to chuck in our two penn'orth about their supposed inefficiency, astronomical cost, associated health problems or the stacked planning procedure that has seen a few do very well out of them, thank you. We're on firmer ground with the aesthetics: parts of the Powys landscape will be royally buggered by yet more, and yet larger, windfarm developments, and the sight of yet more energy (or minerals, water, timber) trickling incessantly east is provoking the most un-neighbourly of sentiment. The politicians in the Bay, startled by the sight of so many Maldwynites pounding on their glass doors, have promised reviews, action, consultation. *Gawn ni weld.*

The dog is rolling in something nasty, and comes back smelling awful. I hold my breath, bundle him down to a peat stream, and force him in. He comes out smelling better, but considerably browner and dirtier. The water is silky smooth though, and on this sultry, heavy August day I long to find a place to dip myself. From the summits, I could see sheets of water almost everywhere, but these invariably transpire to be shallow mawn pools full of oily water and spiky grasses. Far down below, the dark waters of Llyn Llygad Rheidol[9] sulk at the bottom of a bowl, and I gallop down the tussocky slopes, my ankles and knees juddering in complaint, to reach its side. It's no place for a relaxing dip, though. For starters, it's a reservoir now, not that that's always stopped me. More than that, it's so powerfully gloomy, the chilly black water rippled by the wind zipping across it. I seem to have left behind a summer's day and plunged back into the middle of February.

Towering behind the lake is an unexpectedly severe cliff, above which I can see the cairns of the summit of Pumlumon Fawr, where I'd been standing a few hours earlier. This mountain is full of surprises. From most angles, it appears to be nothing more than a

serious of sodden green swells, with no sharp edges. And then suddenly, there's a valley ripping through the bloated flesh, leaving jagged rock cliffs hundreds of feet high and as sheer as anything you'd find in Snowdonia. The path on the map is nowhere to be found, and it's another hard trudge, eyes firmly on every next footstep, down to the Afon Hengwm. Two lads from Aberystwyth are drying off by the side of a deep brown pool, just short of where the Afon Hyddgen joins the Hengwm. I borrow a towel and jump in. The water looks like beer, but feels like liquid satin.

Ruined farmhouses, long abandoned fields and empty animal pens pepper the lower slopes and valleys, as if an unseen plague has crept in and taken all before it. Nowhere is the atmosphere more spectacularly lonesome than in the Hyddgen valley, heading north towards Machynlleth. I've explored this area a few times, on foot and bike, and its vast emptiness – somehow liberating and oppressive all at once – always shakes me to the bones. Two lumps of dazzling quartz sit above the far bank of the river: Cerrig Cyfamod Glyndŵr, his Covenant Stones, according to the OS map (even if they mis-spell 'cyfamod' with a double-m), and according to many standing stone enthusiasts, aligned to a further megalith a kilometre south on the slopes of Pumlumon Fawr.

Most scholars place the actual battle a little further north of Glyndŵr's stones, on land now swallowed by Forestry Commission conifers. Persevere through the sunless clusters, and there are clues to be found. The little valley known as Siambr Trawsfynydd is where it is thought Glyndŵr's army made their camp, and the nearby ring cairn on Esgair y Ffordd supposedly marks the burial ground of the dead. Although the conifers have done their best to conceal it, it is absolutely worth fighting your way through to the bottom of the Hengwm waterfall[10], a long, lazy descent of foam down a striated cliff. Being north facing, it freezes beautifully in the winter and attracts ice climbers. Legend has it that Henry tried to outflank the Welsh by making his troops scramble up the fall to the moorland above. They were, of course, ambushed and slaughtered by Glyndŵr's men. Even if the story is embellishment, this lonely spot will, like so many others around this upland sump at the heart of Wales, send the shiver of centuries down the most sceptical of spines.

DYFI JUNCTION

Aberystwyth Arts Centre café, some time in the early 2000s. Hulking lad, sat with his mam, is leafing through the brochure of upcoming events. *Pwy sy'n chwara' 'te?* asks Mam. Son turns the pages. *Linton Kwesi Johnson*, he replies. Mam screws her face up. *Pwy?* she bellows, *Linton Dovey Junction?*[11] Person at neighbouring table[12] splutters and sprays coffee over his newspaper.

I think of the parallel Welsh dub poet often, and fervently wish he existed. Linton Dovey Junction would be a force to reckon with, his hot rhythms the distant chuckety-chuck of trains coursing through a vast, open bowl of hills, over the gurgle of tidal water and the occasional piercing scream of an overhead jet, layered with the squawk of geese rising in protest at the intrusion. He would speak from the very belly of Wales; would be the voice of us all, and none of us.

The 1863 opening of the railway sliced Powys off from its sea. Literally so, for the tidal Dyfi estuary had to be re-routed at nearby Derwenlas, instantly rendering the old port and shipbuilding centre landlocked and obsolete. Overnight, this westernmost finger of Montgomeryshire changed the direction of its focus one hundred and eighty degrees, from the open ocean of the west to the anglicised

savannah to the east. The modern age had arrived on platform one.

On average, only three or four passengers a day use Cyffordd Dyfi / Dovey Junction railway station. Not because there are so few trains: forty services stop here every day of the week (XSu[13], as they say in the timetable). This is Wales' most remote station: two platforms in the middle of a bog, no road passing within the best part of a mile, only the straggle of houses at Glandyfi within walking distance. One platform, for the succession of tiny halts up the coast to Pwllheli, arcs gracefully towards the river bridge and looks custom-built to house a six-carriage seaside special. The other, for Borth and the buffers at Aberystwyth, is ruler-straight and a third of a kilometre long; it could park the entire length of a freight train. This super-sized version of the station is gleaming new: the massive platform substantially replaced a rickety footpath that led from the main road. Thirty overhead lamp-posts, shiny bike racks, signs galore, bins and seating fresh from the packet. Pass by on the A487 at night, and the whole thing glitters like a space station in the middle of the estuarine black. And still no-one gets on or off the train.

Powys specialised in odd, remote railway junctions, most now a distant memory and pages of old photos on fanatical websites. Talyllyn Junction, between Brecon and Llangorse Lake, now a huge triangle of trees and estate of new bungalows; Three Cocks Junction, up towards Hay, a lorry park and garden centre. You can catch a glimpse of Moat Lane Junction, in the fields near Caersws, from the extant mid Wales line to Shrewsbury, but the platforms and refreshment rooms of this pivotal divide in the Welsh railway system have long been subsumed by mountains of farm equipment. Dyfi Junction alone soldiers on.

As a YouTube song[14] has it, 'What's the function (of Dovey Junction)?' It's where the two mid Wales lines split, so that if you were going from, say, Lampeter to Barmouth, this was where you changed trains. Since all of the lines beyond Aberystwyth were chopped in the 1960s by Beeching, there are only two stops south of the Junction, and the timetables don't dovetail any more either. Changing here, you'll have at least an hour to wait, so nearly everyone continues to the next stop, Machynlleth, four miles up the line, where at least there's a chance of a cup of tea.

Lovely though Machynlleth station is, its buildings and canopies straight out of a Hornby train set, I'd always recommend a thermos and an hour's quiet contemplation at Dyfi Junction. The hills curve round at a respectful distance, broken only by the gap where the estuary mouth spills out into the sea as if over the lip of a jug. You feel utterly alone, yet firmly, indefinably at the epicentre of something. And so you are. This is the point of perfect stillness at the eye of the storm, where north, south and west Wales meet. For fifteen hundred years, the nation's major internal borders have collided here, once three kingdoms, now three counties[15]. In that waiting hour, hop over the fence and across the flood and high tide debris to the river's edge, the westernmost point of Powys as it fades away into reeds and thick mud. There's no triumphant flourish, just a haunting final note hanging in the brackish air.

Be warned though, that the haunting won't stop. Go once, and you can't quite shake the place off. Although little used for its express function, this liminal spot fulfils a far more opaque need for a location that is real, can be pointed to on the map, but which remains beyond the solid, often disappointing certainties of everyday. Holding some essence of Wales, the nation's fulcrum is not the Millennium Stadium or Snowdon or St David's cathedral, but an inaccessible, barely-used railway station in a lonely bog.

That's the function, to answer the song, of Dyfi Junction. Even taking into account imaginary dub poets, it's not been the station's only contribution to our cultural life. Aberdare-born composer

Rhian Samuel composed a jaunty brass scherzo conjuring up the bubbling excitement of holidaymakers en route to the Welsh coast: 'Dovey Junction' premiered at the UNESCO World Music Forum in Los Angeles in 2005, performed by the Borealis Brass Ensemble of Fairbanks, Alaska. In literature, Malcolm Price has featured it in his noir thriller series of Aberystwyth books, for it needs little embellishment to be part of his parallel mid Wales of hallucinatory madness. Gareth F. Williams wrote two novels, *Dyfi Juncshiyn: Y Dyn Blin* and *Dyfi Jyncshiyn: Y Ddynes yn yr Haul*, which told the story, from both sides, of two youngsters from Gwynedd who are stranded overnight on the station platform in September 1965. After a night of passion in the station's waiting room, they arrange to meet back there exactly forty years later.

There can be nowhere as devoid of erotic possibility as the

waiting room's latterday replacement, a Perspex bus shelter, where any lusty thoughts will be whipped out on a steely breeze. In a twenty-first century update of Williams' story, the characters would have to be exhibitionists, not that an audience of seagulls and Canada geese is going to blab. More to the point, they'd need to be contortionists, for the only bench is a cold metal four-seater with unmoveable arm dividers: it has all the libidinous allure of gingivitis. If Larkin was right, and sex really was invented in 1963, it peaked at Dyfi Junction two years later, and it's been steadily downhill ever since.

A distant rumble announced my train, which soon appeared gleaming gold in the evening sunset, dwarfed by the wall of the estuary from Aberdyfi. Birds rose, cattle shifted on the flats, and Linton Dovey Junction cleared his throat for an encore.

ESGAIRGEILIOG

I'm in Powys. But only just. Were my house to slide down the bank on which it is built, to bump its stately way over old shale and slate into the river below, I would have the boundary with Gwynedd scything through my kitchen. I'm looking straight over at that other world now, writing these words in the garden shed. Over there is a sheer, wooded slope; a riverside fringe of beech and ash dwarfed by the poker-straight plantation pines rearing above them. Between the deciduous and the unnaturally evergreen, a busy trunk road. There's been an accident this afternoon. It's Maundy Thursday, the firework launch of the Easter weekend, the tourist season and six month's grimly predictable overtime for the air ambulance. That's been hovering over, trying to find a place to land, while three road ambulances also came screeching through the valley. All that is happening in Gwynedd, although I can see it – even without my specs – in crystal clear detail from here in Powys.

It's a big border, one of the major faultlines in Wales. Not just between two modern counties, but two older ones as well and even, once upon a time, real live kingdoms, all weaponry, chainmail and strategic marriages. On my side with the birdsong and the budding honeysuckle, it's Montgomeryshire, Maldwyn, and Powys. Over there with the plantation conifers and the juddering blue lights of the ambulances, it's Meirionnydd, Merioneth as some still like to think it, and Gwynedd. That's north Wales, this is mid – though

oddly, we're on a loop of the river that means I'm looking south from mid Wales into north Wales. Here, the most consistently Liberal constituency in Britain: since 1880, Montgomeryshire has been represented in Westminster (and now down the Bay too) by a Liberal MP for all but four short years – at least, that is, until Lembit, and then Mick Bates too, dropped it.

The Conservatives captured Montgomeryshire in 1979, in the election that brought Margaret Thatcher to Downing Street. Despite the following election in 1983 being the high water mark of the Tory party, coming as it did in the immediate aftermath of the Falklands War, one of their only losses on the night was Montgomeryshire, which reverted to the Liberals (or 'Liberal-SDP Alliance' as they were known at the time). In May 2010, the Conservatives, represented by former regional AM and Berriew farmer Glyn Davies, took the seat again on a hefty 13.2% swing, one of the largest of the night. This is largely attributable not to a sudden upsurge in affection for either Davies or the Tories, but the hitherto staunch Liberal voters of Montgomeryshire – many of them *capelwyr*, farmers or both – finally losing their patience with maverick MP Lembit Öpik. A year later, the same happened in the National Assembly election. Mick Bates, who'd been LibDem AM for the county since the Assembly's inception in 1999, spent his last few years in the Senedd sitting as an Independent, after being chucked out of the party for assorted misdemeanours, including the drunken physical assault of an ambulance driver. In 2011, new LibDem candidate Wyn Williams was swept away by the Conservative's Russell George, mainly thanks to George's populist promise that he would absolutely resist any new wind farm developments or pylons carrying the power from them: a huge vote-winner. Will the Liberals be back to capture their old stronghold? The jury is out on that one.

Losing the seat twice in a year is quite an achievement when you remember that, even when the Liberal party was down to a taxiful of members in the late 1950s, old Maldwyn kept voting for them, going so far as to provide them with their party leader (not that there was a huge choice: he really didn't want the job)[16]. This is not CND, hairy toes in sandals, protest marches, beardy teacher Liberal voting, heaven forbid. This is dyed-in-the-wool nonconformist Liberalism that's more conservative than the Conservatives. Over there, it's rock solid Plaid, mun. Dafydd El's fiefdom, Cymru dwfn, the National Park.

One of my favourite activities is swimming the border. The Afon Dulas is ripe with pools that call you in and massage you with silky, turquoise caresses. Follow the sun: early morning wake-up dips are best above the waterfall in the Ffrwd; at lunchtime the deep eddies under Pont Evans glow green and inviting and make me feel like a lurking, waterborne troll, invisible to the traffic hurtling by on the main road far above. Loveliest of all are the pools half a mile or so downstream that get blasted by the late afternoon sun. As I glide through the water, under backlit branches of oak, fishes darting beneath my distant feet, the boundary that I'm straddling is the rapidly dissolving one between heaven and earth.

Different kingdoms, councils, counties, constituencies, parishes, electoral regions, languages for the most part, styles of architecture, fire and police authorities. When I first moved here, I had a party that got a little out of hand. Glass, crowbars, rocks, blood and slate slabs out of hand. Very messy. Eventually, a police car whooshed up to the front door, lights whirring excitedly. Copper leaps out, rather in the manner of the opening sequence of *Starsky and Hutch*. I was not anticipating his first question.

"Where are we?"

I tell him, though I would have thought that he'd have an idea himself. After all, someone has called him here, given him the address and everything. I'd like to think too that there was a road atlas in his vehicle, possibly even a satnav. His second question throws a little more light on the conundrum.

"No, I mean which county are we in. Powys or Gwynedd?"

I tell him that too, and on hearing my answer, he starts to get back into his panda car, saying as he does, "ah right, well we're the wrong force. We're North Wales. You want to wait for the Dyfed-Powys boys to arrive. I'm sure they'll be along soon." Meanwhile, the source of our problem, together with a few of his mates, can be heard in the dark distance, wielding his iron bar through the windows of some empty buildings. In my head, he's snarling like the cartoon Tasmanian Devil.

"While you're here, perhaps you could – you know – help us all the same," I offer. "There's some people injured and the bloke who did it is roaming around, completely frantic". Thankfully, he caves in a window somewhere nearby at just that moment, and the harsh crack of shattering glass seems to snap PC Jobsworth out of his gum-chewing indifference. "Oh yeah, OK, I see your point". Dyfed-Powys never arrive, but the brave boys of Gogledd Cymru wrestle His Nibs into the back of their car. He does snarl and tear around in a cartoon Tasmanian Devil fury. In fact, he causes fifteen grand's worth of damage to the car's interior. Off their turf. That'll teach them for not knowing their boundaries.

We quite like living on the edge in this village. It's win-win – gives us plenty of things to mither about, and possibly even more to feel slightly proud of. On the moaning side, there's the perennial complaint of the peripheral, that we're out of the loop, thought of by practically no-one, cared about by even fewer. Even in the fastest car, we're well over an hour from the county council HQ in Llandrindod (but then, to be fair, we were not much nearer when the county in question was Montgomeryshire and the HQ Welshpool). More nebulously, there's the faintly furred identity that comes with border life: the next village up the valley, Corris, is Meirionnydd. Grey blocks, slate mountains, tumbling river, fiercely Cymraeg. Here, it's all a bit more muted, the Maldwyn way, even if we're only a mile distant. The stone's been pebbledashed, the quarries died decades earlier, the river slides through polished pools, and the language stays mainly by the *aelwyd*.

The line leapt from the map and really meant something for a while in the seventies and eighties. Every other village in the valley is on the Meirionnydd bank of the river, and so couldn't order a Sunday pint until the 1989 referendum. Been wet in Montgomeryshire since the fifties, so our pub was the first stop for a whole generation of thirsty Gwynedd residents. It was a gloriously short golden period; there's only been a pub here since 1977. Nora the Shop and her late husband Glyn (still remembered, nearly twenty years after his death, as Glyn Easy: he was enthusiastically bisexual) wanted to extend their front parlour into a bar, sought planning permission and a licence. Never happened here before: this village, since the first quarrymen had arrived to split slate, was strictly chapel. Drinking wasn't something you did, and if you had to, you certainly didn't do it in public. The village split down the middle, worshippers at the two rival chapels coming together to face down the demon bottle. God versus Mammon, no prizes for guessing who won. Roll on thirty years: both chapels closed, started to crumble, were done up, sold as holiday homes. The pub's going great guns over the way. Though it's never reached the heady heights of those 1980s Sundays, tunes thumped out on the piano, lusty singing, lusty everything, trays of sandwiches, some probably rather curly, pool, darts, cards, lock-ins, knock-off baccy, smoke and pheromones you could cut with a knife.

Being on the edge gives us a curious blanket of anonymity. No-one from beyond about ten miles away has the first idea where we are. Many who have lived in this area all their lives wrinkle their noses at the mention of the name, furrow their brow and think that we're somewhere outside Carmarthen, perhaps, they're sure they passed it on the way to Swansea once. Or was it Holyhead?

It's not helped by the fact that no-one is too sure what our name is either. Some say Ceinws[17], some Esgairgeiliog. Ordnance Survey say Ceinws Esgairgeiliog, the signs at either end of the village say ESGAIRGEILIOG CEINWS Gyrrwch yn ofalus Please drive carefully. Some say our end is Esgairgeiliog, everything over the bridge Ceinws. The bridge crosses the Afon Glesyrch, just where it rushes into the Dulas, so the village was known as Aberglesyrch for decades. Julia Gunn, whose family, the Rowlands', have been here from the beginning, and her husband Ray (until his recent retirement, our postman) have written the definitive village book: two hundred A4 pages, nine hundred photographs. Of a place with perhaps fifty houses. They insist that Esgairgeiliog is the proper name, that Ceinws was only used when a post office opened here, for the GPO were frit that mail bound for us would mistakenly end

up in Caergeiliog on Anglesey. An example of such prissy nomenclature comes as a surprise, in this the land of a dozen Llansantffraeds, Tal-y-bonts and Llanfihangels.

Amongst the nine hundred photos are some of the back of my terrace from the late 1980s. Four houses, one big communal garden, rose bushes and azaleas galore all the way down to the river bank. Then we incomers arrived and wanted our own patch, so it was all carved up. Then carved up some more. Down came the rose bushes and oak trees. Up went the fences, walls, leylandii, box hedges, new borders galore. Slightly shady deals were done, land was grabbed. A big patch sold below us for a Midlander to build his dream cottage. The dream went sour: divorce, acrimony, court cases. The house has finally been sold, and with it a little patch of scrub by the river. The new owners have just fenced it off, proud to have a few square feet of moss-covered slate spoil that only they can slide down. Our newest border of all. It looks ridiculous, and every time it catches my eye, especially when they are in residence and their two large dogs are prowling and hollering along the fence, the words of John Clare, writing about the effect of the Enclosures on his little patch of eastern England, boom through my brain:

Fence meeting fence in owner's little bounds
Of field and meadow, large as garden-grounds.

In little parcels little minds to please,
With men and flocks imprisoned, ill at ease.

Notes

1. The Powys border with Glamorgan (now Neath-Port Talbot county borough) cuts across the peak of Mynydd y Drum, to the immediate south-east of Ystradgynlais.
2. Camddwr Bleiddiad = the wolves' leap, for an athletic animal could indeed cross the river here without getting wet.
3. Gwynfor Evans (1912-2005), President of Plaid Cymru from 1945 until 1981 and the party's first MP after success at the 1966 Carmarthen by-election. *For the Sake of Wales* (Welsh Academic Press, 1986) was a reworking of his earlier autobiography in Welsh, *Bywyd Cymro* (Gwasg Gwynedd, 1982).
4. Pumlumon ('five stacks/beacons') is also often named as Plynlimon. That this is given as the anglicised version of the name is curious, for it is probably harder for monoglot English speakers to get their tongue around than the original Welsh name.
5. 'Theatre of the Empire of Great Britain', Speed's county atlas of 1612 and one of the first tomes to link the evolving concept of Great Britain with an imperial ambition.
6. Pumlumon Arwystli, only 11 metres lower than the mountain's summit, nearly two miles away.
7. I beg to differ: see the entry on Staylittle and Dylife.
8. A *cheval-de-frise* is a gruesome relic of medieval warfare: deliberately placed walls of razor-sharp stones arranged in bewildering clusters to delay the progress of any invaders. Following the massive protests of 2011 against the plans for pylons and a sub-station in Montgomeryshire, massive revision of the TAN 8 scheme has been announced by politicians startled at the depth of feeling.
9. Llyn Llygad Rheidol ('the lake of the eye of the Rheidol') is the source of the Afon Rheidol, one of Wales' fastest-flowing. Whereas the Severn takes over two hundred miles to reach the sea from Pumlumon, and the Wye 135 miles, the Rheidol hurtles itself westwards and drops nearly two thousand feet to reach Cardigan Bay at Aberystwyth within twenty-eight miles.
10. Confusingly, this is a different Afon Hengwm from the one in which I swam, just a mile or two to the south. This one is a tiny tributary of the Afon Dulas (and there are two of those, too). Tiny it may be, but its waterfall is dazzling.
11. "Who's playing then?" "Linton Kwesi Johnson." "Who? Linton Dovey Junction?"
12. That'll be me.
13. Except Sundays.
14. By Aberystwyth students Paul Vawer, Mathieu Holladay and Pete Allen.
15. The counties of Powys (Montgomeryshire), Gwynedd (Meirionnydd) and Ceredigion meet here, as did the medieval kingdoms of Powys, Gwynedd and Deheubarth (Dyfed).
16. Clement Davies, native of Llanfyllin, was leader of the Liberal Party from 1945 until 1956. The previous incumbent, the dashing Archibald Sinclair, lost his seat in the Labour landslide of '45, when the Liberals were reduced to a rump of just twelve seats. Six of them were

new to the Commons, leaving a pool of just six from which to find a leader. Davies never wanted the job, and wasn't up to much. Throughout two of the three general election campaigns that he fought as leader, he was hospitalised for acute alcoholism.
17. And there doesn't seem to much consistency in pronunciation either. Some call Ceinws 'kay-nuss' (to rhyme with 'puss'), others 'kye-noose' – another good reason to stick to Esgairgeiliog, in my opinion.

NORTH

Montgomeryshire

COUNTY TOWN

The axis of power in Montgomeryshire, the only county to touch both sides of Wales, has always lain to the east, around the plains of the Severn, or Afon Hafren. Here is the money, the productive land, the easier weather[1], the big houses and the easy transport into England; but here too, of course, are the fortifications and fisticuffs, the often uneasy truce.

The first capital now lies mouldering in a field near Meifod, by the junction of the A495 and the B4389. This is Mathrafal, the royal seat of the Princes of Powys, already past its heyday by the twelfth century. Considered on a par with the royal houses of Aberffraw, for Gwynedd, and Dinefwr, for Deheubarth, Mathrafal was the capital of a shrinking kingdom, once Powys had been split, with the Afon Rhaeadr as the border, between Madog and Gwenwynwyn, the sons of Owain Cyfeiliog. Powys Fadog (the Maelor and upper reaches of the Dee) mutated into the southern tranches of Denbighshire, and Powys Wenwynwyn what we know now as Montgomeryshire.

Only sheep, badgers, rabbits and birds live at Mathrafal now. The princes lie cold in the vast llan at the heart of Meifod village, while the old palace was snuffed out in the middle ages. Six or more centuries on, however, it's still possible to catch a whiff of grandeur in the motte and bailey cloaked in velvet green, and crowned with gargantuan Maldwyn oaks. Far below, the nut brown waters of the Afon Banwy hurtle across striated rocks towards their rendezvous with the Vyrnwy, just downstream. Road junction, river junction, national and regional crossroads. Yet quiet as night, unstirring, unstirred.

Gwenwynwyn and his grandson Owain ('de la Pole'[2]) relocated the borderland omphalos to the east, to Powis Castle, by Welshpool, in the Severn valley itself. Fragments of the early medieval castle survive, albeit entirely eclipsed by the gaudy chutzpah of its later additions, from its purchase by the Herbert family in 1587. Their power was wealth and ostentation more than military might, and the castle was remodelled into a country house of unmatched splendour designed to dominate all before it. Powis is big and red, a fat face of a fortress staring imperiously over the town of Welshpool and looking always 'down country' to Shropshire, to England. Although still the home of the Earls of Powis, it has been in the care of the National Trust since 1965, and, until recently, served as the Welsh

base for Prince Charles when he came to have a few days in his principality. The current Earl of Powis, a strict Christian, refused to allow Charles to share rooms with his then mistress, Camilla Parker-Bowles, so the arrangement came to a rather fractious end. Since making a decent woman out of Camilla, Charles has bought himself a Welsh estate at Llwynywermod, near Llandovery in Carmarthenshire. They have been nowhere near Powis Castle since.

The castle's a grand day out, somewhere to take agnostic aunties still a little suspicious of too-Welsh ways. They will topple like elegantly-coiffed ninepins after a stroll through the magnificent terraced gardens, a promenade through the state rooms and the Tudor long gallery, a cream tea (*how much?*) and the chance to run riot with marmalade and lavender bags in the NT shop. Combine it with a trip around other local outposts of *Country Life* lite – Glansevern Hall gardens for the traditionalists, Andrew Logan's dizzyingly camp sculpture museum at Berriew for the fairy godmothers – and they will be putty in your paws.

If that isn't quite enough, there's always the *de facto* county town itself just down the road, somewhere that always lands the sweetest of sucker punches. Visting Montgomery, says David Barnes in his excellent *Companion Guide to Wales*, "is like calling to see a much-

loved uncle, long retired from a senior position in the civil service, and now well into his anecdotage: an encounter with the well-mannered civility of a bygone age". Like Powis Castle, the town is firmly angled towards the English border, little more than a mile to the east (and for the most part, still coterminous with the ruler-straight groove of Offa's Dyke). Montgomery sits, basking in its own sunshine, on the eastern flank of the first wave of Welsh hills, its back firmly turned to the county that took its name.

For a strange decade or so in the late thirteenth century, when relations between Prince Llywelyn and the English crown were straining towards an eventual war, Montgomery played a pivotal role in negotiations. Regular meetings between the two sides, including some between the monarchs themselves, took place at the ford across the Severn, known as Rhydwhyman[3], two miles north-west of the town. Here, hostages were traded and agreements hammered out, including the 1267 Treaty of Montgomery, wherein Llywelyn was recognised as the rightful Prince of Wales, in return for his swearing fealty to Henry III; numerous high-ranking officials, including a future Pope, were witnesses at the ceremony. Little more than five years later, the war was ignited when Llywelyn failed to turn up at the ford for an agreed rendezvous with ambassadors of the new king, Edward I, leaving them to wait in vain from dawn until dusk on a cold January day.

Like Radnorshire and Breconshire, the county of Montgomeryshire was a creation of the sixteenth century Acts of Union. While Brecon was an ancient, well-established regional capital, the county town choices of New Radnor and Montgomery were not altogether obvious, although both fulfilled the main criteria of the new order, being plantation towns, gathered beneath their beefy Norman castles, and on the plains bordering England. Neither has ever amounted to much, but Montgomery sweeps the board when it comes to charm. There is nowhere quite as winsome in Powys, and that is against some pretty congenial competition. Against too the town's sometimes brutal history, still glimpsed in some buildings. In a town whose population has never gone much beyond a thousand, there are three old gaols[4], all now converted to gingerbread homes decked in wisteria and sugar roses.

The later County Gaol, sited just over the old town wall off the road to Chirbury, was built in the early 1830s. No other buildings were constructed in Montgomery until well into the twentieth century[5]; the Victorian age passed it by entirely and left a fine Georgian time capsule. It is that that so beguiles us today, the redbrick Severn valley architecture in perfect proportion to our twenty-first century covetousness. There's always someone with their nose pressed up against the window of estate agents Morris, Marshall & Poole on Broad Street. Serving the community for 140 years, don't expect much change from three hundred K.

Read the stories in the Old Bell museum ("recognised as the first Heritage Centre in Wales", it claims), fashioned out of a temperance hotel. Better still for history yet in the making, cross the road and visit Bunner's hardware store, the best shop in Wales; established 1892 by youthful entrepreneur Robert H. Bunner (1872-1947), enthusiast for new technology (Telephone Montgomery 4) and bringer of chaos to the Cambrian railway when he ordered a thousand ploughs for delivery. Ironmonger and Cycles it says on the front, but within the labyrinth of stairs, rooms, cellars and yards you'll find everything you ever needed, and plenty you never even heard of. You'll also find Robert's grandchildren and great-grandchildren behind the counter, guiding you straight to the very nail or sprocket you needed, talking animatedly about everything from quadbikes to twine, or serving you petrol from the antique swing-arm pumps out front (the fuel tanks sit directly

beneath the shop, something that is only allowed to continue as the store is not on a main road).

There are some palatial houses dotted around the town, though the best was demolished in the early 1930s. The Herbert family's[6] seventeenth century Lymore Hall was the finest advertisement for sturdy Montgomeryshire oak, at least until its ignominious end on 4th August 1921, when, during a bazaar and fête, the floor of the massive banqueting hall gave way, plunging dozens of townsfolk into the stone cellars below. No-one was seriously injured, though, as the following week's *Montgomeryshire Express & Radnor Times* had it, "some of the ladies showed a tendency to faint, because it was feared that very severe consequences had ensued". The report continued, breathlessly: "With the people who fell into the vault was the fancy stall over which Miss Doris Tomley presided. The young lady, fortunately, did not accompany her stand in its downward track, but was left standing on the edge of the chasm. The Earl of Powis was at the time talking to the Rector of Montgomery. Lord Powis disappeared, but the rector was left on the solid floor. The Earl escaped with very slight injuries, as also did his agent, Mr J. Edmonds, who when in the depths found himself almost inextricably linked with the fancy goods of Miss Tomley's stall".

By then, Montgomery's tenure as county town was also looking near to collapse. The failure of the canal, and then the railway, to come into the town had meant that most of the county's offices had been located in Welshpool, in the shadow of Powis Castle. "[Welshpool] is in reality, though not in name, the capital of Montgomeryshire, containing the assize and sessions courts for the county and the militia head-quarters" said *The National Gazetteer* of 1868, and when the county councils were formed at the tail end of the 1880s, there was no question as to where its headquarters would be. Even on my side of the county, a full hour and a million miles from the plump pastures of the Severn valley, folk always talk about 'going to Welshpool' almost as a euphemism for anything to do with contacting the authorities. Llandrindod barely scrapes a mention.

The expanded county of Powys has absorbed much of the original Powys Wenwynwyn, Montgomeryshire, not least its gorgeous civic motto, 'Powys Paradwys Cymru' (Powys, the Paradise of Wales). It could be said that the name itself is more politically acceptable: Powys, from the Latin *pagus*, or countryside district, the land of the pagans, rather than Montgomery, the name of an invader. But to see the Paradwys Cymru at its loveliest, the old county town still holds the aces. Follow the signs from the castle to the Montgomeryshire county war memorial, 1050 feet up on the top of Town Hill. There, green hills billow out in all directions to the distant purple peaks of Cadair Idris at the far side of the county. On 2nd April 1990, the memorial was ruptured by one of the strongest earthquakes ever recorded in Britain, whose epicentre was between nearby Clun and Bishop's Castle. That this heart-breakingly beautiful countryside lies on one of our deepest faultlines comes as no surprise at all.

WELSHPOOL: RELOCATION, RELOCATION, ARYAN NATION

Someone's been busy scratching out the letter l from the signs. Welshpoo. Very droll. Until 1835, it would have been straightforward Poo, because the 'Welsh' prefix was only then added to distinguish the town from Poole in Dorset. According to the *New*

Statesman, though, it's Weimar that you'll most likely mix it up with. In early 2004, the left-leaning London periodical published a very strange piece about the former county town of Montgomeryshire[7]. Freelance journalist Jack Jameson wrote of being stranded for the night here when his car broke down. Walking into a pub, he found something of a Nazi rally going on, all spittle and jackboots in the soft borderland hills. His descriptions were precise, his language apocalyptic. The Welshpoo hit the fan.

Where was this pub? Everyone quickly discounted the Royal Oak: the town's principal old coaching inn was surely just too venerable, too stately for 'Deutschland über Alles' and Heil Hitler salutes. It just didn't quite fit with duchess potatoes and an aspirational wine list. My money was on one of the blowsy old boozers strung out in a cheap necklace the length of the handsome High Street (in truth, the town's main shopping street has five different names in quick succession along its half mile length, only one of which is High Street. At other points, this fine boulevard is named Broad Street, Chapel Street, Mount Street and Raven Street). The Mermaid, the Green Dragon perhaps, the Pheasant or the Talbot. The Pinewood could be a little basic, but *that* basic? Or perhaps the mystery bierkeller was one of the unknown bars (the Crown? The

Grapes? The Angel?) tucked away down the narrow side streets. There was no shortage of suspects. Although the article gave us clues – the pub, it said, "had a large, wood-panelled lounge that opened on to a terrace and garden" – it was all rather obliquely laid on. Deliberately so, stated the *New Statesman*'s then editor Peter Wilby when challenged by the Welsh media, for "we didn't want to make things difficult for that particular publican". Gosh no, you can see his point.

Until it became clear that neither the pub nor 'that particular publican' actually existed at all. Jameson was nobbled into an appearance on BBC Wales' *Dragon's Eye*, where he offered an enigmatic explanation for his article. "It is, in fact, not a news story," he told presenter David Williams. "It is an allegorical story. It is trying, by use of allegory and symbolism, to draw a comparison between certain happenings in mid Wales and what happened in Weimar, Germany, in 1933." Asked if the pub actually existed, he replied: "If the pub does exist, it is, indeed, no more than a composite – something which is put together from a number of different instances." Well, who hasn't had a night like that when they all blur into one?

The clumsy comparison that he was attempting to make was all about the arrival of the British National Party (BNP) in this part of the world. The BNP leader, Nick Griffin, had moved into a farmhouse up a dead-end lane near Llanerfyl, fifteen miles west of Welshpool, in the early 1990s – specifically "to escape multicultural Britain" as he acknowledged in a *Guardian* interview in 2000. He's not been the only one. The former BNP Deputy Chairman, Simon Darby has followed his leader and relocated to the Welshpool area too, in his case the village of Trewern on the road to Shrewsbury. The BNP's merchandising arm is listed as being based locally. During the Conservative party leadership election in 2001, Nick Griffin's father Edgar, who also lives in Welshpool, was sacked as a vice-president of Iain Duncan Smith's campaign and then booted out of the Conservative party when a journalist called the BNP hotline and found that it was Griffin Senior who answered. In subsequent interviews, Edgar Griffin stated that the BNP's policies were 'very, very moderate' and that "many, many Conservatives I believe are letting their subscriptions lapse and join the BNP. That's what I hear, a little bit of pillow talk from my lady wife," he said. His lady wife has stood as a BNP candidate. Rural Powys, and it seems Montgomeryshire in particular, has become the new home hotspot for English racial supremacists. Relocation, Relocation, Aryan Nation: coming soon to the Sky Nostalgia Gold Plus channel.

That they become the immigrants they so despise at home is an irony that seems not to trouble them. This is especially true in the Dyffryn Banwy, the gentle valley to the west of Welshpool, centred on the small town of Llanfair Caereinion[8], where the Welsh language is traditionally strong, but much under threat from a steady influx of monoglot English outsiders. Despite twenty years in the Bro Banwy, Nick Griffin himself has never bothered to learn Welsh, though he has been happy enough to push his teenage daughter on to the screen to stumble through BNP party political broadcasts for S4C.

Looking at the map, I notice a public right of way going straight through Griffin's farmyard. Could there be a clearer invitation for a good nose? Ideally, I should have organized a parade of drag queens or chanting imams to accompany me (sadly, this is probably an either/or option), but I make do with novelist Niall Griffiths instead. I doubt that he's ever worn a burqa or a basque, but he jumps at the chance for a bit of 'fascist-baiting' as he calls it. We acclimatise to Llanerfyl with a quick stop at the village church, as I want to show him the humungous ancient yew tree that fills half the graveyard, its massive, scaly branches plunging off in all directions. Dark and twisted, it suits the mood.

Parking on the lane near to the Griffin des res, the first unexpected surprise is a field full of llamas looming through the morning mist. "Bloody foreigners, coming over here, taking our fields", we chorus. We attempt an old holloway up to chez Griffin, but it's blocked and muddy, so revert to the longer route via the tarmac lanes. This takes us straight through a neighbouring farmyard, where untethered dogs race around us, roaring their disquiet. Niall is better at placating them than I am, and they let us pass. We're both a little shrill and sweaty after that.

Further up the lane, we pass Nick Griffin's immediate neighbour, out working in his garden. Slightly stiff good mornings are proffered; he must have seen all sorts wandering past. He's added his and his wife's names to the garden gate, which perhaps points to too many occasions of mistaken identity, either by BNP boneheads or their fired-up opponents: you wouldn't fancy either knocking on a dark night. The lane climbs up the lower slopes of Cefn-llys Isaf and straight into the Griffins' yard. There's supposed to be a public footpath off to the right, through their garden, but there's no sign of it and no opening for it either. There's an old byway on the other side of the yard however, so we saunter through, sending their caged rottweiler into a frenzy. He slavers and jumps, bouncing off the mesh as he loops round in furious circles, his baritone bark echoing off the hills. The chickens look a great deal friendlier.

There are a couple of cars in the yard, but no sign of life in the house. We're both disappointed and quietly relieved. It's a Tuesday morning after all, and Nick Griffin himself is perhaps at his day job, as an MEP for the north-west of England (for a party that sets such store by an individual's provenance, the BNP leader is pretty casual about carpetbagging himself into any part of the country that looks potentially rosy for his venal ideology. Griffin grew up in Suffolk, has lived in Montgomeryshire for nearly two decades, but has stood for election all over the place: for Westminster in Croydon North West (for the National Front in 1981 and 1983), and for the BNP in West Bromwich West (2000), Oldham West and Royton (2001), Keighley (2005) and Barking (2010), plus in the 2007 National Assembly election for the South Wales West region, and finally succeeding in getting elected as an MEP for the North-West of England in 2009 on 8% of the vote). They'll know we passed though, for there are CCTV cameras, security lights and alarms winking on every barn and gable. We wander through a gate and on to the old byway. The rottweiler's still raging; the cameras still rolling.

"So what were you going to say to them, if we got challenged?" asks Niall as we turn around and head back through the farmyard. I suddenly realise that I'd never even thought of that. What would I say? "Er, hello…", probably, while pretending not to recognize him. A properly British riposte; my youthful anti-fascist activist self died a little further at the realisation. And then I think of Jack Jameson's ridiculous article in the *New Statesman*, designed to prick the righteous indignation of the metropolitan left, at the same time shoring up their own lacy patchwork of snobbery and prejudice.

The laziness of it staggers me; if Mr Jameson had bothered to check, he'd have found that rural Montgomeryshire has, in fact, consistently (yet with characteristic politeness) rebuffed the occasional overtures made by the BNP since their leadership decamped here to live. During the Foot and Mouth crisis of 2001, Griffin and his cohorts took to leafleting Welshpool livestock market (the largest in the region), but with little success. There was a video on YouTube of them running stalls in Newtown and Welshpool, but it made for truly pathetic viewing. And they have never contested local seats in any election. To have so willfully misrepresented the truth of rural Wales in pursuit of an easy headline seems every bit as shallow and bigoted as anything the BNP are capable of, and had the unenviable by-product of handing them an open goal. Did he not think anyone hereabouts would read or question it? Evidently not. Like the ancient yew in the churchyard of St Erfyl, foolish, reductive thinking can grow in both directions at once. Either way, it only darkens clear skies.

GWLAD Y PLYGAIN, GWLAD Y PYNK

Who better to discuss the finer points of hymn-writing with than an unreconstructed punk? Rhys Mwyn, né Rhys Thomas of Llanfair Caereinion cynt, is meeting me at Pont Llogel, a speck of a place in the woods, on the B-road between Llangadfan and Llanfyllin. Blink and you'd miss it, as the old adage has it, but somehow we manage to miss each other, having arranged to rendezvous in 'the Forestry Commission car park'. Pont Llogel is nothing more than a scatter of farms, a half-derelict Victorian schoolroom and – miraculously – a tiny petrol station-cum-shop straight out of the era of sticky leather seats and saluting AA men. It does, however, have two FC car parks, and we plump for different ones. Only after half an hour of waiting and wondering (no mobile signal, of course) do we both simultaneously take a wander and collide in the lane.

Rhys is a taut bundle of excitable energy. He always is. The hair may be greyer, but the sharp sardonism and bright eyes glitter as fiercely as they did when he fronted bands such as Anrhefn and Hen Wlad Fy Mamau. We've arranged to walk the Ann Griffiths Trail to her memorial chapel at Dolanog, five or so miles away, and start by reading the comely bronze alloy memorial to her, a large open book, covered in leaves and birds. Even the logos of multiple funding agencies look strangely cute cast in metal. Despite having grown up in the area, Rhys knows little about the celebrated hymn-writer, and is characteristically puppy-eager to discover more. We pool our knowledge: that she died shockingly young (in 1805, at 29, weeks after her infant first child had died), that she was prone to dancing and singing herself into an ecstatic trance, that her hymns

tend towards mystical vision and an almost erotic yearning for the Christ figure[9], that many of her finest verses came to her when working in the fields, and that she never wrote any of them down (their survival came thanks to the memory of her maid, Ruth Evans). She sounds like the kind of girl Rhys would have had pogoing sweatily at one of his local gigs.

Pont Llogel is only three miles from the Vyrnwy dam, but the rectilinear brutality of the reservoir and its attendant conifer forests soon fade away. As we walk to Dolanog along the banks of the Afon Vyrnwy, sidling by clear and brown like a fine ale, he tells me of his efforts, quarter of a century ago, to bring punk to the Dyffryn Banwy. "I grew up in a brilliant era, in a way. Politically, it was all get involved, do-it-yourself, that whole fanzine ideology. I ran this thing called the Welsh Underground Festival, which was mainly putting gigs on in local village halls. We soon exhausted the supply of venues, as we'd get banned every time after going to any one of them. Not that we did anything wrong – it was just 'oh no, we can't have this', and that was that. The amount of times I put my hand down toilets to dredge out cigarette stubs so that we didn't get banned, but they'd still find some small pile of puke within a five mile radius of the hall, and that would be it. Banned again." That didn't stop him managing to get the mighty Crass, the punk high priests themselves, to play a gig in Llanerfyl village hall. Well worth the inevitable outrage.

He could have left it at that; going to gigs in Shrewsbury and putting on the odd local one by sympathetic visiting bands, but his greatest need was to see if he could force a shotgun marriage between the spirit of punk and the Cymraeg culture in which he'd grown up. "I felt that this fire, this energy all needed to happen in the Welsh language, but even feeling that surprised me. All my girlfriends in the early days were from English-speaking families, but deep inside I knew we needed a Welsh language version of Patti Smith or whoever". This was, perhaps, his need to splice together the two major ingredients in his own make-up, to find the overlap where there was none apparent, to see if there were others out there who felt the same way. I've heard the same thing from gay friends who grew up in this area: although to most, the gap remained unbridgeable and they almost always had to leave in order to do anything about their sexuality.

Rhys paints a vivid portrait of his upbringing. "In an area like Montgomeryshire, it was such a conservative culture. School, Llanfair Caereinion High, for me was being bullied by farmers, all of them *bochau cochion a dwylo mawr*[10]. I just found the whole thing highly, highly depressing, and awful, and intimidating, hurtful, cruel and horrible, you know. Listening to John Peel was the only sanctuary, knowing that there were thousands of others out there, but I knew that we had to do these things in the Welsh language, and no-one was doing it, so we had to do it ourselves". Thirty years on, the humiliation still crosses his face, the sudden shadow of clouds drifting through a rolling hillscape.

He loves coming back ("I was so looking forward to today"), but only for a visit. "There's a brilliant sense of old here, and I like the idea of time being able to move slower, and I think it does in this part of Montgomeryshire. The pace is slower, everything is slower. The question to me is whether I could ever come back, and I think the answer is no. I left for real reasons – bullying was part of it, and so was narrow mindedness. I don't want to be unkind, but it was like being in the middle of the rednecks. It wasn't healthy in any sense. And now I'm 48, and I've still not really got over it all. I'd still be uncomfortable going to a local pub and seeing people I knew from those days. There are people of course, like Siân James and Gwyn Jones[11], and they are able to do their thing from here, having set up their studio in Llanerfyl With new technology, they could be anywhere, so it is easier than it was, say, even fifteen years ago. But it's not for me".

Not that he's averse occasionally to returning and poking the area with a sharp stick. His ample musical tastes and – let's be honest – prodigious talent in winding up the habitually offended brought him back at Christmas 2008, in order to lay on an 'updated' *plygain* by folk singers, to be recorded for BBC Radio Cymru, and with a film crew from S4C's *Sioe Gelf* also on hand to capture the inevitable harrumphing. "There's no copyright in Cymraeg", he cheerfully declares, and his interest in plygain was utterly genuine. "The whole idea was to come back and rediscover, redefine something that I've missed. It's mine as much as anyone else's". Combative carols from the überpunk impresario; what could possibly go wrong?

North-east Montgomeryshire, this area of tough old roots, slow tractors, hirsute cheekbones and the legendary *mwynder* Maldwyn[12] is the heartland of *plygain*, that ancient free-form Christmas carol service of unaccompanied harmony singing. Mwynder was in short supply all round: Rhys knows all too well that the best way to publicise a gig, any gig, is a modicum of controversy drip fed into the eager gullets of the press. This he provided by if not exactly ripping up the *plygain* rule book, then certainly scribbling on a few of its pages and then showing them to *Y Cymro* and the *Daily Post*. Nothing too revolutionary – a bit of instrumental accompaniment, a few reworked chords, some casual clothes, but even such modest modernisation was enough to ruffle local feathers. That he planned to put on his event in the totemic hilltop church of Llanfihangel-yng-Ngwynfa, self-declared capital of *plygain,* only made matters worse. With a sense of grinding inexorability, some locals objected to this 'pop *plygain*', and, at the last minute, permission to use the church was denied, whereupon a replacement venue was found in the church of nearby Llangedwyn. It was a manufactured storm in the tiniest of teacups, but faithfully, breathlessly aired across all branches of the media.

Llanfihangel-yng-Ngwynfa ('St Michael in Paradise') is a tiny village a few miles north of Dolanog. It was here that Ann Griffiths' family originally worshipped, although after her conversion, at a fair in Llanfyllin at Easter 1796, she decided that the established church offered her little, and she became an enthusiastic member of the local Methodist congregation in nearby Pontrobert. Her infant daughter, who died after only a few days, was buried in

Llanfihangel churchyard and Ann herself joined her just a couple of weeks later. Her memorial, a large obelisk, is the most obvious gravestone in the churchyard. For such a totemic church, and in such a lofty spot, the plain Victorian building there today is a brutal disappointment. Llanfihangel-yng-Ngwynfa's other claims to fame are as the home of the last remaining parlour pub in the district (The Goat, second home to many *bochau cochion a dwylo mawr*), and when it was named recently as the hardest village in Wales for non-Welsh speakers to pronounce properly.

We reach Dolanog, curled up quietly in the afternoon sunshine, and eat our sandwiches sitting on a wall opposite the Ann Griffiths memorial chapel. Built in the Arts and Crafts style and opened in 1905, the chapel manages to be both severe and strangely sweet at the same time. From there, it's a stiff climb over Allt Dolanog, and down to her old home at Dolwar Fach, the ultimate destination for the many pilgrims who continue to traipse in her footsteps. Despite the overwhelming sensation that this area is still, settled, has barely changed for eons, even Ann Griffiths found herself straddling unexpected boundaries. The established church, under the iron grip of the Wynnstay squirearchy, was doing all it could to squash the rising tide of nonconformism, whose earliest manifestation can still

be seen in the tiny old Quaker meeting house of 1700, tucked up in a fold of the fields towards Pontrobert. It was part of the Dolobran estate, home from the fifteenth century of one of Montgomeryshire's most celebrated families, the Lloyds, early industrialists, staunch Quakers and, once they'd moved to Birmingham, founders of the bank of the same name. Furthermore, although she spoke precious little English, this is a border area where cultures have collided for centuries. Canon Allchin noted that Dolwar Fach was a meeting place for two types of religion and two forms of culture at a crucial period in Welsh history, and goes further by stating that it was also a notable meeting place of time and eternity, of heaven and earth.

While Ann Griffiths is justly lauded and so amply commemorated in her home patch, another, older daughter of the district, no stranger either to erotically-charged religious poetry, goes almost unremarked. Gwerful Mechain preceded Ann by three centuries; in her poetry, she too mixed heaven and earth – though her earth was darker, rougher and quite likely to be kicked in your face, while her heaven was far more explicitly orgasmic. She took on, in battles of waspish *englynion* and *cywyddau*, many of her male contemporaries, notably Ieuan Dyfi and Llywelyn ap Gutun, and wrote poems attacking domestic violence towards women. Sir O.M. Edwards recorded that many country folk in Wales could, even towards the tail end of the nineteenth century, recite reams of Gwerful's work off by heart, four hundred years after it had been written.

In the same circle of fifteenth century Powys bards was Dafydd Llwyd of Mathafarn, three or four decades older than Gwerful and definitely her teacher, possibly her lover. This latter assumption comes from the fact that Dafydd and Gwerful wrote *englynion* to each other, discussing in some detail each other's genitals. But Gwerful was not shy of such topics, as her most celebrated poem, 'Cywydd y Cedor'[13], also known as 'Cywydd y Gont'[14], fulsomely demonstrates. In this, she chastises male poets for their overly coy ways of describing the beauty of women, and cuts to the quick, and to the quim:

> Duw er ei radd a'i addef,
> diffrwyth wawd o'i dafawd ef:
> gadu'r canol heb foliant
> a'r plas lle'r enillir plant,
> a'r cedor clyd, rhagor claer,
> tynerdew, cylch twn eurdaer,
> lle carwn i, cywrain iach,
> y cedor dan y cadach.

> He pays homage to God's greatness,
> fruitless eulogy with his tongue:
> leaving the middle without praise
> and the place where children are conceived,
> and the warm quim, clear excellence,
> tender and fat, bright fervent broken circle,
> where I loved, in perfect health,
> the quim below the smock.[15]

Is that a little dig too at those who give inadequate cunnilingus? Certain bards, perhaps? It certainly sounds that way, and as she shoots down sexist wordsmiths, she piles on the praise for the "silk, little seam, curtain on a fine bright cunt", the "very proud forest" and "faultless gift", before shuddering to the glorious conclusion that:

> breisglwyn merch, drud annerch dro,
> berth addwyn, Duw'n borth iddo.

a girl's thick grove, circle of precious greeting,
lovely bush, God save it.

One day, please god, let that too be cast in bronze and placed in a Forestry Commission car park.

A NEW TOWN FOR MID WALES

A new town, not *the* Newtown, though the two ended up intimately related. A New Town for Mid Wales was the name of a government report issued in July 1966, calling for the establishment of a Montgomeryshire megalopolis, a linear Severnside sprawl, fourteen miles long and with a population of 70,000. Biggest in Wales it would have been, outside the southern triplets of Newport, Cardiff and Swansea. A space-age town centre was to be built on the high ground to the immediate north of Caersws[16], although the development was to surge both up and downstream along the Severn, with the existing towns of Llanidloes and Newtown as its bookends. According to the report, it would be "a novel type of new town, combining traditional manufacturing functions with recreational and resort functions": Milton Keynes Wells.

Such a plan formed the basis of *The Fight for Manod*, the little-known third novel in Raymond Williams' *Border Country* trilogy. Dr Matthew Price, socialist academic and Williams' alter ego, is sent by the government for a year to live in the area designated for the new city, Manod. He and his firebrand colleague, Peter Owen, uncover a sinister network of global capitalist finance, spearheaded locally by corrupt councillors, already profiteering out of the idea and destined to do so even more should the plan go ahead.

Although not published until 1979, Williams began *The Fight for Manod* in the 1950s. The mid-Wales new city plan, in both fiction and history, reeks of post-war paternalism, pipe-smoking planners carving up the country regardless of local nuance. In Williams' novel, Robert Lane, who'd appeared in *Second Generation*, the second book of the trilogy as a University lecturer, has now become the man in the ministry who commissions Price and Owen to spend a year in Manod. When they return to see him near the end of their tenure, Lane wearily explains why, without the new city, the area is doomed:

Because in terms of U.K. resources – in the ordinary way our only accessible resources – Manod and places like it are simply nowhere on any list. Yes, they're disadvantaged regions, yes, they have a case for assistance. But compared with the inner cities and with the old declining industrial areas they just don't begin to compete. They are marginal problems, in the strictest sense. In public policy, now, they simply have to be left, while we rebuild the inner cities and reinvest in manufacturing.

In reality, the idea was not, as we'd perhaps prefer to imagine, Big Bad London imposing its iron will on a defenceless rural outpost. There were plenty here, as Raymond Williams so forensically detailed, eager to sign up too, and to their own considerable advantage. The new town plan had been first floated at the tail-end of the 1950s, by the Mid Wales Industrial Development Association, which comprised of four representatives of each of the five Canolbarth county councils (Montgomery, Radnor, Brecon,

Cardigan and Merioneth[17]) under the chairmanship of economist Professor Arthur Beacham. Most were substantial landowners (the four Montgomeryshire representatives include the well-known county surnames of Hamer and Brymer-Griffith), on the bench and decorated with an assortment of Establishment gongs, and many stood to make massive personal profits from any large-scale development. In their 1964 report, *Mid Wales – its Problems and Prospects*, they were scathing in their assessment of the chances for the region as it stood, identifying not just "the low level of population in the area [and] its general distribution in small and scattered centres" but also "the quality of the remaining population (after years of selective migration)". They slyly reiterated this point, while pretending that it came from elsewhere: "The area has perhaps become so used to its brightest elements migrating that there are some who appear to think that migration and success are synonymous – and that those who stay are not quite 'with it'!"

Things start to smell even more rancid when, in the same report, they identify without qualm or qualification where they saw the new population coming from: "the Association has always enjoyed the closest liaison with the Birmingham Overspill Committee and before approaching the government to ascertain its current attitude towards the establishment of New Towns, invited the Chairman of the Overspill Committee and senior officials of the Birmingham Corporation to join in discussion with the MP for Montgomeryshire, the Rt. Hon. Clement Davies. From the discussions which took place, the Association felt confident that the establishment of a New Town in Mid Wales would command the support of the Birmingham Corporation as a substantial contribution to the solution of the city's overspill problems." And this is the stuff that they saw fit to publish. Heaven only knows what was being said, and traded, behind closed doors.

Clem Davies must have been a sick old man by the time any such meeting took place, as he'd died two years earlier in March 1962, having been the county's MP since 1929. Shoehorning his name posthumously into the report looks like a grubby attempt to give the plans legitimacy. But the tide was turning. Even Davies' successor as Liberal MP for Montgomeryshire, Emlyn Hooson, was firmly against the new town proposal as outlined by the MWIDA. In 1965, he and Liberal colleague Geraint Jenkins produced their own document, *The Heartland: A Plan for Mid Wales,* in which they agreed to the need for a new town, but "not simply as an overspill device to help Midland cities". "The further west the town, the better," they wrote, going on to say that "it is essential that the town should serve Wales and its people, and not be a mere satellite of another area". To that end, they proposed that Aberystwyth should be at least trebled in size, and have built an airport and "panoramic coast toll road", including new bridges over the Dyfi and Mawddach estauries.

It's hard to imagine that a west coast corniche would, as they hoped, "have immense attraction to holiday-makers, for it would open up the wonderful panoramic views along the coast": it would surely have turned out like all the other 1960s auto-obsessed eyesores and errors. But at least they were thinking about Welsh solutions for a Welsh problem, unlike the new Labour government[18]. Despite having established the post of Secretary of State for Wales as something of a sop to growing Welsh consciousness, the government were keen still on the Caersws plan and encouraged it at every turn. In early 1966, Harold 'white heat of technology' Wilson won a far more comfortable majority at the second general election inside two years. In Wales, Labour almost swept the board, winning all but four seats, on a share of the vote of 61%. When the report recommending the new city finally emerged in July, the Labour machine, at its seemingly impregnable height, was foursquare behind it.

But something else happened in July '66: Gwynfor. Plaid Cymru's first MP won an unexpected victory in the Carmarthen by-election. With memories of the campaign against the creation of a reservoir in the Tryweryn valley near Bala still fresh in the national memory, the idea of drowning a further Welsh valley, but in bricks and Brummies rather than water, suddenly appeared far too high-risk, and by mid 1967, the plan was dead. Instead, existing settlements were to be given steroid boosts of population and industry, in particular Newtown, which has more than doubled in size since then to around 13,000 inhabitants, making it the largest town in Powys.

That Newtown became a designated new town seems almost inevitable, although the joke – such as it is – on the signs that welcome you in is that the town has been new since the thirteenth century. All the same, it fell easily into promoting itself in those heady early days of boosted status, churning out brochures and plans to lure in businessmen searching to relocate their factories and warehouses. "A new town where business is a pleasure," klaxoned one early seventies PR magazine from the Mid Wales

Development Corporation. Why? "Because it is so pleasant and easy to drive to Newtown on excellent, traffic-free roads", it went on. Or that "shopping is a sheer delight" and that "with two libraries, a cinema, an amateur theatre, an art gallery and two hotel ballrooms, Newtown has no leisure time problem."

Forty years on, one of the libraries has gone, the hotels have lost their balls, but the cinema's still going strong, Theatr Hafren is the regional capital of tribute bands and the modernist art gallery (Oriel Davies, after the sisters of nearby Gregynog) is bold and sometimes brilliant, if usually empty. You can add too a crawful of pubs, from the morose to the boisterous via the pleasant enough, a few curry houses and Chinese takeaways, a rash of kebab shops (one filling its window with the boast that it is "the ONLY place in Wales where you'll find Double Doner Kebabs"), numerous benches on which to smoke weed and swig cider and a couple of sticky-floored nightclubs. Too old myself, but that never used to stop twinkletoed former MP, Lembit Öpik, a regular denizen of

Crystals. On a website[19] discussing the town's after-dark options, opinion varies seismically. To Claire from Llandrindod, "crystals is borin its alright for da old clubbers who like boring music lols", but for Wayne "you don't have to be wearing Armani or Gucci to get a conversation with a women, a bottle of WKD will usually suffice", which I think is a compliment. Between them, those two statements certainly make more sense of Lembit's fondness for the place. Jade from Aber points out that "there's absoloutely no fun to be had on a dancefloor where you're not allowed to drink on!", something Sam, Amy and Katie from Coleg Powys seem to be in accord with ("newtown is great but only if your hammered. try spendin the night in crystals when ur sober, zzz"). Last, and most poignant, word should go to Rob: "I really like going out in newtown. Its like hollywood to me because i live in lanni".

More than any other town in Powys, its largest is the one that could be anywhere. There are few tethers mooring it to Wales, a fact that provides both its oomph and its cynicism. The oomph produced Robert Owen, pioneer socialist, and Pryce Pryce-Jones, rampant capitalist. Owen is commemorated in a small, worthy museum on the main street in which I was the first visitor for two days[20]; Pryce-Jones by the massive curving Victorian warehouse that muscles out the town skyline, a cathedral of consumerism now half-full of dowdy catalogue shops. One is called Phoenix Furnishings, which is never a good sign. If I was a Business Adviser (unlikely), I'd seriously counsel against using the name Phoenix for anything (unless it was based in Arizona). That hint of past bankruptcy or scandal does not do much for a customer's confidence.

And the town's cynicism? It's the sameyness, the me-too aspirations that have Newtown forever squaring up against Shrewsbury, Telford, Brum or Aberyswyth, and forever finding itself wanting[21]. The rootlessness that seems to float in the ether, undercutting even the slender tendrils that bind the town to its Maldwyn soil. Even against Welshpool, far nearer the border, Newtown seems unsure of its identity and character. Every couple of years, someone suggests changing the name to help combat the anonymity of being one of a hundred or so British Newtowns (albeit the oldest, it is proudly claimed; like being the tallest dwarf). Invariably Newtown-upon-Severn is the favourite, though this sounds far too English, say a few, who then go on to ask what's wrong with Y Drenewydd, the ancient Welsh name seen on maps four hundred years ago? Suddenly, the faultline looks a little too sharp, too rusty, and the

issue is quietly forgotten for another couple of years.

Distant view 1: the 1922 half-inch Bartholomew map of the area. Barts were the first cartographers to use colour shading to denote height, from the deep green of the valley floor, through lighter greens and then ever darkening browns to the mountain tops[22]. You can see exactly where the new city would have gone, filling the map's lighter shades, its centre at Caersws in the middle of a tricorn-shaped basin, the valleys of the Severn and Trannon. Dotted lines, marked as Roman Roads, converge there too, for Caersws was the largest fort in mid Wales. So do drovers routes, turnpike roads and the railways.

Distant view 2: from the high lane between Dolfor and Kerry, looking over Newtown, nearly a thousand feet below. The letters spelling out PRYCE JONES on the top of his Royal Welsh Warehouse stand proud, a prosaic Hollywood; sunlight glints off the Severn, coiled around the town's heart. New estates, housing and industrial, fade into the distance and suddenly, there it is, the 1960s city snaking away, packing out the valley floor and clambering up the lower slopes either side. A Montgomeryshire Bilbao, it briefly looks like…

(Distant view 3: Matthew Price to Peter Owen in *The Fight for Manod*: "You feel it here, do you? Something different. Something other. Some altered physical sense.")

…but then the sun sets and the concrete turns to dust, curling up on a gentle breeze into a clear, starlit sky.

LLANIDLOES

It's all in the fabrics, darling. Only a town that's used to dealing in reams of the stuff could come up with the outfits on display. First Friday of July, get a costume (even better, make one), get to Llanidloes. The streets are closed off, pubs creak to the rafters, music bounces off the walls and wigs, and over the next few hours, you'll clock more bizarre sights than in an average month, even by the rainbow standards of smalltown Powys life. The Queen and Ali G sharing a bag of chips. A cloister of nuns having a pint and a fag outside the Unicorn. Fred Flintstone chatting up one of the Sheila's Wheels girls, while a disconsolate cornflakes packet looks on.

Those are the best, the inanimate outfits, especially the group efforts. A few years ago, there was a gang of six lads as tampons, one of them doubling up as the box ('Highly Irregular' it said) in which they all gathered periodically. As it were. People come as strawberries, cupcakes, volcanoes, walls, cans of baked beans, trees, planes, cars, buildings. There'll be a few windfarm turbines this year, bet you, with a big sign round their necks saying NO! My favourite ever was a faintly Dadaist group of half a dozen or so, who came as a suburban living room. One carried a roll of carpet, which, every so often, he'd throw down on to the road, whereupon the others would arrange themselves in speedy formation. Someone dressed as a standard lamp shot into the corner, and stood stock still. Another went down on all fours as a table, upon which someone dressed as a television sat. Two blokes in matching padding slotted together and became a sofa. They all held their positions for a minute or two, before snapping back out of it, rolling the carpet back up and vanishing into the crowd.

And oh, the men in frocks. It's as if the Rebecca Riots had never ended. Hippy boys getting in touch with their feminine side, Betty Boop eyes and Monroe lips framed by a dirty cloud of dreadlocks. Lairy lads in glittery slutwear, unable to stop grappling their fake boobs and pointing them at everyone as if they were loaded

weapons. Best of all, squat Maldwyn farmers squeezed into Laura Ashley cast-offs, zips and floral swirls straining to contain arms like flitches of pink ham. Alongside them their wives, liberated from Merched y Wawr twinsets in über-macho apparel: combat fatigues, camouflage war paint, stompy boots and with a plastic gun to wield with giggly intent. All great fun, and all great foreplay.

I've not been to Fancy Dress these last few years, so I'm not sure whether Laura Ashley's abandonment of the area has had any discernible effect on the quality of drag. In the 1990s, the night was an alternative advert for the Queen of Carno, a welcome departure from her usual parade of willowy English roses. For forty years, Laura Ashley was Powys in fabric, or at least, the version of Powys that sells beyond its borders: fragrant, wholesome, rustic, eternally sunny, the *Country Diary of an Edwardian Lady* brought to life.

Born in Merthyr, Laura Ashley brought her husband Bernard and their young children back to Wales in 1961, settling first on Machynlleth's main street in a shop and flat above. They opened the shop, but stock was limited: tea towels and aprons mainly, overprinted with Victorian hand bills and advertisements. In 1967, they needed to expand and moved to Carno, first to an old social club and then to the recently-closed village railway station. The

Development Board for Rural Wales could scarcely believe their luck, as the station complex soon grew into a major international headquarters, the darling of their brochures. Ladies in farmhouses all over Montgomeryshire made good pin money from stitching hems and frilly borders over the kitchen table, sheep shearers were employed as pattern-cutters, and locals were free to come to Carno and help themselves to seconds and off-cuts, not just frocks and aprons, but wallpaper and paint too. In the 1970s, the houses on even the roughest pebbledashed estates of Newtown or Mach had interiors like a Fulham deb's boudoir.

Things went absolutely ballistic when, in 1980, Lady Di posed for That Shot, the backlit see-through skirt and the cute little kiddies on a perfect English summer's day. It was, of course, an Ashley skirt and the empire swiftly conquered the Americas. Anyone could be a princess, thanks to Laura Ashley. By the time Diana walked terrified up the aisle a year later, to be wed to a man she'd met only thirteen times previously, Ashley's had five thousand outlets worldwide, a gorgeous global machine whose elfin heart beat from Powys. In 1985, poor Laura Ashley died on her sixtieth birthday, after plunging down a staircase in her daughter's Warwickshire home. The company started to go the same way without her, and by the late nineties was in serious trouble. Eventually, the Malaysia-based MUI Asia Group bought them out.

Bit by bit, they pulled out of the area that spawned them. The extensive Carno factory, with the old village station still at its core, closed in early 2005. Weeds sprang up, rocks were dumped at the entrances to deter joyriders, the Welsh Development Agency promised action but never found any, and the forest of For Sale signs for years afterwards made Carno a particularly gloomy stretch of the A470. In January 2008, the store on Llanidloes' Great Oak Street closed too. Opened in 1976, it had been the first proper outlet in Wales and was held proudly, if over-optimistically, as the flagship of the entire empire (the earlier tea towel flogging interlude in Machynlleth doesn't count here, and people in Llanidloes still get quite sniffy if you remind them of it). There's still an Ashley presence in Newtown: a town centre shop, though that appears threatened[23], and up on the Vastre industrial estate, a distribution depot and call centre. My boyfriend worked at the latter for a brief spell in the nineties, but couldn't get along with spending his days being shouted at by Solihull matrons.

But what goes round, comes round – after a fashion. Laura

Ashley's original, tiny shop at 35 Heol Maengwyn in Machynlleth is now a Cymro-Swedish interiors outlet (acres of fabric a specialism) run by two formidable young women with expansive horizons. In many ways, it is something of the natural, twenty-first century successor to Ashley's, but functional and funky, rather than fey and floaty[24]. The old Llanidloes shop, true to form, now ploughs a more conventional post-Ashley furrow as Wedding Belles at Laura's, its windows full of waterfalls of white tulle, which will either enchant you or make you feel a bit poorly. The town is a home too for Welsh quilting, which is a great deal more interesting than it sounds. Every year, an exhibition of quilts in put on at the Minerva arts centre, staring down the fine main street of the town. The artwork that can be woven into quilts is an eye-opener for those of us who think of them merely as something to get a bit of kip beneath. Of course, there are the questionable Gaian dreamscapes as woven by the pewter-ringed hands of old New Agers, but much more besides: dazzling geometry, cosmic patterns, landscapes to fall into, leitmotifs that take an old theme and tjuze it up for the modern age.

Fabric everywhere, skeins and sheets of it, folded back and forward through the years. Everyone needs clothing, and Montgomeryshire has long been able and willing to supply it. There

has to be some use for all those bloody sheep for starters. Llanidloes was one of the major centres of flannel production; you can see it in the artisan cottages that pack the rickety side streets in the town centre, or the riverside mill now full of half-empty flats. Once massive mechanisation came, and the industry was concentrated in ever more gargantuan factories and mills in the north of England, the mid Wales flannel industry spluttered and died. Even the coming of the railways failed to halt the exodus of jobs, as hoped. In fact, it precipitated it, as trains coming in from the east were laden high with cheaper flannel goods from Yorkshire and Lancashire. The flannel industry of Llanidloes and Newtown, let alone the hand-looms and tiny mills of the Carno, Banwy and Rhiw valleys, could never compete.

Aside perhaps from the lofty ambitions of Pryce-Jones in Newtown, the Montgomeryshire flannel industry didn't much help itself either. Conditions were dreadful, practices restricted. Truck shops were the norm, where employees were paid in tokens that they had no choice but to spend in the shops run by their bosses, and usually at inflated rates. Looking at the small, self-assured town today, one that is regularly called the prettiest in the region by visiting guide book writers, it is hard to imagine that this was a crucible of violent political protest, but a perfect storm of recession, the hated new Poor Laws, Chartist agitation and bosses' greedy intransigence ensured that, in the late 1830s, Llanidloes seethed and burned. It smoulders still, though rest assured that the prettiest fire blanket is on hand.

STAYLITTLE AND DYLIFE

Popular legend has it that the English name of Staylittle[25] comes from an old blacksmith, so lightning fast in his work that travellers needed only to 'stay-a-little' hereabouts while their horses were re-shod. Don't believe it. The name is a warning passed down from the ancestors, for there is nowhere in gentle Montgomeryshire so devoid of warmth and invitation than this place strewn across the pock-marked hills like wayside litter. It might as well be called Pissoff.

Its starkness is all that people remember. Mention Staylittle, or its surly twin Dylife, the old lead mining community now shrivelled to a handful of cottages and a lonesome pub[26], and most people will wrinkle their faces and come out with a story about sudden blizzards, dead sheep, ghosts, flash floods or gale-force winds as they took the mountain road one day from Llanidloes to Machynlleth. It is possibly the most famous unclassified road in Wales: epic, legendary, terrifying at times, but everyone has to try it. The views are never anything less than breathtaking, especially from the semi-circular memorial erected to the memory of Wynford Vaughan-Thomas. There he is, immortalised in slate, his arm pointing out the peaks that you can see on a fine day, which it probably isn't. Best bit of graffiti ever, a few years ago: scratched into the slate, alongside the usual LUFC and Cymru Am Byth!, the neatest little aphorism accompanying the great WVT's chiselled list of achievements. CWDYN TAEOG it read, 'servile scrotum' if you like. 'Forelock-tugging ball bag', if that wasn't such a biological impossibility. Oh to be damned with such elegant economy.

Back in Staylittle, there are Quakers' Gardens marked on the map, for the scabby isolation of this place had its uses, especially for those fleeing persecution in the towns and valleys far below. A web of dotted green lines on the OS indicate a fair choice of paths to explore the area, to try and find the homes, the gardens and the graves of those whose determination to withstand the sickly

pressures of approved piety had forced them up onto this bleak plateau. The web on the map may look inviting, but it doesn't translate to the ground: I cannot find one single path in the place that it should be. No signs, no stiles, no step-gates, nothing visible except rolls of barbed wire, padlocks and puddles slick with something unidentified, yet rancid. Snowdrops – snowdrops! It's April – are shivering in the brisk wind. They're not the only ones.

My search for dead *crynwyr* comes to a feeble end in a muddy farmyard. There's a dead sheep, two collies straining on chains and a small, feral child who vanishes into a barn as soon as we momentarily lock eyes, all swilling around in a vat of shit and oil. For a second, I have been transported into the pages of a Niall Griffiths story.

That said, I can't quite leave the place alone. It has that effect on most people: the grim fascination of this forsaken wold gets under the skin in a way that nice, gentle, green places rarely do. It's the abandonment more than anything, the sense that light and life have slipped into the next room, leaving only the cold ashes for us to poke around in, undisturbed by now. We seem to need that, more than ever. Discarded places like Dylife are a blank canvas on which we can project whatever we wish, and when you're in that particular mood – fractious, aching – the only company you want is skylarks and ghosts; you will find your way here and stomp, squelch some track to a brighter horizon. I've stayed up here a couple of

times in my camper van, after a few pints and a bit of dinner in the Star Inn. It's always a night full of the weirdest, swirliest dreams.

Michael Brown is addicted to the place. He's been coming here since the family holidays of his childhood, this stark moonscape a world away from the fecund Herefordshire of his upbringing. He returns as often as possible, and has explored miles of adits and tunnels, squeezed into flooded pit openings, dug out rusty nuggets and emerged plastered in the slime of yesterday, and deliriously happy. Having written a superb book about the place[27], Michael is taking me out to explore, but first we meet for a beer at the Star, shivering above the lonely road. He's good company, if quite reserved. Not when we get out into the detritus of the lead mines, though. Then, it's as if someone has plugged him into a power source. He becomes animated, eyes gleaming. I'm quite nervous, tending towards claustrophobia, but his enthusiasm bats it aside as we burrow down into an old adit and hunch below the dripping walls of rock.

That's far enough for me, but for Michael and many others, it is just the beginning. They have burrowed far into this riddled, scraped-out mountain, coaxing out more and more of its history with each shovelful. He shows me a rusty something, and a corroded something else, but I'm more intrigued by the social side, tales from this one-horse, two-bit shanty town that grew up almost overnight and vanished with equal speed, thirteen hundred feet up on the frozen watershed of Wales. At its height in the 1860s, Dylife contained around fifteen hundred inhabitants, three pubs (official), a church and three chapels, though by all accounts, the pubs won. Far from any outpost of authority, Dylife was a genuine Welsh Klondike, a den of drink, debauchery and death.

The place touches me even more deeply when I walk through one May day on a hike across the whole width of Montgomeryshire. This was my attempt at inventing a Welsh Coast to Coast, starting in time-honoured fashion with my feet in water at one edge (the Caebitra stream, the English border between Bishop's Castle and Montgomery), and then heading west to wash them again in the tidal waters of the Dyfi. Having wheezed my way up on to the Dylife plateau from the Severn plain, then the Trannon valley and Llawryglyn – quite literally llawr in its glyn – down below, the contrast hits me like a slap. I follow the track from Staylittle and across the grimy moor, pausing for a sit down and sandwich at the old Roman fortlet, Penycrocbren. As the name so morbidly specifies, this was where the gallows were built to execute Siôn y Gof (Siôn Jones), from Ystumtuen, near Devil's Bridge, who had come to work at Dylife around 1720. Weeks went by, and his family back in Ceredigion had heard nothing of or from him, so his wife, accompanied by their two children, made the long journey to see him. Siôn meanwhile had been knocking off a maid at Llwyn-y-Gog farm, and in walking his wife and children back after their visit, murdered them by pushing them into a deep, disused shaft. The crime was discovered months later, and Siôn was condemned to hang. As the resident blacksmith, he had to build his own gallows. The gibbet and skull, unearthed in the 1930s, were placed first in the window of a Machynlleth chemist, but are now in the St Fagan's Museum near Cardiff. On this windswept plateau, his corpse remained for years, hanging as a warning, quietly rotting. Lovely spot for a cheese'n'pickle.

The path (at this point part of the Glyndŵr's Way National Trail) continues westwards, across more tussocks and dereliction, clipping above the sharp, scarred valley of the Afon Clywedog, crossing it on

a footbridge and then heading north towards the steely disc of Glaslyn, the biggest natural lake in Montgomeryshire. This is the watershed of mid Wales: to the right, the Clywedog[28] flows down to the Severn and England, while to the left, the Afon Dulas, emerges from the lake to plunge down the sheer-sided cwm of Esgairfochnant on its way to the Dyfi and the Irish Sea. Here too is the linguistic and cultural watershed, the dividing line between the readily anglicised east and the defiantly resistant west.

After a quick dip in the lake, it suddenly occurred to me that I should go and seek the source of the Clywedog, about half a mile away. This, after all, trickles down to join the Severn at Llanidloes, so that if I found its first seepage up on this lonely moor and dropped in a feather, it would stand a theoretical chance of passing through the Worcestershire towns of my childhood within a few days. Looking at the map when planning the walk, it seemed that the total length of the Clywedog to the confluence at Llanidloes was more than the Severn alone from the slopes of Pumlumon to the same spot. According to an 1839 encyclopædia[29], the Clywedog is "a river of about the same length as the Severn itself", but I measured it to check, using the time-honoured method of a good Ordnance Survey, a ball of string and some breath-baited concentration. The distance from the headwater of the Clywedog to Llanidloes is 14 miles; that of the Severn from Pumlumon 11. Britain's longest river could be three miles longer yet.

So how is it decided which river is the main one, and which the tributary? With modern science, the answer is usually to do with the total drainage area; the greatest wins. But such knowledge and technique were not available when the Severn and the Clywedog were identified; it was more of an aesthetic and cultural evaluation. Culturally, because Pumlumon is an easier reference point for the source of our greatest river, and the Wye rises there too. Aesthetically, because the convention was that whichever river appeared to be the straighter, or the more predominant, at the confluence, would generally be the one given primacy; this is certainly the case with the Severn at Llanidloes. The Clywedog comes in at an angle, and is about two-thirds of the width of its supposedly senior sister (another factor that often made the difference). Yet the Severn here is wide, but very shallow, and the volume of water coming out of the Clywedog looks at least as great, if not greater. That's hard to prove since the building of Llyn Clywedog in the 1960s, explicitly to regulate the flow on the Severn and help prevent flooding downstream, but that in itself suggests that the Clywedog is potentially a mightier river than the upper Severn.

Its headwater is also a whole lot prettier than the oily drops oozing from slabs of wet peat on the side of Pumlumon. In a field of prickly grass yards from the mountain road, I catch a faint gurgling sound on the breeze, and head in its direction. Louder and louder it gets, and then suddenly, there's a torrent of clear, urgent water springing from the ground below. It tumbles out excitedly, chattering and singing its way off on its great journey, two hundred and twenty-three miles to the Irish Sea[30]. I thought of the lethargic, dirty puddles of Pumlumon, and it was no contest. This is my source.

MACHYNLLETH

On a finger of Powys, poking out between the west coast counties of Meirionnydd (Gwynedd) and Ceredigion, Machynlleth's haughty isolation only fuels a very fine opinion of itself. In what other country would a distant town of just over two thousand souls be ranked so highly in the national discourse? "Prifddinas Hynafol Cymru / The Ancient Capital of Wales" trumpet the signs ushering

you in. Remember though that this status comes from its place as the site of Owain Glyndŵr's 1404 parliament, the apogee of his all-too-brief surge of power. The whole shebang would have been over and done with in a week. Seven days, over six centuries ago. Like putting 'Qualified Antiques Expert' on your CV, on the strength of having collected stamps for a fortnight when you were eight. Very bold. Very Machynlleth. And who would dare disagree?

Even if the title is hyperbolic, the status feels real enough. Machynlleth is the first bridging point on the Dyfi estuary, that deep nick in the coast that perfectly splices north from south Wales. Here, accents, views and outlook change. Whole words too in Welsh. It's not hard to imagine a little sentry box on the bridge, and a customs point where you swap your 'gyda' for an 'efo', trade in a 'mas' for an 'allan', deftly reverse your 'nawr' into a 'rwan'; all fully reimbursable at a 1:1 rate on your return.

If you can return, that is. Three days of rain and the shelves of the town's shops will be empty, for everyone knows that the Dyfi bridge will be out before long. Fed by numerous mountain streams, the wide, placid river rises with startling speed, the residents of the bridge-end cottages move their electricals upstairs and the traffic is forced off on lengthy detours down grumbling back lanes. In between downpours, lorries regularly take chunks out of the bridge's crumbling masonry, and the temporary traffic lights are up again. 'Pan Welwch Golau Coch, Sefych Yma'[31] is a phrase scored wearily in local hearts, and contemplated far more often than Prifddinas Hynafol Cymru. When the name of Machynlleth is heard in the media, it's generally as yet another warning in the traffic report, between the Brynglas tunnels and the Gabalfa. At least Radio Wales can pronounce the place: it usually causes a pause, a nervous giggle and a slight mangling from London.

Jan Morris once told me that the only book she has ever written which failed to elicit so much as one letter from a reader was *A Machynlleth Triad*, her bilingual collaboration with son Twm that had them imagining the town at three key points in its history: Glyndŵr's fifteenth century convocation, a loose now (early 1990s) and at some time in the not-too-distant future, when it had become the small, self-assured capital of an independent Welsh republic. Those of a nationalist bent – and Machynlleth is always where any aspiring Plaid Cymru candidate for the otherwise hopeless Montgomeryshire seat garners their greatest support – held the book tight to their hearts, even if it never encouraged any of them to write and thank the author[32]. The Brave New Wales conjured in its final trilateral is exquisitely portrayed and powerfully evangelical, but nothing ages as fast as a vision of the future, and so it is here.

For if you want to peer into the crystal ball for the Machynlleth of Christmas Future, look no further than the town's ongoing spat with the mighty Tesco empire. Until 2010, Powys contained not one single branch of Britain's biggest supermarket chain. Friends from elsewhere could not believe it when I told them that the nearest Tesco was a good hour away (in Porthmadog). I imagined a vast wall map in Tesco HQ, little flags posted to signify every branch in Britain, and this great void at the heart of Wales. Every time one of the more ambitious rising managers of the empire passed it, he vowed to fill the gap with little flags, like some wartime general pushing his tanks across a vast table plan of enemy lines. At a stroke, Tesco announced their intention for a five-pronged attack into Powys, with stores at Newtown, Welshpool, Ystradgynlais, Llandrindod and Machynlleth[33]. There was mumbled opposition everywhere, but nothing on the furore that erupted in Machynlleth.

The other four Powys stores are up and running, but still the Tesco-owned old cattle market site in Machynlleth remains under a stubborn carapace of weeds. The application was eventually thrown

out because of concerns over traffic, but they came with a revised plan in September 2011 and seem determined to succeed. Between the initial announcement and the eventual first refusal, campaigns for both sides appeared in the town – or, more specifically (and inevitably), on Facebook. The anonymity and Dutch courage of the internet meant that people spewed bile into their keyboards that they would never have used in person, on the pavement outside the Spar. Posters appeared, stones were thrown, windows broken and veiled threats made. *The Independent* magazine ran a feature in September 2009 entitled 'The Lost Villages of Britain', with the sub-head 'Can our Rural Communities Survive in the 21st Century?'. Despite the fact that calling Machynlleth a village is a smacking offence hereabouts, it used the town, and its battle with Tesco, as a prime part of the narrative. Native son, jeweller Kelvin Jenkins, stated baldly that "Tesco is splitting our population down the middle" and that "the extent of the venom over this has shocked me... the rip in the community will take a long time to heal".

The force most ferociously unleashed in the campaign was the much sat-upon hatred towards middle-class English rat race refugees who have made Machynlleth their Welsh Nirfana. The proximity of the Centre for Alternative Technology, up in their disused slate quarry since 1974, has kept the spark of mutual antipathy glowing for nearly four decades, but the Facebook campaigns both pro- and anti-Tesco were a gallon apiece of kerosene on the embers. The Independent put it relatively diplomatically ('Many of those in favour of the Tesco plan argue that the protestors are trying to hold on to a quaint "olde worlde" vision of Machynlleth, which they believe is unprogressive'), but no such exegetical modesty in cyberspace. The town had rather liked to congratulate itself on its comparative indigenous-incomer cohesion, but the Tesco frenzy showed, in the starkest possible terms, what a fragile – and far more complex – unity it was. There are some great comical by-products of this schizophrenia. It's always fun to watch the newest vegans in town head off to the annual Countryside Fair, expecting it to be full of people bending willow and singing folk songs, and then fleeing in horror when confronted by the hunt pack of beagles and lots of fat fellas shooting.

Tesco revealed the Machynlleth district to be cleft, like Jan Morris' book, in three. There are the Cymry Cymraeg, many hailing from the villages and farms that cluster around the town. The English-speaking locals, born and bred Mach, who live on the newer estates at the east end of town and down in the Garsiwn[34], and whose ancestors often came here from England, Ireland, Scotland and beyond for work on the railway[35]. And the blow-ins, the incomers, most of whom came to town deliberately to escape clone town England. When it came to the Tesco question, strange alliances brewed: the Cymry Cymraeg fairly evenly split (generally becoming more anti the nearer to the process of food production they were), the English-speaking locals almost universally for it and the incomers almost equally universally anti.

Fast forward a few years, and instead of finding Jan Morris' winsome capital, let us rework Future Machynlleth according to its rather more likely fate as a Tesco delivery truck driver's least favourite outpost. He swings in from Newtown, cursing the caravans and tractors that clog the route and delay his satellite-calibrated progress. A mile from the eastern end of the town, a new roundabout pushes him on to the arterial road that sweeps down to the new river bridge, the price of Tesco's admission into the district[36]. The signs steer him into the Parc Manwerthu Glyndŵr, not that he's ever noticed that. He does however notice dayglo signs advertising Final Sale Reductions in the window of the Celtic Crafts superstore across the way from Tesco, and curses the fact that he's already running behind schedule and won't have time to look for a

birthday present for his wife, back in Telford.

New roads have begat new housing estates too, Ystad Hen Brifddinas on the north-eastern flank of town and Parc Maen Llwyd to the west, between the old Aberystwyth road and the river bank. Machynlleth's population, which had hovered between two and two and a half thousand for 150 years, has doubled in less than ten. Local families, mainly the children of Bryn-y-Gog and Cae Crwn[37], occupy the couple of dozen affordable homes within their limits. Commuters – working in Aberystwyth, Newtown, even Shrewsbury and Birmingham – and retirees from the West Midlands fill the substantial remainder, those presumably declared unaffordable by default.

It is Wednesday, market day since 1291. The axis of the town moving north to the retail park has left a few gaps along Heol Maengwyn, but the market stalls fill them in temporarily. Tesco promised that their arrival would help the main street boom, but few supermarket punters bother to combine their big shop with a sidle along the narrow pavement into town, mainly because signs warn them that if they occupy a car parking space for longer than two hours, they have agreed to pay £70 for the privilege[38]. There's no butcher's or bakery any more, and the Co-op has become a

Netto, but a new rash of charity shops has made Machynlleth a favourite hunting ground for Aberystwyth students looking for the perfect fancy dress outfit.

Dividing the main street from the retail park is the jagged crag of Pen yr Allt, known more fondly as Mach Mountain. As you stand on Heol Maengwyn, cast your eyes up to the big, whitewashed slogan that has been regularly – and mysteriously – painted on its face since the 1990s. CYMRU RYDD! it declares. Free Wales! There is no truth in the rumour that it is soon to be changed to Buy One, Get One Free Wales!

LLANBRYNMAIR

Talking of the escapades of Samuel Roberts, Victorian Radical minister and founder of a disastrous Welsh colony in Tennessee, Jan Morris makes an uncharacteristic slip-up in placing him in 'Llanbrynmair, Gwynedd'[39]. It's an entirely understandable mistake. Sat in her Llanystumdwy study, she typed the name Llanbrynmair, and the image that sprang to mind was of a Meirionnydd-like landscape and the sensation of a stubborn, bulwark fastness. Both could easily make you slide the word Gwynedd in without thinking, for Llanbrynmair does have the feeling of an exclave of the muttering, mountainous north-west dropped like a lump of grit into the heart of the *mwynder* Maldwyn. That it breeds a Gwynedd-like chippy insularity is immediately explained if you raise your eyes over the village and look to the east: there, slashed through the hills, is the Talerddig gap, the favoured route of every invader coming from the Severn plain. Like Dolwyddelen, Dolbadarn or Castell-y-Bere, this was the last redoubt.

There should be a castle here too, you think, and there was. No masonry now, but still the imposing grassy tump of Tafolwern, where the castle of Owain Prince of Cyfeiliog[40] once sat, its gaze straight up the gap to the east (and allowing too a weather eye to be kept on the Twymyn valley to the south and the passes to the north and west). Tafolwern is a favourite haunt of Dr Nicholas Fenwick, a Farmers Union of Wales official and translator of a hitherto lost text about the area, the *Darlundraeth o Fachynlleth a'i Hamgylchoedd* of 1854[41]. Nick takes me up there one Sunday afternoon, and I can see why the place excites him so much. The position is perfect. The

Twymyn and Rhiw Saeson rivers almost meet just south of the mound, with just the width of a country lane separating their sweeping meanders. This, Nick believes, was the main gatehouse into the castle complex, for the rivers then arc out around the site, before meeting for real just to its north. Not only did this give an uninterrupted view up to Talerddig and any advancing hordes, it is a near complete natural moat. Nick's young daughters, Myfanwy and Morfudd, scamper excitedly around the mound, the streams and the sessile oak woods that cluster on their banks. The steam from their laughter curls up into the wintry air, hanging just that little bit longer than expected, like playful will-o'-the-wisps dancing in the moss-draped branches. This is a place beyond time, a crossroads of history, and it completely enchants me. The main A470 lies only a couple of hundred yards to the north, and there's a vast caravan park between us, but none of that seeps into the eyes, ears or consciousness.

By comparison, the village itself of Llanbrynmair, just up the lane, feels like a gatecrasher, and so it is. It came into existence only when a new turnpike road was built from Machynlleth to Newtown in 1821, replacing the old hilltop drovers route further south. As a staging post for the mail coach, the new settlement became known by the name of its coaching inn, the Wynnstay Arms[42], for the name of Llanbrynmair was used for the original village two miles south, on the other side of Tafolwern. Only when the railway arrived in 1862 – the Talerddig gap, as ever, proving to be the greatest obstacle to its progress – did the new settlement start to outflank the old. The name of Llanbrynmair followed the population, and became grafted on to the new village.

The old village, known now simply as Llan, has endured all the same, perhaps better than would be expected. The newer village might have the pub, the shop, the school, the community hall, the bus stops, the railway, some workshops and industrial units, but it could never compete with the original church, settled deep into its eponymous llan on the bryn (hill) dedicated to Mair (Mary). In 1868, the new settlement built a church, dedicated to St John, but it was little admired, little used and fell into ruin after only a century, finally being demolished and replaced by a 1970s bungalow.

As the Victorians were fussing around building the new village and its unloved church, its medieval predecessor escaped their restorative zeal, and it remains one of rural Montgomeryshire's most intact and impressive, particularly for its setting. Here is a church that seems to crown its modest hill with the lightest, yet at the same time deepest, of touches. It sits in a landscape of many apparently similar green swellings, happy to be part of the crowd but not averse either to pulling rank and demanding deference. It is impossible not to afford it just that, for as you climb through the circular churchyard, sat high above the road, the church seems to grow in stature in a way far greater than a mere change of perspective. Every sheep-contoured slope and distant farmhouse seems to be taking its cue from this hallowed spot.

The church is locked, but out of nowhere looms a local man, who guides me to the house of the key-holder. We chat by a roaring fire in his parlour. I tell them where I live, less than ten miles away. Both men are lifelong parishioners of Llanbrynmair, but neither has ever visited my village: it is beyond their pale, across at least one invisible divide. Key in hand, I explore the church in the effusive company of the man I first encountered. He's not been to church since the day his mother died; he could keep the pretence up no longer. In his boyhood, he'd been a regular bell-ringer here, and as I'm examining the stark, sober interior of the large, single-cell church, I hear the bells start to clang out across the wide valley. Heading up into the tower, I find him chirruping with glee as he tugs the ropes of the three seventeenth century bells. They, and he, are in fine voice.

And like many a Gwynedd bastion, the voices of this singular parish have been carried far beyond its limits, although the bells of the established church were positively hushed next to the sonorous clamour of the nonconformist *capelwyr*. Samuel Roberts (1800-85), he of the misguided colony in Tennessee[43], was the minister of the Hen Gapel[44], and became a national leader for pacifist and abolitionist causes. A later member of the same congregation, Iorwerth Peate (1901-82), founded the Welsh Folk Museum at St Fagan's, near Cardiff. Both had their eye on the Talerddig gap. In the 1850s, Roberts was desperate to see the railway come through it, and wrote angrily about the delays that held it back. Ninety years later, Peate warily eyed the secularising, anglicising influences pouring through it, and dedicated his life to countering them. Now, we thank the gods that the railway line still exists, and that it hasn't been turned instead into a dual carriageway, speeding in yet more caravans and jetskis from the Midlands.

A crossroads, a bulwark, an exclave of Gwyneddness in Powys, a place apart. Hard and hard-living too: Llanbrynmair has never been a soft option. A never-quite town, equally inconvenient for Machynlleth and Newtown, this "self-centred and self-contained community", according to Alun D.W. Owen in his memoir *A Montgomeryshire Youth*, pleases no-one but itself. Even the name raises quiet hackles in other parts of the old Cyfeiliog district. Folk are quite simply a little bit scared of the place, have heard stories of bloodied noses, broken limbs and drunken bust-ups, have been warned off by their well-meaning parents. Whispers abound that the drip-drip of lead into the local water supply has had noticeable, and terrible, effect on the parishioners. Native boy Alun Owen spells it out: "Indeed, to walk through the village square on a warm Saturday evening after, say, a day at the seaside was not unlike making one's way through a fieldful of bullocks." The bullocks still graze, the bells still ring. And the gap is forever minded.

RED AND GREEN

Our new house, Rhiw Goch, the Red Hill. Looking out over the Iron Age hillfort of Fron Goch, the Red Breast. There are many splashes of coch on the map, but we're moving in through May, and red is nowhere to be seen. All is green. Green in every direction, and in an infinite variety of shades, from the feathery lime of the beech in first leaf to the dark, army camouflage of ivy in sunless corners. Green so luminous that it tinges the sky. I realise that 'green' must be the most overused word in this book, but it cannot be helped. No Powys landscape can be described without recourse to it and its easy suggestibility. Titania, queen of the fairies in *A Midsummer Night's Dream*, talked of "the quaint mazes in the wanton green", and as I look around this new world, one so unknown, yet destined to become so familiar, her words float in the damp[45] sky, coiling around bulbous oaks and wind-racked thorns. The Wanton Green is here, now.

I'm drenched in it. The green of this corner of Montgomeryshire is soothing, yet sometimes suffocating too. I walk out into it unprepared, and it batters me, eats me whole and spits me back out again, a spent husk. I have never known such greenness, an endless rippling sea of it crashing in all directions. It gives me the unsteadiness of sea legs too: chlorophyll as chloroform.

Paradoxically, the green seems deeper the murkier the skies above it. On a bright day, the glowing patches drifting across the fields and the playful, dappled sunlight in a wood are phosphorescent in their loveliness, but in a way that pirouettes across my vision with fairy grace. Go out under leaden skies, or at dusk, and the depth of the green sucks you in like quicksand, holds you under and allows no escape. It has much the same effect as those blue fairy lights recently so popular at Christmas, which seem almost to give out some kind of anti-light, pulling your vision down into its unfathomable depths, rather than pushing it out into illuminated clarity. There is form for this chromatic ambiguity. In Welsh of course, *glas* traditionally meant both blue and green; *gwyrdd* was only coined latterly to differentiate the two hues. Place-names demonstrate etymology better than anything, and despite it being the overwhelming background colour of the country, the only names in Wales that include *gwyrdd* are modern concoctions, usually newbuild estates called Cae Gwyrdd and so on. No shortage of places with *glas* or *-las* in their names though. There's only one word to cover both green and blue in many Asian languages too, as well as Euskara, the Basque tongue and surely the true winner of the hotly-contested title for the 'oldest living language in Europe'[46].

In the spectrum of colour, green lies in the middle, between the colder shades of blue, indigo and violet, and the warmer tones of yellow, orange and red. That fits too. Having hovered on borders and boundaries, the 'fold in the map', for so long, my new home is firmly in the middle; there are no edges to hang on to for safety. It lies in a plump, settled landscape whose identity has remained unperturbed for centuries. And green, the middle colour, the still place at the heart of the spectrum, is its natural colour.

Green is good, we know that. Green is clean, sustainable, fresh, bright, natural. We hear it all the time: greenwash sprayed with all the finesse of a tom cat over every clumsy pronouncement, lofty promise and spurious claim. 'For the sake of the environment': a phrase that has almost become as hollow and inverted as 'for your safety and security…'. But green is also nauseous or naïve, and moving here, I catch myself feeling both. Friends profess their jealousy at our new place dug deep into its bower; they too are green.

I've sometimes joked that my love for Wales was ignited at my birth, when Tom Jones was top of the charts for a month and a half with 'The Green, Green Grass of Home'[47]. I imagine that on that Sunday evening, a week before Christmas nearly half a century ago, I emerged in Solihull Maternity Hospital, and somewhere in the distance, The Voice was booming out of a tinny transistor. "Hair of gold and lips like cherries / It's good to touch the green, green grass of home". Destiny was set.

We were never a bookish household. The one set of bookshelves in my childhood home was a Middle England read-by-numbers: the *Complete Works of Shakespeare*, the complete works of James Herriot, annuals of Giles cartoons, an untouched set of hardback Dickens, a whole shelf of Readers' Digest condensed novels and an assortment of Lovely Britain-style books, Christmas presents from book clubs mainly. Lavish with illustration and maps alike, I lost weeks combing through those books, imbibing their clipped histories and sense of promise. One made a particular mark on me, the 1980 *Sunday Times Book of the Countryside*, diagrams, maps, photos and text galore, and an introduction by John Fowles. One sentence in the introduction to chapter nine ('Seasons in the Countryside') never left me: "Not for nothing did the Apollo 11 astronauts on their way to the moon in 1969 comment upon how green the British Isles seemed when viewed from space". The words are written in white over a double-page photo of luxuriant greenery, a grey farm wallowing in the most wanton green imaginable: hills, trees, hedges, fields bursting with rude health. The rhododedrons are flowering too; it is late May, early June. And you note from the caption, we are in "characteristic lushness seen here near Newtown, Powys". Of course. The middle kingdom is the middle colour, and this is the start of my biggest adventure yet.

My lights change to green. Go for it.

Notes

1. The eastern side of Montgomeryshire receives considerably less than half of the rainfall that falls in the north and west of the county.
2. Pole = (Welsh)Pool
3. Rhydwhyman is a typical borderland corruption of the Welsh name, Rhyd Chwima, the 'rushing (or swift) ford'.
4. Four if you include the castle. The oldest gaol – on the slope behind the town hall – was built in 1735, about the same time as the smaller House of Correction, on Pool Road. The new County Gaol, of 1830, complete with its hugely impressive entrance arch, is at the bottom of Gaol Road.
5. Even the railway passed it by. There was a Montgomery station on the Cambrian line, but nearly two miles north-west of the town. Trains on the line still run today (the service between Birmingham and Aberystwyth/Pwllheli), though the station closed in 1965, and is now a private dwelling.
6. The same family that owned Powis Castle, and dominated life for centuries in the upper Severn valley. The Herbert tomb of 1600 in Montgomery's parish church is staggering: Sir Richard and his wife lie in effigy, with his shrouded cadaver lurking beneath. Their eight children – including the mystic poet George Herbert – look on angelically.
7. Entitled 'Weimar in Wales': http://www.newstatesman.com/200401050012
8. Afon Einion is an alternative name for the Afon Banwy.
9. The physicality of her adoration can be seen in the lyric of one of her most famous hymns, 'Wele'n sefyll rhwng y myrtwydd'. Christ is 'Gwyn a gwridog, teg o bryd' (White and flushed, fair of face'). She looks forward to 'Henffych fore / Y caf ei weled fel y mae' ('morning greetings, that I shall see him as he is'), and the hymn concludes with the rousing ambition 'O! am aros / Yn ei gariad ddyddiau f'oes' ('Oh! to linger / In his love for all of my life').
10. "red cheeks and big hands".
11. Siân James is the vivacious folk singer from Llanerfyl, who commands any room, of any size, in which she performs. With her musician husband Gwyn Jones, she has established a thriving recording studio, Recordiau Bos, in an old chapel in her home village.
12. "the mellowness of Montgomeryshire".
13. Ode to the pubic region.
14. Ode to the cunt.
15. Text and translation from Dafydd Johnston's *Canu Maswedd yr Oesoedd Canol / Medieval*

Welsh Erotic Poetry.
16. The new city plan was the main reason that Caersws kept its railway station, when, in the mid 1960s, Carno, Montgomery and Llanbrynmair lost theirs along the same line.
17. The spellings of the day.
18. The election of October 1964 had returned the first Labour government since 1951, albeit with a wafer thin majority of just four seats.
19. www.bbc.co.uk/wales/mid/sites/newtown/pages/clubbing.shtml
20. Even the lady behind the desk – the town Mayor no less – said "Robert Owen? I just find him boring." Her subjects seem to agree with her.
21. In the nineteenth century, at the height of the town's textile trade, Newtown even played up to the hubristic moniker of being 'the Leeds of Wales'.
22. And for higher mountains than these, purple and eventually snow-white for the summits.
23. At the time of writing (June 2011), rumours are circling that the days of the Newtown shop are numbered. Certainly, looking at the list of Ashley stores these days, Newtown stands out as an anomaly. The vast majority are in the south of England, in the well-heeled commuter towns of the Home Counties especially, plus the inevitable outlets in mega-malls such as Bluewater, Meadowhall, Merry Hill, Westfield and Bicester Village. The company's 2011 Annual Report states that "our store realignment programme continues in 2011, based on our stringent property selection criteria". In the previous year, the "store realignment programme" had seen two open and sixteen close.
24. See http://www.wix.com/machdeco/annifyr#!biography
25. The Welsh name is Penffordd-las, 'the head (or end) of the green road', which possibly refers to the Roman highway that bumps grumpily over the moor through the village.
26. There's a third tiny settlement up here as well: the Forestry Commission hamlet of Llwynygog, built between 1949 and 1951. The plan was for eighty houses, a school, a shop and a village hall, but only twenty houses, and no amenities, were ever built. The bleak, truncated spirit of the place continues.
27. *A History of the Dylife Mines and Surrounding Area* by Michael Brown (published 2010), a much-expanded version of Michael's 2006 book *Dylife*.
28. In its upper reaches, known as Nant Goch.
29. *The Penny Cyclopædia of the Society for the Diffusion of Useful Knowledge.*
30. Had it flowed west instead, the water could reach the Irish Sea within fifteen miles.
31. When you see a red light, stop here.
32. Nor, for that matter, enrage those of a furiously unionist persuasion to take up their pens in order to berate her for her fanciful thinking.
33. The other area that Tesco were concentrating on at this time was the Highlands and islands of Scotland, which, taken together with the thin soil of Powys, does rather spell out the full scope of their ambition for ubiquity. Inverness, the modest capital of the Highlands, has four branches. Every little helps.
34. The Garsiwn, a name that comes from a Cymricisation of the word 'garrison', is the lowest patch of Machynlleth, both topographically and figuratively. On the western flank of the town down below the clock tower and Heol Doll (Toll Street), it housed the worst of the flannel weavers' hovels, the town's principal tannery, the tip, the municipal gasworks and was cited in numerous nineteenth century sanitary reports as the epicentre of any outbreaks of disease.
35. When the railway finally arrived in Machynlleth on 3rd January 1863, the town's direction of focus changed overnight. Until then, it looked west to the sea, via the port and shipbuilding yard of Derwenlas. The railway necessitated the re-routing of the Dyfi estuary at Derwenlas, and the port died. And from then Machynlleth looked east, its new iron railroad umbilically connecting it to the Midlands of England. In the decade that followed the opening of the railway, the town's population ballooned by 25%, all from beyond the

hitherto tight confines of the Dyfi valley. In-migration is no new thing.
36. Big supermarket developments frequently include their building of new infrastructure as part of the deal. Welshpool, Newtown and Llandrindod received re-worked roads and a whole new traffic system; Porthmadog got a new secondary school. The price for Tesco in Machynlleth will almost inevitably be a new Dyfi bridge and roads to whoosh the traffic around the town's perimeter, where all routes lead not to the clock tower but into their own gargantuan car park.
37. Bryn-y-Gog and Cae Crwn are the two big post-war estates built on the eastern edge of the town to relieve pressure on the crowded Victorian terraces of the Garsiwn to the west.
38. As is the case at the Tesco store in Porthmadog, and many others.
39. In her magisterial book, *Wales: Epic Views of a Small Country*, a revamp of her earlier *The Matter of Wales*.
40. Cyfeiliog is the ancient name of this western portion of Montgomeryshire, always a pivotal place in Welsh history. In the twelfth century, the castle at Tafolwern was its capital, Owain its Prince. Invasion through the Talerddig gap was not a one-way affair: Owain surged east and conquered the upper Severn valley, founding Y Gastell Goch, the red castle, known now as Powis Castle, near Welshpool.
41. *The Portrait of Machynlleth and its Surroundings* was a book expanded from the essay that won the Machynlleth Literary Society's prize in 1854. It was, in fact, the only entry in the competition, but that is not to take away from its quality. Remarkably, its author Evan Jones (under the pen name of Caradwc o Lancarfan) was only seventeen at the time. Nick Fenwick's translation into English of Jones' work was published in 2009 by Coch-y-Bontddu bookshop of Machynlleth.
42. The prevalence of the name Wynnstay hereabouts is thanks to the Wynn family's status as Lords of the Manor of Cyfeiliog since 1750.
43. Samuel Roberts was the ringleader of Llanbrynmair's second wave of emigration to America. The first groups, in 1795, settled relatively successfully in Pennsylvania and Ohio. Roberts' expedition, in 1856-7, headed south to Tennessee, a slave state. This immediately put the abolitionist Welsh nonconformists at odds with their host area, but this was nothing compared with the main problem that the land they believed to be theirs by dint of having been 'bought' legitimately, transpired to be much disputed. The onslaught of the American Civil War finished the project off for good.
44. Old chapel, up a side lane at Dolfach, a mile east of Llanbrynmair village. Founded in 1739, Montgomeryshire's second such meeting house, it provided the area's nonconformist worshippers with their first dedicated chapel, although regular (and growing) congregations had been gathering since the 1670s in a lean-to at Tŷ Mawr.
45. And 'damp' probably runs 'green' quite close in the overused stakes.
46. Although vainglorious boasts that Cymraeg is 'the oldest living language in Europe' are mercifully fewer on the ground these days, they still pop up with tedious predictability. It isn't.
47. 'The Green, Green Grass of Home' by Tom Jones went to number one on the 3rd December 1966 and stayed there for seven weeks. Although often thought of as a simple tale of joyful homecoming, that element of the song is soon revealed to be a fantasy, for the protagonist is in fact on death row, and is only dreaming of home. The *hiraeth* inherent in Jones' interpretation of the song must also have chimed with the national mood in the wake of the Aberfan disaster on 21st October 1966.

WORKS CONSULTED

AA, *Touring Guide to Wales*, 1975
Barfoot, James, *Plas Machynlleth*, 1996
Barnes, David, *The Companion Guide to Wales*, Companion Guides 2005
Bebb, W. Ambrose, translated by Marc K. Stengel, *A Welsh Hundred: Glimpses of Life in Wales*, Authorhouse 2008
Booth, Richard, *My Kingdom of Books*, Y Lolfa 1999
Briwnant-Jones, Gwyn, *Picturesque Dyfi Valley*, Gomer 2002
Briwnant-Jones, Gwyn, *Railway through Talerddig*, Gomer 1990
Brown, Michael, *Dylife*, Y Lolfa 2005
Bullough, Tom, *The Claude Glass*, Sort Of Books 2007
Burnham, Helen, *Clwyd and Powys*, Cadw/HMSO 1995
Butler, Lawrence & Knight, Jeremy K., *Dolforwyn Castle / Montgomery Castle*, Cadw 2004
Caradawc o Lancarfan (translated by Nicholas Fenwick), *A Portrait of Machynlleth and its Surroundings*, Coch-y-Bontddu Books 2009
Chatwin, Bruce, *On the Black Hill*, Jonathan Cape 1982
Christiansen, Rex, *Cambrian Lines* (British Railway Pictorial), Ian Allen Publishing 2004
Condry, William, *Exploring Wales*, Faber & Faber 1970
Conradi, Peter J., *At the Bright Hem of God: Radnorshire Pastoral*, Seren 2009
Davies, David Wyn, *A Mach Lad*, Machynlleth & District Civic Society 2007
Davies, David Wyn, *The Town of a Prince*, Machynlleth Rotary Club 1991
Davies, Dewi, *Bridges of Breconshire*,
Davies, John, *A History of Wales*, Penguin 1994
Davies, John and Delyth, Marian *Cymru – y 100 lle i'w gweld cyn marw*, Y Lolfa 2009
Davies, Russell, *Hope and Heartbreak, A Social History of Wales and the Welsh 1776-1871*, University of Wales Press 2005
Davis, Paul, *Sacred Springs*, Blorenge Books 2003
Edlin, Herbert L. (Ed.), *Cambrian Forests*, HMSO 1959
Evans, A.T.D., *Border Wanderings*, A.T.D. Evans 2008
Evans, Gwynfor and Delyth, Marian, *Cymru o Hud*, Y Lolfa 2001
Evans, Gwynfor, *For the Sake of Wales*, Welsh Academic Press 2001
Farr, Martyn, *The Secret World of Porth-yr-Ogof*, Gomer 1998

Gardner, Don, *The Vagabond Books of Mid Wales*, assorted, 1960s-70s
Gerald of Wales, *The Journey Through Wales / The Description of Wales*, Penguin 1978
Godwin, Fay and Toulson, Shirley, *The Drovers' Roads of Wales*, Whittet Books 1987
Griffiths, Anthony, *Elenydd*, Gwasg Carreg Gwalch 2010
Griffiths, Beryl H., *Merched Gwyllt Cymru / Wild Welsh Women*, Gwasg Gwynedd 2007
Griffiths, Brian S., *The Secret and Sacred Beacons*, Gwasg Carreg Gwalch 2001
Gruffydd Rhys, Ann, *Nansi Dolwar: Stori Ann Griffiths*, Gwasg Bryntirion 2005
Gunn, Ray and Julia, *Esgairgeiliog Ceinws in pictures and words*, Efel Productions 2003
Hart, David et al., *Border Country*, Woodwind Publications 1991
Haslam, Richard, *The Buildings of Wales: Powys* (Pevsner Guides), Yale University Press 1979
Howse, W. H., *Radnorshire*, E. J. Thurston 1949
Hughes, Wendy, *The Story of Brecknock*, Gwasg Carreg Gwalch 1995
Hughes, T. J., *Wales's Best One Hundred Churches*, Seren 2006
Humprheys, Melvin and others, *Llanfyllin Portrait of an Age*, Llanfyllin & District Civic Society 2002
Humphries, John, *Freedom Fighters: Wales' Forgotten War 1963-1993*, University of Wales Press 2008
Jenkins, Simon, *Wales: Churches, Houses, Castles*, Allen Lane 2008
Johnston, Dafydd, *Canu Maswedd yr Oesoedd Canol / Medieval Welsh Erotic Poetry*, Seren 1999
Jones, Cyril, *Maldwyn, Cyfres Broydd Cymru*, Gwasg Carreg Gwalch 2003
Kilvert, Francis, *Diaries*, Jonathan Cape 1969
Llewellyn, Alun and Vaughan-Thomas, Wynford, *The Shell Guide to Wales*, Michael Joseph 1969
Milton, David, *The Elan Valley Way*, Meridian Books 1999
Moore-Colyer, Richard, *Roads & Trackways of Wales*, Landmark Publishing 2007
Morris, Chris, *A Portrait of the Severn*, Tanners Yard Press 2006
Morris, E. Ronald, *Atlas Hanesyddol Maldwyn*, Y Lolfa 1988
Morris, Jan, *Wales*, Penguin 2000
Morris, Jan and Morys, Twm, *A Machynlleth Triad*, Penguin 1993

WORKS CONSULTED

Musson, Chris, *Wales from the Air – Patterns of Past and Present*, Royal Commission of the Ancient and Historical Monuments of Wales 1994
National Trust, *Powis Castle* 2000
Owen, Alun D.W., *A Montgomeryshire Youth*, Compton Books 2000
Powysland Club, *The Montgomeryshire Collections*, annual
Ray, Rebbecca, *A Certain Age*, Penguin 1998
Ray, Rebbecca, *Newfoundland*, Hamish Hamilton 2005
Richards, Alun John, *Fragments of Mine & Mill in Wales*, Gwasg Carreg Gwalch 2002
Roberts, Dewi, *A Powys Anthology*, Gwasg Carreg Gwalch 2003
Roberts, J.E. and Owen, Robert, *The Story of Montgomeryshire*, Educational Publishing Company 1916
Sager, Peter, *Wales*, Pallas Guides 1991
Salter, Mike, *The Old Parish Churches of Mid Wales*, Folly Publications 1991
Stone, Moira K., *Mid Wales Companion*, Anthony Nelson 1989
Thomas, Roger, *The Brecon Beacons National Park*, Webb & Bower 1987
Thomas, W.S.K., *Journeys into Brecon's Past*, Gomer 1996
Wakelin, Peter and Griffiths, Ralph A. (Ed.), *Tysorau Cudd: Darganfod Treftadaeth Cymru*, Royal Commission on the Ancient and Historical Monuments of Wales 2008
Ward Lock & Company, *Llandrindod Wells and Central Wales*, 1910
Watkins, Alfred, *The Old Straight Track*, Abacus 1974
Welton, Ann & John, *The Story of Montgomery*, Logaston Press 2003
Whittle, Elisabeth, *The Historic Gardens of Wales*, Cadw/HMSO 1992
Williams, Raymond, *The Fight for Manod*, Chatto & Windus 1979
Wilson, Colin, *Wales Leisure Atlas*, Hamlyn 1981

THE PHOTOGRAPHS

Streetscape, Presteigne	18
The Cornewall Lewis Monument, New Radnor	19
Atop Powys County Council HQ, Llandrindod Wells	22
Llandrindod Wells	23
Sign on the A44, Penybont	25
To the races, Penybont	26
The Committee and prizeware, Penybont trotting races	28
Crossroads of a nation, Rhayader	30
One of many pub options, Rhayader	32
Drinking fountain, Elan Village	35
Radnor 2000 memorial below Caban Coch dam, Elan Valley	36
Old saw, Safn-y-Coed	39
Lane, Llandeuddwr Common	42
Royal Welsh showground	44
Rhulen church	47
Disserth church	48
Footpath above Llanbadarn-y-Garreg	51
Forestry Commission landscaping	52
Llanstephan bridge	53
Sugar Loaf station	55
Heart of Wales railway at Builth Road	57
Offa's Dyke, near Montgomery	65
Sycarth	68
Oak at Sycarth	69
Breidden Hill, quarry and Rodney's Pillar	72
Harry Tuffin's, Churchstoke	75
Bookshop, Hay-on-Wye	78
Pavement, Hay-on-Wye	79
View from Llandefalle churchyard	83
Infantryman statue at the Dering Lines, Brecon	89
Brecon library	91
The Beacons	93
Beacons lay-by on the A470	94
Partrishow church	96
Field near Crickhowell	98
Powys, Texas at Penwyllt	101
Old railway station, Penwyllt	104
The 'dual carriageway' on to the Epynt from Llywel	106

THE PHOTOGRAPHS 207

The FIBUA mock German village, Epynt	108
Oak wood at Llangammarch Wells	111
Old garage, Builth Wells	113
A470, near Cwmbach Llechryd	115
Llywelyn memorial, Cilmeri	117
Goat Inn, Llanfihangel-yng-Ngwynfa	122
Ynyscedwyn iron works, Ystradgynlais	132
Camddwr Bleiddiad on the Afon Irfon	135
Glaslyn, on the slopes towards Pumlumon	137
Pumlumon stream	140
The way to Dyfi Junction	142
Dyfi Junction station	144
View above Esgairgeiliog	146
Forestry above Esgairgeiliog	150
Gardens, Powis Castle	155
Montgomery	156
Bunner's store, Montgomery	158
Llama farmers in Dyffryn Banwy	160
Dam at Lake Vyrnwy	165
Llanfihangel-yng-Ngwynfa church	168
Ann Griffiths memorial, Pont Llogel	169
Newtown station	172
Newtown	175
Pryce-Jones warehouse, Newtown	177
Butchers, Llanidloes	179
Laura Ashley's grave, Carno	181
Llanidloes	182
Wynford Vaughan-Thomas memorial, Dylife	184
Rusted iron barrel, Dylife	185
Dylife	187
Glynd?r memorial, Y Plas, Machynlleth	189
Machynlleth	191
Outside the Co-op, Machynlleth	193
Hillside above Llanbrynmair	195

THE AUTHOR

Mike Parker was born in 1966, and lived in Worcestershire, London, Cambridge and Birmingham before moving to mid Wales in 2000. He'd been co-writing the *Rough Guide to Wales* for nearly ten years by then, and since landing in y Canolbarth, has written and presented seven series of travelogues for ITV Wales (*Coast to Coast* and *Great Welsh Roads*). Other books include *Neighbours From Hell?*, about the attitude of the English towards the Welsh, *Map Addict*, a bestselling love letter to the Ordnance Survey, and *The Wild Rover*, in which he explores the tangled history of the humble footpath and its place in our life, landscape, culture and history. He also does occasional stand-up comedy, acting and broadcasting. After ten years in Esgairgeiliog in the Dulas valley near Machynlleth, Mike recently moved to the Montgomeryshire boondocks in the parish of Darowen.

INDEX

A470 8, 29, 113-16, 195
AA Touring Guide to Wales 121
Abberley Hill 128n
Abbey Cwmhir 117; Happy Union (pub) 124
Abercamlais 104
Abercraf 103
Aberedw 46, 48-54, 116
Abergavenny 97, 99
Abergwesyn 136
Abergwesyn Pass 133-4, 135
Aberystwyth 18, 142, 143, 174
Allchin, A.M. 169
Allt Dolanog 168
Ann Griffiths Trail 164
Ashley, April 86n
Ashley, Bernard 179
Ashley, Laura 179-181
Atkinson, Tiffany 32

Afon Bachawy 51
Bailey, Joseph 99
Baldng, Claire: *Britain by Bike* 66; *Ramblings* 66
Afon Banwy 154
Banwy valley 182
Barnes, David: *Companion Guide to Wales* 46, 121, 155-6
Basini, Mario 100
Bates, Mick 146
Battle 125n
Beacham, Arthur 173
Beeching, Richard 56, 143
Begwn hills 46, 83
Berriew 9, 146, 155
Berwyn mountains 9
Birmingham 13, 34, 35-6, 37
Bishop's Castle 76, 159, 186
Black Mountain 93
Black Mountains 50, 83, 93, 94-5, 97
Blue Guide to Wales 121
Booth, Richard 77-81, 122; *My Kingdom of Books* 79-80
Borrow, George: *Wild Wales* 138
Breconshire 7, 12, 13, 34, 38, 82, 89, 98, 99, 101, 107, 124, 157, 172
Brecon 7-8, 49, 71, 88-92, 103, 105, 142, 157; The Bulwark 88-89; Brecknock Museum 125n; Brecknock Shire Hall 88; Cathedral 89-90; Christ College 90; Dering Lines 88; Plough chapel 90; St Mary's church 89; South Wales Borderers Museum 88; The Watton 88; *Pubs:* Boar's Head 90; Bull's Head 90; Camden Arms 90; Clarence 90; George 90; Gremlin 90; Old Cognac 90; Punch Bowl 90; Puzzle Tree 90; Wellington 90; Wheatsheaf 90
Brecon Beacons 50, 92-7, 114, 131
Brecon Beacons National Park 92-3
Brecon Jazz Festival 91-2
Bredwardine 86n
Breidden Hills 71-72
British National Party 161-4
Brown, Michael 185-6
Brycheiniog 125n
Brynmawr 130
Bucknell 66
Bwlch-yr-Efengel (Gospel Pass) 94
Builth Road 56
Builth Wells 8, 49, 58, 105, 109, 111, 112, 113, 115, 116, 124; Castle 8-9; Wyeside 8
Bullough, Tom 32, 48-54; *The Claude Glass* 51-2
Bunner, Robert H. 157
Burton, Ernest 73
Burton, Uriah 73

Afon Caebitra 186
Caersws 115, 171, 177; Moat Lane Junction 143
River Cain 85n
Camddwr Bleiddiad 136
Capel-y-Ffin 94-5
CARAD 33
Cardiganshire 173
Carmarthenshire Fan 50
Carno 179-80; Ty Brith 123
Carno valley 182
Castell-y-Bere 194
Castle Idris 66
Cefn-Coed-y-Cymer 130
Cefnllys 59n
Cefn-llys Isaf 162
Centre for Alternative Technology 191-2

Charles (Prince of Wales) 9, 155
Chatwin, Bruce 95; *On the Black Hill* 46, 48, 51, 126n
Chirbury 157
Churchstoke 74-7; Harry Tuffin's 74-7
Cilfaesty Hill 85n
Cilmeri 9, 56, 116-20; Llywelyn memorial 119-20; Prince Llywelyn (pub) 118
Claerwen 37
Clare, John 150
Clatter 115
Cleobury Mortimer 76
River Clun 66
Clun 159
Clun Forest 65
Afon Clywedog 186-8
Clyro 46, 51, 81-4
Commins Coch 115
Condry, William: *Exploring Wales* 121
Cooke, George Alexander: *Topography of Wales* 23
Cope, Julian 70-1
Cordell, Alexander: *Rape of the Fair Country* 100
Corn Du 93
Corndon Hill 76
Corris 148
Corwen 67
County Times 59n
Craig Goch reservoir 38
Craig-y-Nos 102-4
Craven Arms 76
Cregina 46
Cribarth 103
Crickhowell 97-101; Crickhowell Resource and Information Centre 126n
Cross gates 24
Crug Hwyel 126n
Cwm Twrch Uchaf 130; George IV (pub) 130
Cwmdeuddwr: Triangle (pub) 124
Cwmgiedd 131
Cwmllinau 114
Y Cymro 167
Cyfeiliog 12, 197
Cynghordy 56
River Cynllaith 67

Dafydd Llwyd 170

Daily Mail 78-9
Daily Post 167
Dan-yr-Ogof showcaves 103
Darby, Simon 161
Darlundraeth
Davies, Clement 173
Davies, Damian Walford 81-4
Davies, Deborah Kay 32
Davies, Glyn 146
Davies, Gwendolyne 175
Davies, John: *A History of Wales* 121
Davies, Margaret 175
Defoe, Daniel 125n
Delves, Paul 76
Denbighshire 7, 154
Derwenlas 141
Development Board for Rural Wales 79, 180
Devil's Bridge 186
Devil's Staircase 133-6
Dingle-du Bank 66
Dock Leaves 125n
Dolanog 164, 165, 167, 168; chapel 164, 168
Dolau 56, 57
Dolbadarn 194
Doldowlod 114
Dolfor 177
Dolobran 169
Dolwar Fach 168
Dolwyddelen 194
Dovaston, John 73
Afon Dulas 145, 147, 149, 187
Dyffryn Banwy 162, 165
Dyfi Estuary 7, 141, 174, 186, 187, 189
Dyfi forest 37
Dyfi Junction 141-145
Dyfnant forest 37
Dylife 183-188; Star Inn 124, 185

Edward I 116, 157
Edward VII 37, 126n
Edwards, O.M. 170
Afon Edw 49
Afon Einion 200n
Afon Elan 32
Elan Valley 34-8, 41, 105; visitor centre 36
Elan village 34-5, 37
Epynt 37, 105-9; Capel y Babell 107; Drovers Arms 105; military use 105-9

INDEX

Erwood 113-16
Esgair y Ffordd 141
Esgairfochnant 187
Esgairgeiliog 123, 145-51; also know as Ceinws 149
Evans, Gwynfor 136, 174
Evans, Rev J.M. 47
Evans, Ruth 165
Evans, Theophilus 110

Faenor 130
Felindre 66
Fenwick, Nicholas 194-5
Florence, Norman 80
Florence, Peter 53, 80
Foot and Mouth epidemic 108-09, 163
Forestry Commission 52, 141, 145, 164, 170
Free Wales Army 50, 118-19
Fron Goch 198

Fforde, Jasper 32
Fforest Fawr 93, 131

Garlick, Raymond 125n
Garth 112
Guardian 161
George, Russell 147
Gerallt Cymro (Gerald of Wales) 95, 120; *Itinerarium Kambriae* 121
Gigrin Farm 33
Gill, Eric 95
Glandyfi 142
Glansevern Gardens 155
Glantwymyn 123; Dovey Valley Hotel 123
Glanusk House 126n
Glaslyn 187
Afon Glesyrch 149
Glyndŵr's Way National Trail 186
Glyndyfrdwy 67-8
Gogin 66
Golden Valley 64
Green, Gordon 112
Green Man festival 100-01
Gregynog 175
Griffin, Edgar 161
Griffin, Nick 161-3
Griffiths, Ann 164-9,
Griffiths, Niall 162-3, 184
Afon Grwyne Fawr 95, 96

Gwenwynwyn 154
Gwerfyl Mechain 169-171; 'Cywydd y Cedor' 170
Gunn, Julia 149

Hafren forest 37
Hamer, George Frederick 173
Prince Harry 99
Hay on Wye 9, 46, 77-81, 82, 84, 94, 112, 124, 143; Three Tuns (pub) 122
Hay Bluff 83
Hay Festival 53, 77, 81
Heart of Wales Railway 54-9, 110
The Heartland: A Plan for Mid Wales 173-4
Afon Hengwm 140
Henry III 157
Henry IV 128n
Henry V 67-8, 120, 141
Herbert, Christian (6th Earl of Powis) 158
Herbert, John George (8th Earl of Powis) 155
Hereford 7, 12, 38,
Herefordshire 7, 64, 82
Herman, Josef 131, 133
Hooson, Emlyn 173
Housman, A.E. 82; *A Shropshire Lad* 82
Hughes, Simon 90
Humphreys, Emyr: *The Taliesin Tradition* 64
Afon Hyddgen 140

Ieuan Dyfi 169
Father Ignatius (Lyne, Rev J.L.) 95
The Independent 191
Iolo Goch 67
River Irfon 8, 109, 136
River Ithon 26, 31, 85n, 117-18

James, Sian 166
Jameson, Jack 160, 161, 163
Jenkins, Geraint 173
Jenkins, Kelvin 191
Jenkins, Simon 95; *Wales* 121
Jones, Carwyn 109
Jones, David 95
Jones, Dolly 121
Jones, Evan: *Darlundraeth o Fachynlleth a'i Hamgylchoedd* 194
Jones, Gwyn 166
Jones, Rhys 121

Jones, Roy 121
Jones, T. Harri: 'Llanafan Unrevisited' 121

Kerry 177
Kilvert Country 82
Kilvert, Francis 81-4, 95; *Diaries* 51, 82
Kington 46
Knighton (Tref y Clawdd) 46, 57, 58, 65, 66, 85n

Landor, Walter Savage 95
Lane, Flossie 123, 128n
Lee, Bishop Rowland 16
Legg-Bourke, Shan 99-100
Legg-Bourke, Tiggy 99, 100
Leighton Hall 64
Leintwardine 85n, 123
Lewis, Sir George Cornewall 19
Lewis, Gwyneth 9
Lhuyd, Humphrey: *Cambriae Typus* 65
Livesey, Richard 119
Logan, Andrew 155
Ludlow 38, 85n
River Lugg 19
Luttrell, Narcissus: *Brief Historical Relation of State Affairs* 16
Lymore Hall 158

Llanafan Fawr 120-5; church 120; Red Lion (pub) 120, 121-2, 125
Llanbadarn-y-Garreg 49, 50
Llanbister Road 56
Llanbrynmair 115, 194-7; Hen Gapel 197; St John's church 196-7; Wynnstay Arms 196
Llandefalle 126n
Llandegley 112; International Airport 12, 24-5
Llandeuddwr Common 41
Llandinshop 66
Llandovery 54, 57
Llandrindod Wells 8, 16, 19, 21-4, 27, 56, 57, 58, 109, 111, 112, 159, 190; Coleg Powys 22; Gwalia Hotel 17, 22; High Street 16-17; Holy Trinity church 21, 59n; Metropole Hotel 21; Norton's Garage 22; Pump House Hotel 16-17, 22; Radnorshire Museum 59n; Rock Gardens 8, 22-4; St Michael's church 59n; Welsh Assembly Government office 22; Ye Wells Hotel 22

Llaneleu 126n
Llanelwedd 42-5
Llanerfyl 161, 166; St Erfyl's church 162, 164
Llanfair Caereinion 162, 164, 166
Llanfair Hill 66
Llanfihangel Rhydithon 57
Llanfihangel-yng-Ngwynfa 123, 167; The Goat (pub) 123, 168; St Michael's church 167, 168
Llanfilo 126n
Llanfyllin 164, 167
Llangadfan 124, 164; Cann Office 124
Llangammarch Wells 8, 16, 58, 107, 109-10, 111-12; Ffynnon Drewllyd 110; Lake and Pump House Hotel 109-10
Llangasty-Talyllyn 126n
Llangedwyn 67, 167
Llangollen 7
Llangorse Lake 126n, 142
Llangurig 29, 39, 115
Llangynllo 56
Llanidloes 7, 124, 171, 178-83, 187; Great Oak Street 180; Minerva arts centre
Llanmynech 86n
Llanrhaeadr-ym-Mochnant 9
Llansantffraed 71
Llansantffraed-in-Elvel 71
Llansantffraid Cwmdeuddwr 71
Llansantffraid FC 85-86n
Llansantffraid-juxta-Usk 71
Llansantffraid-ym-Mechain 71, 73
Llanstephan 51
Llanwrtyd Wells 8, 55, 57, 58, 109, 110-112, 133-4, 136, 148; Dol-y-Coed Inn 110; Neuadd Arms 112
Llanwrybryn 186
Llanynys 117-18; St Llyr's church 117
Llowes 84
Lloyd-Lewis family (of Rhayader 61n
Llwyn-On reservoir 114
Llwynygog 201n
Llwynywermod 9, 155
Llyn Clywedog 188
Llyn Llygad Rheidol 139
Llyswen 39; Griffin (pub) 125
Llywel 107
Llywelyn ap Gutun 169
Llywelyn Fawr 117
Llywelyn the Last 9, 49, 116-20, 156;

INDEX

Llywelyn's cave 49-50

Machynlleth 9, 12, 13, 29, 69, 74, 76, 140, 143, 179, 180, 181, 188-94, 196, 197; Celtic Crafts 192; Heol Maengwyn 193, 194; Parc Manwerthu Glndwr 192; Tesco 190-2, 193
Madog 154
Maldwyn 145, 147, 148, 167, 176, 179, 194
Mallwyd 114
Marchant, Ian 20
Marsh, Richard 56
Mathafarn 170
Mathias, Roland 90; *The Flooded Valley* 125n
Mathrafal 154
Mawddach estuary 174
Meifod 154
Meirionnydd 43
Merioneth 145, 173
Merthyr Tydfil 7
Mid Wales Development Corporation 174
Mid Wales Industrial Development Association 172-3
The Midlands 7
Moel y Golfa 73
Monaughty Poeth 66
Monmouth 99
Monmouthshire 98
Montgomery 65, 154, 155-9, 186; Broad Street 157; Bunner's store 157-8; castle 159; County Gaol 157; Old Bell museum 157; Town Hill 159; war memorial 159
Montgomeryshire 7, 9, 12, 13, 38, 39, 69, 82, 123-4, 139, 141, 145, 146, 148, 149, 154-200
Montgomeryshire Express & Radnor Times 158
Morgan, Derek 39-41
Morgan, Jeff 126n
Morgan, Tommy 126n
Morgan, Veronica 39-41
Morgan, William 9, 20
Morris, Jan 95, 194; *A Machynlleth Triad* 190, 192; *The Matter of Wales* 121
Morys, Twm 124, 190
Mudiad Amddiffyn Cymru 61n
River Mule 85n

Mwyn, Rhys 164-7
Mynydd Bwlch-y-Groes 107, 108
Mynydd-y-Bryn 69
Mynydd y Drum 130
Mynydd Troed 50

Nant-y-Moch reservoir 138
National Eisteddfod 76, 103, 123
National Gazetteer 159
National Theatre of Wales 109
National Trust 154
Neath and Brecon Railway 102
Nether Skyborry 66
New Radnor 16, 17-19, 157; castle 17-18, 121; Lewis Memorial 19
New Statesman 161, 163
Newbridge-on-Wye 114
Newcastle 66
Newfoundland festival 31-2
Newsom, Joanna 100
Newtown 7-8, 74, 171-8, 180, 182, 190, 193, 196, 197; Crystals 176; Oriel Davies 175; Robert Owen Museum 176; Royal Welsh Warehouse 177; Theatr Hafren 175; Vastre industrial estate 180
Norton, Tom 22-3

Ogof Ffynnon Ddu 102
Old Radnor 16; Harp Inn 59n, 124; St Stephen's church 59n
Offa's Dyke 64-6, 156
Offa's Dyke National Trail 65-6
Opik, Lembit 146, 175-6
Oswestry (Croesowallt) 7, 64
Owain Cyfeiliog 154, 194
Owain Glyndŵr 18, 65, 67-68, 119, 137, 141, 189, 190; Covenant Stones 140-1
Owain de la Pole 154
Owen, Alun D.W.: *A Mongomeryshire Youth* 197
Owen, Jamie 90
Owen, Robert 176

Painscastle 46
Parker, Mike: *Great Welsh Roads* 36, 107; *Map Addict* 11; *Rough Guide to Wales* 10, 66, 105, 112
Parker-Bowles, Camilla 155
Patrishow 95-7; St Issui's church 96-7; St Issui's well 95

Patti, Adelina 102-4
Peate, Iorwerth 197
Pen Cerrig Calch 100-1
Pen yr Allt 194
Pen-y-Fal 126n
Pen-y-fan 93
Penpont 104
Pentiken 66
Pentrebach 107; Shoemakers Arms 107, 125
Penwyllt 101-5
Penybont 24-9, 112; Fleece Inn 60n; market 25; Severn Arms 25, 124; Thomas Shop 25; trotting racecourse 25-9
Penycrocbren 186
Piper, John 95
Plygain country 12, 164-71
Pont Llogel 164, 165
Pontrobert 167, 169
Pontsticill 130
Powell, Chris 33
Powis Castle 154-6, 159
Powys 7, 11-13, 22, 24, 98, 143, 145, 157
Powys County Council 17, 22, 148
Powys fadog 154
Powys Wenwynwyn 154, 159
Presteigne 16, 17, 18, 19-21, 22, 30, 46, 124; Broad Street 19-20; Radnorshire Arms 20
Price, John 60n
Price, Malcom 144
Price, Mary 60n
Pryce-Jones, Pryce 176-7, 182
Pumlumon 38, 136-41, 187-188
Pumlumon Arwystli 138
Pumlumon Fawr 139, 140

Radnor Forest 16, 17
Radnorshire 7, 16-62, 71, 82, 83, 89, 157, 174
Ray, Rebbecca 31-3; *A Certain Age* 31; *Newfoundland* 31
Rebecca Riots 30-1, 37, 178
Roberts, Samuel 194, 197
Robeson, Paul 131
Rodney, George Brydges 72
Rodney's Pillar 71-2, 73
Rowland, Elizabeth 86n
Rowlands, Ray 149
Royal Welsh Show 42-5, 113

Afon Rhaeadr 154
Rhaeadr Gwy 29
Rhayader 16, 29-33; 34, 38, 71, 114, 115, 124
Afon Rheidol 151n
Rhespass 66
Rhiw valley 182, 195
Rhos Fiddle 66
Rhulen 46-4; Black Hill 48; Red Hill 48; St David's church 46-8
Rhydspence 38
Rhydwhyman 156
Rhys, Gruff: 'Epynt' 105

St Bridget 70-1, 72, 73
Safn-y-Coed 40-2
Sager, Peter: *Pallas Wales* 121
Samuel, Rhian: 'Dyfi Junction' 144
Sandby, Paul 95
Scargill, Arthur 81
River Severn 38, 64, 71, 85n, 137-8, 154, 156, 159, 171, 177, 186, 187-8, 194
Severn, John Cheesement 60n
Shan Cothi 45
Shell Guide to Wales 92, 121
Shelley, Percy Bysshe 37
Shrewsbury (Amwythig) 7, 12, 55, 64, 143, 166
Shropshire 7, 66, 76, 82
Siambr Trawsfynnydd 141
Siddons, Sarah 91
The Silent Valley 131
Sion y Gof 186
Smith, Ian Duncan 161
Sparkes, John 128
Speed, John: *Theatrum Imperii Magnae Britannicae* 17, 136
Start, Daniel 62n
Staylittle 183-8; Quakers' Gardens 183-4
Sugar Loaf 54-6, 57, 58
Sugar Loaf (mountain) 98
Sycarth 67-70

Tafolwern 194, 196
Talerddig gap 194, 196, 197
Talgarth 50, 126n
Talybont reservoir 125n
Talybont-on-Usk 125; Star Inn 125
Talyllyn Junction 142
River Tanat 85
Tarren yr Esgob 95

INDEX

River Tawe 131
River Teme 66
Tenbury Wells 85n
Thomas, George 56
Thomas, Joshua 95
Thomas, Rhodri Glyn 62n
Thomas, R.S.: 'Reservoirs' 105
Three Cocks Junction 84, 143
Tintern 99
Tirabad 107
Tomley, Doris 158
Trannon valley 177, 186
Treaty of Montgomery 156
Tretower 97
Trewern 161
Treweryn valley 37, 174
Tuffin, Doris 74, 76
Tuffin, Harry 74, 76
Turner, J.M.W. 95
Twm Tobacco 50
Twymyn valley 194, 195

Usk 99
Usk valley 88, 97

Vaughan-Thomas, Wynford 183
Vyrnwy dam 165
Vyrnwy valley 37, 71, 85n, 105, 154, 165

Wales Tourist Board 79
Walton Plain 17
Ward Lock guides 37, 109, 12
Webb, Harri 7, 13
Welsh Development Agency 180
Welshpool 7-8, 64, 65, 124, 148, 154, 159-164, 176, 190; Broad Street 159; Chapel Street 159; High Street 159; Mount Street 159; Raven Street 159; *Pubs*: Angel 160; Crown 160; Grapes 160; Green Dragon 159; Mermaid 159; Pheasant 159; Pinewood 159; Royal Oak 160; Talbot 159
Western Mail 100
Whitehead, Nicholas 24-5
Wilby, Peter 161
Wilhelm II 110
Williams, Dai 131
Williams, David 160
Williams, Gareth 144-5; *Dyfi Juncshiyn: Y Dyn Blin* 144; *Dyfi Juncshiyn: Y Ddynes yn yr Haul* 144
Williams, Glyn 92
Williams, Kirsty 128n
Williams, Raymond: *The Fight for Manod* 171-2, 178; *Second Generation* 171
Williams, Roger 119
Williams, Wyn 147
Wilson, Harold 174
Woodbury Hill 128
Wordsworth, Dorothy 95
Wordsworth, William 95
Wroxeter 64
River Wye 29, 31, 32, 38-9, 41, 53, 83-4, 115, 124, 188
Wynne-Rhydderch, Samantha 32

Ynyscedwyn 132
Ystumtuen 186
Ystradgynlais 12, 99, 130-3, 190